The
Church

The Church

*A Theological
and Historical Account*

Gerald Bray

B

Baker Academic

a division of Baker Publishing Group
Grand Rapids, Michigan

© 2016 by Gerald Bray

Published by Baker Academic
a division of Baker Publishing Group
P.O. Box 6287, Grand Rapids, MI 49516-6287
www.bakeracademic.com

Printed in the United States of America

Library of Congress Cataloging-in-Publication Data
Names: Bray, Gerald Lewis, author.
Title: The church : a theological and historical account / Gerald Bray.
Description: Grand Rapids, MI : Baker Academic, 2016. | Includes bibliographical references and index.
Identifiers: LCCN 2015040638 (print) | LCCN 2015042600 (ebook) | ISBN 9780801030864 (pbk.) | ISBN 9781493402557 (ebook)
Subjects: LCSH: Church history. | Church.
Classification: LCC BR145.3 .B73 2016 (print) | LCC BR145.3 (ebook) | DDC 262—dc23
LC record available at http://lccn.loc.gov/2015040638

16 17 18 19 20 21 22   7 6 5 4 3 2 1

Contents

Preface

Since ancient times, almost all Christians have confessed their belief in the "one, holy, catholic, and apostolic church," as the Nicene Creed puts it. At the time the creed was composed, that definition of the church was not particularly controversial, and for centuries thereafter hardly anybody thought seriously about what it meant. The church had its quarrels, but although some of them proved to be intractable and led to permanent divisions, most people continued to think that with a little goodwill on all sides, the differences could be patched up and the visible unity of the ancient church restored. It was not until the Protestant Reformation in the sixteenth century that this assumption was seriously challenged, although even then the Reformers continued to insist that the words of the creed expressed their understanding of the church, and they hoped that their proposals would bring back the unity and purity that everyone wanted.

Yet whether they realized it or not, the Reformers were developing conceptions of what the church was that differed from what was commonly believed at the time. They were not interested only in cleaning up corruption or getting rid of obvious abuses in the traditional system. They wanted a church structure that was based on their understanding of New Testament principles, which they believed had been abandoned or forgotten in the course of time. In England there was a serious attempt to marry this new biblical understanding with the traditional pattern of the church, and those who promoted that combination believed that they had hit on the best of both worlds. Unfortunately, as they soon discovered, traditionalists did not accept their doctrines and the more radical Reformers chafed at what they thought were surviving relics of the past that should have been completely rejected.

The result was a civil war in which different visions of the church competed with one another. In the end, the original compromise was reinstated, but it could no longer claim a monopoly, and the English-speaking world became a place where rival groups of Christians developed their own ecclesiologies in the form of what we now call "denominations."

For better or worse, these denominations are still with us today, with the result that people who are of one mind on the other articles of the creed find themselves interpreting its statement about the church in ways that reflect and perpetuate these post-Reformation divisions. The entire Christian world is affected by this, but whereas in other countries there is usually one dominant church or tradition, it is in those that have been directly affected by the fallout from the English Reformation that ecclesiological issues are most likely to affect the daily life of the average worshiper. It is not for nothing that labels such as "episcopal," "presbyterian," and "congregationalist" are commonly used to define particular churches—it is their polity, more than their doctrine, that sets them apart from one another. This is even true of "baptists," since the refusal to baptize infants is as much a statement about the nature of the church as it is about the state of a newborn child in the mind of God.

This book is not a history of the church, nor is it an exposition of the church's doctrine. Rather, it is an attempt to understand how and why the different Christian bodies that now exist have come to understand the church in the ways that they have and why they persist with their own interpretations of ecclesiology even when they know that by doing so they are perpetuating the disunity of the Christian world. The eccentric Anglican ecumenist William Palmer (1803–85) believed that the church was like a tree that over time had grown and produced different branches. To his mind, the Roman Catholic Church, the Eastern Orthodox churches, and the Anglican Church were the most important of these, and he hoped that they would be able to recognize one another, if not actually reunite, on the basis of their common foundation in the original trunk.

Palmer's "branch theory" of the church did not win much favor at the time and is now regarded as a curiosity rather than as a serious model for ecclesiology, but properly understood, it has more to commend it than might appear at first sight. It is certainly true that over time, the church has grown and expanded across the world. In the process it has split into different branches, not naturally (as Palmer thought) but as the result of conflict, misunderstanding, and political expediency, as well as of incompatible doctrines. The sad fact is that if the church is the body of Christ, it has the wounds to prove it. Many people have written about this history, almost always from their own denominational standpoint, which they want to justify in light of theology, history, and practical experience. Sometimes they portray their own spiritual forebears as saints and heroes who were persecuted, or at least misunderstood, by their contemporaries, who are cast by default in the role of villains. This black-and-white approach is now in retreat, particularly in academic circles, but no one is entirely free of bias, and the old fault lines are often still visible, if only in the way the subject is approached and examined.

As a result, very often ecclesiology is an exposition of what a particular theologian thinks the church ought to be, and not of what it actually is. Sometimes the apologists for a particular position solve this problem simply by excluding from the church those who do not fit their picture of what the church ought to be. The most obvious examples of this can be found in the Roman Catholic tradition, whose theologians, in line with official church teaching, have frequently asserted that anyone not in communion with the see of Rome is outside the church. Others may be more generous when dealing with Christian groups that are not of their own persuasion, and even the Roman church has moderated its stance since the Second Vatican Council (1962–65), but those who feel strongly that their model of the church is the right one are bound to find it difficult to do justice to other points of view. Only by setting them in historical context and trying to see why each tradition has become what it now is can we gain some perspective on this and look for common elements that underlie our differences and may help us to overcome them. There is no prospect that the church will recover its ancient unity any time soon, and perhaps it never will. But if we can understand one another, we can at least come to terms with one another's traditions and perhaps even learn from them. That is the aim of this book.

Given the nature of the subject, it is only right that the author should disclose his own ecclesial identity. He is an ordained priest of the Church of England and is of the Evangelical persuasion within that church. Over the years he has worked, and at various times has worshiped, with Presbyterians, Baptists, Plymouth Brethren, Churches of Christ, Roman Catholics, and Eastern Orthodox and has learned to appreciate them all without abandoning his own denominational allegiance. He hopes that something of that depth of commitment to one tradition that allows for a corresponding breadth of sympathy for others will convey itself to the reader of this short introduction to the doctrine of the church. When all is said and done, Christians are men and women who have been born again of the Spirit of God and who belong to the church because that Spirit has united them in the body of Christ. The lifeblood of that union is love, and it is when we learn to love God that we begin to understand who he is and what his purposes for his people are. It is my prayer that he will bless you as you read these pages and open your eyes to the wonder of the grace by which he has reached out to a world of sinful human beings and called his chosen ones to be his church, now and in eternity.

Gerald Bray
August 20, 2014

1

The Origins of the Church

The Church and the Old Testament People of God

Unlike the world, the Christian church was not created out of nothing. Its beginnings can be dated to the period immediately following the death and resurrection of Jesus Christ, who was its inspiration and perhaps even its founder. Whether Jesus deliberately intended to establish a body of followers who would carry on his teaching after his departure has been disputed in modern times, but the belief that he did was universal for many centuries. It is hard to explain why Jesus chose and trained a body of disciples if he had no thought of perpetuating his ministry. The New Testament tells us that it was at the feast of Pentecost, seven weeks after the resurrection, that Peter stood up in Jerusalem and proclaimed that the ancient prophecies had been fulfilled. God's Holy Spirit was then poured out on the three thousand people who believed his message, and the church as we know it was brought into being.[1]

The Pentecostal outpouring of the Spirit was understood by those who took part in it to be a fulfillment of the promises that God had made to their ancestors, promises that could be traced back to Abraham, Isaac, and Jacob. Israel itself was the name that God had given to Jacob because he had fought with God and prevailed—an extraordinary statement that

1. Acts 2:14–41.

1

demonstrates how privileged Israel's relationship to God was.[2] The biblical accounts do not hide the fact that Israel was closely related to the surrounding nations, some of which were also the offspring of Abraham and Isaac, though they make it clear that these other nations had not been chosen by God. Somewhat surprisingly perhaps, the language they spoke came to be called Hebrew, a word apparently taken from the otherwise unknown Eber (or Heber), who was a great-grandson of Shem, one of the sons of Noah.[3] Why this was so is never explained, but the use of this term has never been questioned. For a time, the name Israel was used to describe the ten northern tribes that broke away from the kingdom centered on Jerusalem, which was then called Judah after the name of its dominant tribe. But after the ten tribes were taken into exile, the terms "Israel" and "Judah" merged to the point where they became virtually synonymous, a situation that still obtains today.[4]

This was the situation that prevailed in the time of Jesus. Israel was a single Jewish nation, based in Palestine but with a significant Diaspora population in both east and west. The easterners were mainly located in Mesopotamia, where they had remained after the Babylonian exile. The Old Testament books of Daniel and Esther remind us that these Jews played a significant role under the Persians, and several centuries later they would flourish again as major contributors to the development of the Talmud, a repository of Jewish learning that is of central importance for later Judaism. But in the New Testament, the voice of this Diaspora community is virtually silent. It is possible that the wise men who came to find the baby Jesus had heard of Jewish messianic hopes from members of that community, but if so, nothing is said about it.[5] Babylon is mentioned in the New Testament book of Revelation, but it is generally agreed that this is symbolic and not intended to refer to the historical city. Peter greeted the people he wrote to from "Babylon," but again, most commentators take this as a code word for Rome as there is no evidence that Peter ever went to Mesopotamia.[6] But on the day of Pentecost, we are told that there were pilgrims from what was then the Parthian Empire, the successor state to ancient Persia, and we can assume that some of them must have become Christians at that time.[7] But what happened to them

---

2. Genesis 32:28.

3. Genesis 10:24; 1 Chronicles 1:18. In Luke 3:35 he appears as one of the human ancestors of Jesus.

4. Thus, the modern state of Israel is a Hebrew-speaking nation populated mainly by Jews.

5. Matthew 2:1–2.

6. 1 Peter 5:13.

7. Acts 2:9.

afterward is unknown, and we have to say that the eastern Diaspora played no significant part in the emergence of the Christian church.

It was very different with the western Diaspora. This had emerged after the time of Alexander the Great (336–323 BC), whose conquest of the Persian Empire brought Palestine into the orbit of the Greek, and later of the Roman, world. Jews were soon to be found in significant numbers in Alexandria and in the other major cities of the Mediterranean. They became Greek speakers, and within a few generations had translated their Scriptures into that language. By the time of Jesus, they were producing great scholars, of whom Philo of Alexandria (d. AD 50) was the most important. He wrote commentaries on the Bible that were widely read in the early church, though they do not appear to have had any impact on the New Testament writers themselves. Saul of Tarsus was one of these Diaspora Jews, and it was in large measure because of him that the early church expanded into the Greco-Roman world.

In the late nineteenth century it was fashionable to portray the birth of Christianity as a kind of fusion between Jewish and Greco-Roman culture, but this hypothesis is no longer tenable. The New Testament was written in Greek, but the Gospels are clearly centered in Palestinian Judaism. We do not know whether Jesus spoke any language other than his native Aramaic, but even if he could speak some Greek, there is no sign that he ever ministered in it or that he was familiar with Greek literature and philosophy. His teaching can be fully explained within its Jewish context, which is where the surviving records place it, and modern scholars generally respect this. Today, it is the links between Jesus and his Jewish background that dominate academic discussion of the origins of Christianity. Greco-Roman influences were certainly present later on, but they are usually regarded as secondary and unconnected with Jesus himself.

It is now universally agreed that Jesus was born a Jew, that he chose his disciples from among his own people, and that the first Christian believers were for the most part also Jews.[8] The Gospels tell us that Jesus occasionally ministered to individuals who were not Israelites, but such cases were exceptional and were perceived as such at the time. When he got into controversy with the Samaritan woman at the well, Jesus did not hesitate to tell her that "salvation is from the Jews," a statement that explicitly denied the claims of her own religious group.[9] He could also be quite harsh toward non-Jews (or gentiles, as they are usually known) who approached him for help, though

8. This seems so obvious to us that it is easy to forget that in the early twentieth century, anti-Semites and those under pressure from them (as in Nazi Germany, for example) tried to disprove it, or at least did their best to ignore its implications.

9. John 4:22.

when they did so, he normally responded to them positively and could even observe that their faith was greater than anything to be found in Israel.[10] In sum, Jesus made it clear that he was sent to the Jews and not to others, but when others came to him of their own free will, he did not turn them away.

This approach was to be of particular relevance for the early church. One of the most significant controversies it had to face was whether non-Jews could become Christians without first becoming Jews. The Samaritans, whose beliefs were a kind of syncretistic and primitive form of Judaism, belonged in a special category, and we know that Jesus was prepared to reach out and embrace them to some extent.[11] Shortly before his ascension into heaven, Jesus commissioned his disciples to take the gospel to Samaria, which they duly did, but at first the Samaritans were baptized in the name of Jesus only and did not receive the Holy Spirit.[12] We are not told why this was so, but it may be that Philip, who evangelized them, thought they were second-class Jews and therefore ought not to receive the full blessing promised to Christians. That is speculation, of course, but we know that it was an anomaly, because when the apostles in Jerusalem heard about it, they rushed down to Samaria and put things right by laying hands on those who had been inadequately baptized.

Their attitude toward gentiles, on the other hand, was distinctly less welcoming. Over the years, a few gentiles had become familiar with Judaism and attached themselves to synagogues as "God-fearers," so they were among the first non-Jews to be evangelized. Cornelius, a Roman centurion stationed at Caesarea Maritima on the Palestinian coast, was a test case, which is why his story is recounted at great length in Acts 10–11. He was a gentile who was very sympathetic to Jews and had done as much as any outsider could to make himself acceptable to them. An angel of God appeared and told him to seek out the apostle Peter, who was staying in nearby Joppa at the time. Peter, however, was not prepared for an encounter with someone like Cornelius. Before the two men could meet, God had to teach Peter in a dream not to consider anything unclean—a reference to Jewish food laws, but one that could easily be extended to cover gentiles. When Cornelius's messengers arrived, Peter agreed to go with them, but although he understood that what was happening was of God, he still went somewhat reluctantly. Only when he heard Cornelius's story did his resistance break down, and he preached the gospel to gentiles for the first time.

10. Matthew 15:21–28; 8:10. See also Luke 4:27.
11. See Luke 17:16. But there were limits to this. When Jesus sent his disciples out to preach, he expressly forbade them to have any dealings with the Samaritans. See Matthew 10:5–6.
12. Acts 1:8; 8:14–17.

Cornelius and his household believed in Jesus, and the Holy Spirit fell on them (which had not happened to the Samaritans), so Peter baptized the entire household. He had been won over by these events, but the members of the Jerusalem church were another matter. When Peter reported back what had happened, they resisted him until he explained the situation, whereupon they accepted it in much the same way that Peter had. But we know that was not the end of the story, because later on, when Peter was in Antioch having fellowship with gentiles there, members of the Jerusalem church appeared and put pressure on him to desist—which he did.[13] That provoked a dispute with Paul, which was finally resolved in the gentiles' favor, though with certain conditions attached. Gentiles could join the church, but they were expected not to offend Jewish Christians by eating meat that had been sacrificed to idols or that had been killed in a way that contravened the Jewish food laws.[14]

A tug of war was going on at this time between those who thought like Paul and the so-called Judaizers, who seem to have set up a kind of rival mission in order to counteract his "liberal" policies.[15] Today, Jewish Christians are a small minority in the church, and much of this ancient controversy sounds petty and irrelevant to us, but its significance should not be minimized. The fear of the Judaizers was that gentile converts would take the church away from its Jewish roots, and they were not entirely wrong to think that. Non-Jews almost never learned Hebrew, the language of the Old Testament, and had little or no feeling for Jewish laws and customs. The Judaizers were wrong to oppose letting them become church members, but they were right to believe that the church could not just walk away from its Israelite inheritance. Somehow, Christians had to come to terms with that ancient tradition, whose promises they claimed to have inherited, without becoming enslaved to it.

The difficulty that Paul had to face was that the church was not just a continuation, in slightly modified form, of ancient Israelite tradition. As Jesus told his disciples, the law of Moses and the message of the prophets were authoritative until the time of John the Baptist, but in Jesus's ministry a new era had begun.[16] Jesus claimed that those who knew how to read the Hebrew Scriptures properly would find that they spoke about him—in other words, that their true meaning would only be understood as they were read in light of the revelation that he proclaimed in his teaching and worked out in his life and ministry.[17] He even said that not a single letter of the law would be overturned;

13. Galatians 2:11–14.
14. Acts 15:22–29.
15. Acts 15:1–2; Galatians 2:4–5.
16. Luke 16:16.
17. John 5:39–40.

it would all be explained and fulfilled by him.[18] At the very least, this meant that the Hebrew Bible would continue to be regarded as a sacred text whose message would inspire Christians as much as it had inspired generations of Jews before them. The first two generations of the church had no other sacred Scripture, or at least not a body of literature that was clearly recognized as such.[19] Even if most of the writings that now form the New Testament were in existence as early as AD 70, Christian writers hesitated to quote them as authoritative until the middle years of the second century—more than three generations after the events they described.

Throughout this period, the Old Testament (as Christians call the Hebrew Bible) remained the basic reference text of the church; defending it as a revelation that God intended for them rather than for Jews who rejected the claims of Jesus was a major preoccupation of Christian writers.[20] When Marcion (d. 144?) sought to break away from this tradition by rejecting the Old Testament and substituting a rump collection of New Testament texts divested of all trace of Judaism in its place, he was roundly condemned and refuted by most Christians, who were just as opposed to potential Judaizers as they were to him.[21] Like it or not, Christians could not get away from the Old Testament, but neither could they allow it to be interpreted by Jews in a way that excluded their own claims for Jesus as the one who fulfilled its prophecies.

There were two reasons for this. First, it is impossible to understand the New Testament without having a good idea of what the Hebrew Scriptures are all about. This is true even of a book such as Revelation, which never quotes the Old Testament directly but is incomprehensible without it. Second, the New Testament makes it plain that Jews before the time of Christ could have a saving relationship with God through their faith in his promises to them, even if they were not fully aware of how those promises would be fulfilled and would have to wait until that happened before they could fully benefit from them.[22]

18. Matthew 5:17–20.

19. An exception to this can be found in 2 Peter 3:15–16, where the letters of Paul are classified as "Scripture" and are clearly recognized as having authority in the church. Many scholars have used this as evidence that 2 Peter must be a late, pseudonymous work dating from the mid-second century, but even if they are right, this would still be the earliest evidence that part of what we now know as the New Testament was regarded as canonical Scripture.

20. See, for example, Justin Martyr, *Dialogus cum Tryphone*, where he argues the case for the Christian interpretation of the Old Testament against the famous rabbi Tarphon.

21. The most famous work of this kind is Tertullian, *Adversus Marcionem*, which was written about AD 200 and has come down to us in five books. On Marcion, see H. Räisänen, "Marcion," in *A Companion to Second-Century Christian "Heretics,"* ed. A. Marjanen and P. Luomanen (Leiden: Brill, 2008), 100–124.

22. Hebrews 11:39–40.

A key figure in the early church's self-understanding was Abraham. Jesus taught his disciples that Abraham had foreseen his coming and rejoiced in it, though he did not tie his remark to any particular Old Testament text.[23] Perhaps he was thinking about the tithe that Abraham offered to Melchizedek, the king of Salem, who is presented as a type of Christ in the Epistle to the Hebrews.[24] Or he may have been thinking of the sacrifice that Abraham was asked to make of his son Isaac, only to be told at the last minute that God would provide something better—presumably his own Son.[25] We do not know, but it is clear that the first Christians claimed Abraham as their ancestor in the faith every bit as much as contemporary Jews did, but in a different way. Jews claimed him as their physical ancestor, but Christians insisted that Abraham's real descendants were those who shared his faith. This was made explicit by the apostle Paul, who did not hesitate to remind his readers that Abraham had been given the sign of circumcision because of his faith in the promises of God, and that it was that faith which was Israel's true justification.[26]

The law of Moses presented a greater challenge for the early Christians because Jesus apparently rejected significant parts of it, including the food laws and the observance of the Sabbath, both of which had become sacrosanct in strict Jewish circles. Jesus justified his attitude by pointing out that Moses had given the law because the Israelites had shown themselves to be incapable of maintaining the high standards of Abraham. As he explained it, the law was a barrier against further spiritual decline, not a light that was meant to lead Israel to a higher truth.[27] He also said that the law had to be internalized in order to be properly understood. Thus, whereas Moses had said that murder was wrong, Jesus went further and told his disciples that even to harbor an evil thought against someone else was a sin.[28] By pointing his hearers to the principles underlying the law, Jesus could deepen the force of its application and at the same time override specific details (such as strict observance of the food laws) that got in the way of that. It was by reading the law in this way that Jesus taught his disciples how to reconcile the obligations imposed on the ancient Israelites with his own teaching.

Jesus and his disciples claimed that they were adding nothing to the Hebrew Bible but were merely showing how it ought to be interpreted. From that point of view, it might be said that they were preaching the true message that had

23. John 8:56.
24. Genesis 14:17–24; Hebrews 7:1–2.
25. Genesis 22:1–14; Hebrews 11:17–18.
26. Romans 4:1–12.
27. John 7:19–24; Matthew 19:7–8.
28. Matthew 5:21–26. The same principle applied to committing adultery, Matthew 5:27–30.

been overlaid and corrupted in the course of time. But after all was said and done, how much did the Christian church look like its Jewish parent? Were the similarities between them enough to encourage mutual support and dialogue, or were they merely superficial resemblances and more likely to cause misunderstanding than harmony?

From the very beginning, Christians saw themselves as the true heirs of the Old Testament people of God and regarded Jews who had not accepted Christ as blind to the truth. However, even as severe a critic of that blindness as the apostle Paul did not hesitate to recognize that all Jews, including those who had rejected the gospel, remained beloved by God for the sake of their ancestors. Paul taught that this blindness was actually a blessing for the gentiles, because it provided an opportunity for the apostles to preach the gospel to them. When that mission was completed, God would remove the blindness of his chosen people and integrate them into the church, so that "all Israel" would be saved in the end. It is not clear whether by "all Israel" Paul meant believing Jews and Christians combined, or whether he meant everyone who belonged to the Jewish people, whether they had any faith or not. Either way, God would eventually honor the promises he had made to the patriarchs.[29]

In the meantime, the church, as the offspring of Israel, had to come to terms with that legacy and learn to appreciate to what extent it was the same and in what ways it differed from its apparently wayward parent. Let us take a quick look at Israel's heritage and see how far (and in what ways) the church could appropriate it.

When God called Abraham to leave his family and his people, he told him to go to a land that would become his inheritance, even though he had never seen it. As part of this calling, God promised Abraham that he would receive the following:

1. His descendants would become a great nation.
2. He would be blessed and become a blessing to the whole world.
3. Those who supported him would be blessed, and those who did not would be cursed.[30]

To what extent had these promises been fulfilled in the time of Jesus? Nobody can doubt that Israel had become a nation, though whether it could really be called "great" was problematic. After a brief sojourn in the land promised to Abraham, Israel had gone down to Egypt to escape famine

29. Romans 11:1–32.
30. Genesis 12:1–3.

conditions and eventually been enslaved. More than four hundred years passed before that condition was altered, and then it was only by a mass exodus following a persecution that amounted to attempted genocide. Under the leadership of Moses, the people of Israel abandoned the fertile banks of the river Nile for the challenges of the desert, where their faith and commitment to the God whom they served would be tested to the limit. Finally, after a generation of wandering, they were able to enter the promised land, but it would be several more centuries before they were firmly established there. It was not until about 1000 BC, nearly a full millennium after Abraham, that they established a kingdom under the leadership of David, whose descendants would rule over them "forever," according to God's promise to him.[31] But no sooner was that promise given than it appeared to be broken. After the glorious but ruinously expensive reign of David's son Solomon, his kingdom fell apart, and only the tribes of Judah and Benjamin were left as his grandson's subjects.

The kingdom of Judah struggled on for a few hundred years, usually as a pawn in the diplomatic struggles of the great powers of the day, but in 586 BC it was finally extinguished. A remnant was left in the land, but most of the people were transported into exile in Babylon, from which they did not return for almost two generations. They were then able to rebuild the temple in Jerusalem, but apart from a century or so (roughly 150–63 BC), Judah (also known as Judaea) never again became an independent state. In Jesus's day, the Jews had spread across the known world, but their homeland was subdivided and ruled by client kings in the name of the Roman Empire. They had survived and spread, thanks to the liberal policies of Persia and Rome, but to call them a "great nation" surely strains the facts.

Whether they had been "blessed" is equally problematic. Subjects of David and Solomon saw God's hand at work in the establishment of the great kingdom of Israel and counted it a blessing, as would the returning exiles who were allowed to rebuild the temple, but in the bigger picture it is hard to see how anyone could regard a nation subjected to foreign rule as "blessed" in the sense that God had intended when he made his promise to Abraham. Nor (and for the same reason) could Israel be regarded as much of a blessing to others. In fact, so defensive and ingrown did it become that it was more concerned to keep others out than to attract them. The Diaspora communities tolerated the presence of gentile "God-fearers" in their midst, but there was little attempt to absorb them into the Jewish nation, and active proselytism was rare. On the contrary, the most zealous Jews were those who wanted to

31. 1 Kings 11:36; 2 Kings 8:19.

practice the Mosaic law with such precision that even other Jews might find it hard to gain recognition as such from their coreligionists.

Finally, there was little or no sign that gentiles who supported the Jews would be blessed and those who did not would be cursed. It is possible to read the story of Esther in that way, but that was the exception that proved the rule. On the whole, there was no advantage accruing to non-Jews by supporting Israel and little sign that those who abused them suffered for it. Sadly, the Jews were entering a period in their national history when discrimination and persecution would become the order of the day, and nobody would experience any divine retribution for their behavior toward God's chosen people. Perceptions vary, of course, and it is true that Jews through the ages have always thanked God for his blessings toward them, but from an objective standpoint it is hard to see that the promises made to Abraham have ever been fulfilled in Israel.

The calling of Abraham was extended to his descendants, but only through the privileged line of Isaac, whose birth was a miracle that lay outside the normal expectations of human generation. Abraham had other children, notably Ishmael, born to him by his slave concubine Hagar, but they were sent away with a separate inheritance and were never reckoned among God's chosen people.[32] In the next generation a similar thing occurred with Esau and Jacob. By an act of trickery it was Jacob, the younger brother, who inherited Isaac's birthright, and Esau was cast out.[33] He became the founder of the Edomite kingdom, and the close relationship of his descendants to Israel remained an important factor in later times. For example, the prophet Obadiah reproached Edom for not coming to Judah's aid in time of trouble, and the Herodians who ruled the Jews in New Testament times were of Edomite (Idumaean) origin.[34]

After Solomon's death, Israel split into two rival kingdoms, the northern one, which embraced ten of the twelve original tribes, and Judah (with Benjamin), which retained the capital at Jerusalem and the legitimacy that went with being the guardians of the temple there. As the tribe of David, Judah's right to claim the inheritance of Abraham was never questioned, but the history of the northern kingdom was more complicated. Lacking a worship center of their own, the northern kings felt obliged to establish two on the borders of their territory—one at Dan in the north and the other at Bethel, not far from Jerusalem—in an attempt to prevent their subjects from going to offer sacrifice in Solomon's temple. We cannot be sure what happened inside the kingdom

32. Genesis 25:6.
33. Genesis 27:1–45.
34. Obadiah 10–14.

itself, but it appears to have been more susceptible to outside pagan elements than Judah was, and none of its kings was regarded as satisfactory by the chroniclers who recorded their deeds. On the other hand, Elijah and Elisha, two of the greatest Israelite prophets, ministered in the north, and even in New Testament times there were Israelites who claimed descent from one or other of the northern tribes.

Quite what happened after the disappearance of the northern kingdom in 722 BC is uncertain, but eventually a variant form of Judaism established itself in the region of Samaria. The Samaritans claimed to belong to the Old Testament people of God, but they refused to join in the temple worship at Jerusalem and were rejected by those for whom the temple was central to worship. By the time of Jesus, Jews had no dealings with Samaritans, and although Jesus did not adhere to that pattern, he was in no doubt that it was to the Jews that salvation belonged. By then, the pillars of mainline Jewish religion were three:

1. The *priesthood* that went back to Aaron, the elder brother of Moses, and which existed as long as the temple and its sacrifices continued to operate. After the destruction of the temple in AD 70, the priesthood collapsed, although there are still people who claim that Jews who bear the name Cohen belong to it and would be expected to take over the management of the temple should it ever be rebuilt.

2. The *law* given by Moses. It was contained in the Torah or Pentateuch (Genesis to Deuteronomy) and interpreted by the priests with the help of a growing body of commentary literature, starting with the targumim, which are essentially running commentaries on the texts, and developing from them into the Mishnah and the Talmud, which form the basis of later Judaism.

3. The *Scriptures*, which consisted of the prophetic books and the so-called Writings in addition to the law of Moses itself. The prophetic canon was definitely closed by Jesus's day, but there was some uncertainty about the writings, particularly about the book of Esther, which never mentions the name of God and may have been suspect for that reason. There was also a discrepancy between the Hebrew canon, which corresponds to the modern Old Testament in its Protestant form, and the Greek translations, which included a number of extra books known collectively as the "Apocrypha." These are now accepted as canonical by the Roman Catholic and Eastern Orthodox churches but are rejected by Jews and Protestants.

How fundamental each of these pillars was to the Jewish religion can be deduced from the way they appear in the New Testament. The Hebrew Scriptures were authoritative beyond question, and the Torah enjoyed special prestige. But the commentary tradition that had grown up around it was more suspect, and we get the impression that Jesus was opposed to its very existence.[35] That may be an exaggeration, but there is no evidence in the Gospels that he had any sympathy with rabbinical teachings that purported to interpret the Mosaic text in light of contemporary circumstances. The priesthood was also important but less fundamental, and the task of teaching religion to the people fell mainly on the scribes, the rabbis, and assorted groups such as the Pharisees and the Sadducees, who had no official recognition in the temple establishment, although many Sadducees belonged to it.

In the course of its history, the people identified as Israel gradually became relatively smaller and narrower. Even if there were more Israelites in the time of Jesus than in the time of David, this was only because the natural increase in the population of Judah and their dispersal across the world produced growth in terms of absolute numbers. Otherwise ten of the original twelve tribes had been lost, and there was a steady outflow of Jews into the surrounding pagan world. It is true that there was also a trickle of gentiles into the Jewish community, but they were never numerous enough to make up for the losses. Jews remained a significant presence in Palestine and were probably still the majority population there in the mid-second century AD, but successive rebellions diminished their influence, scattered their leadership, and deprived them of their traditional homeland. They continued to be a common sight in many cities around the Mediterranean basin and in Mesopotamia, but they were a minority. When the Christian church became the leading religious movement in the later Roman Empire, the synagogues were unable to offer any compelling alternative to it.

Deciding who was a Jew was not easy. A male had to be circumcised— without that, he would not be accepted in any Jewish community.[36] Jews were also expected to observe the food laws and ceremonies of the Mosaic law, but this seems to have gone by the board in many Diaspora communities, and the impression we get is that many Jews were content to leave it that way. Observing the commandments to the letter was difficult at the best of times, and a minority in an alien environment would have found it harder than those who lived in Jewish-majority villages in Palestine. Knowledge of Hebrew, on

35. Matthew 15:2–6.
36. See Acts 16:3.

the other hand, was neither here nor there. The rabbis learned it, of course, but ordinary people spoke Greek or Aramaic, supplemented (though only to a very limited degree) by particular Hebrew words and expressions such as *amen* and *hallelujah*. Most of those who heard Peter speak on the day of Pentecost in Jerusalem must have been Jewish, but as the text indicates, they all heard him speaking to them in their own languages, which were those of the Jewish Diaspora regions.[37]

The major festivals such as Passover were widely celebrated, but most of what the modern world has come to think of as Jewish culture is of much more recent origin. On the surface at least, there would have been little to distinguish most Jews from Christians, and although the continued practice of Jewish customs among those who were converted to Christianity occasionally caused problems, these were quickly resolved and did not resurface. This suggests that the practices were not deeply rooted in popular culture, whatever their symbolic or theological importance may have been. What kept Jews together was a sense of belonging that was bolstered by prejudice as much as by religious practice. Jews were regarded as odd by gentiles, and they returned the compliment, generally keeping to themselves and marrying within their own community.

How many of these Jews could be classified as "believers" is impossible to say. It was one thing to avoid contact with pagans but quite another to take on board the faith of the Old Testament in any coherent or comprehensive way. In the time of Jesus there were devotional movements such as that of the Pharisees, which promoted a strict observance of the law of Moses, and the Sadducees, who from our modern perspective were the theological "liberals" of their time because they rejected such beliefs as the resurrection of the dead.[38] There were also fringe bodies such as the Essenes and the Qumran community, who practiced forms of asceticism and withdrawal from the world. But these groups were a small minority. Most Jews must have been more like Joseph, Mary, and the disciples of Jesus—ordinary people with a conventional faith that was seldom challenged or put to the test. The existence of sacred writings ensured that literacy rates among males were higher than average, but although in every synagogue there were men who studied them, there is little sign that this made much difference in the devotional life of the wider community. When Paul preached the gospel at Beroea, he noticed that the people there consulted the Scriptures to verify whether what he was saying about them was true, but the fact that Luke

37. Acts 2:7–11.
38. Matthew 22:23.

recorded it indicates that such diligence was unusual and far from the norm in most places.[39]

What we do know is that there were a number of Jews who paid little attention to their ancestral faith and whose lives made a mockery of the law of Moses. As the apostle Paul put it, they were a disgrace to their nation because their behavior belied the principles that were supposed to identify them. By no means all who called themselves Jews shared the spirit of the Mosaic law, and this contradiction in terms called the nature of Israel into question. Was it a people who were physically descended from Abraham, or was it made up of those who believed as Abraham believed, whether they were his actual offspring or not? Jesus did not hesitate to tell his fellow Jews that there had been gentiles in ancient times who had received God's blessings when Israelites who needed them just as badly had been passed over. Naaman, the Syrian general who was cured of leprosy, was an outstanding example of this, as was Ruth the Moabitess, who was one of his own ancestors. Faith and nation overlapped but were not coterminous, and for Jesus and his followers it was the former that really counted. Yet a certain ambiguity remained. To be born into a Jewish family was a great advantage, although it required a higher degree of spiritual responsibility. Those who knew the truth from birth had a duty to live by it, and if they did not do so, scandal was the inevitable result, because Jews were a people set apart in significant ways, whether they wanted to be or not.[40] The Christian church would be different, but to what extent and with what effect?

Was Israel the Old Testament Church?

At different times in its history, the Christian church has looked back to ancient Israel and seen in it a model for its own life. Following the legalization of Christianity in the Roman Empire (in 313) and its establishment as the state religion (in 380), church leaders looked to the Old Testament for models of how a Christian society ought to be governed. The emperors became sacred rulers along the lines of the kings of Israel and Judah. They were anointed in a coronation ceremony that was deeply religious in nature and were given a place of great honor in the church, sometimes even being regarded as equal to the apostles (*isapostoloi*).[41] The Christian clergy were organized into an

---

39. Acts 17:11.
40. Romans 2:17–24.
41. This was especially true of Constantine I (306–37), who legalized Christianity, and Justinian I (527–65), who built the great church of Hagia Sophia in Constantinople.

order of priests on the Aaronic model and given a tithe of all produce for their maintenance, just as the ancient Levites had received.[42] Even church services took on an Old Testament flavor, as the Lord's Supper was transformed into the memorial sacrifice of the Lamb who was slain for the sins of the world—*Agnus Dei, qui tollis peccata mundi,* as the great medieval Communion hymn put it.[43]

The links thus created were possible because the Old Testament was allegorized to make it fit the needs of the Christian church. For example, Jacob's vision of a ladder ascending to heaven was interpreted to mean that while Israel was asleep in the house of God (Bethel), Christians had woken up and were climbing the ladder, along with the angels and archangels. Echoes of this interpretation remain in the prayer of consecration in the Anglican Book of Common Prayer, where it is "with angels and archangels and all the company of heaven that we laud and magnify thy glorious Name." Visitors to Chartres Cathedral in France will discover that the magnificent stained-glass windows are arranged in two matching series, one devoted to the Old Testament and the other to the New. There is a deliberate correspondence between them, so that the story of the Good Samaritan, for example, is placed opposite the story of the sale of Joseph into slavery in Egypt. The logic behind this is that in the Old Testament, the unfortunate victim was condemned to slavery, whereas in the New Testament he was rescued by a figure generally regarded as an image of Christ.

In keeping with Christian tradition, Jewish allegorical parallels are always presented as partial and inferior to the Christian ones, but the fact that they are there at all tells its own story. Christians saw themselves mirrored in the Old Testament, privileged to be able to put right by the gospel what had gone wrong under the law of Moses. To what extent was this perception valid?

In one sense, there can be no doubt that Christians saw their experience of God as the fulfillment of the Old Testament promises. That the gospel was superior to the law went without saying—if it were not, there would be no reason for anyone to become a Christian. The apostle Paul did not hesitate to describe the relationship between the synagogue and the church by comparing the former to Hagar, Abraham's slave concubine, and the latter to Sarah, his legitimate wife. Their sons were both Abraham's offspring, but the former (Ishmael) was cast out, whereas the latter (Isaac) inherited his father's blessing.[44] So it was with the church. Jews could claim to be the children of

42. Numbers 18:21.
43. "Lamb of God, that takest away the sins of the world."
44. Galatians 4:21–31.

Abraham but were slaves to the law and so had been cast out, whereas Christians were the children of the free woman. They were so similar in one way, yet so different in another.

What Paul mentions in passing was developed in a systematic way by the author of the Epistle to the Hebrews, who begins his argument as follows: "Long ago, at many times and in many ways, God spoke to our fathers by the prophets, but in these last days he has spoken to us by his Son."[45] After a lengthy exposition of what this entails, he brings his argument to a head by pointing directly to the great men and women of faith whose lives are recorded in the Old Testament and who serve as examples to us who come after. Yet great though they were, he still concludes: "All these, though commended through their faith, did not receive what was promised, since God had provided something better for us, that apart from us they should not be made perfect."[46]

So there we have it. The saints of the Old Testament were great servants of God and, in the final reckoning at the end of time, will be counted among the righteous, just as we shall be. Yet at the same time, they were different from us. They looked ahead to the blessings that we have received and enjoy in a way that they did not. Their lives followed a different trajectory, and they were subjected to burdens and limitations that no longer apply to us. Did they constitute a church of their own, which was the ancestor of the Christian equivalent? Can we now regard them as Christians, even though they lived before the coming of Christ and did not use that term to describe themselves?

Here we are to some extent dependent on the definitions of words. Both ancient Israel and the later Christian church were called "the people of God," and if that is what we mean by the word "church," then Israel must be included. But the New Testament does not go that far. The differences between the historic institutions of Israel and those of the early Christian movement were just as significant as their similarities, and the way in which Christians used the word "church" is indicative of that. They recognized that, for all the similarities and connections between them, Christianity was not just a branch of Judaism. If it had been, the disciples of Jesus would never have formed such distinct (and distinctive) worshiping communities. The fact is that although they remained Jews, their spiritual experience could not be contained within the bounds of traditional Judaism. Furthermore, it was possible (and soon became the norm) for gentiles to believe in Christ and enjoy the same experience of him without becoming Jews. There was something new here, and it

45. Hebrews 1:1.
46. Hebrews 11:39–40.

is this that the term "church" expresses. The main reasons why we usually do not (and probably should not) include Israel under the umbrella term of "church" can be set out as follows:

1. Israel and the church both possess a written revelation from God, which is central to their life and faith. The Christian church has absorbed the Jewish Scriptures as its own, but in a different way. First of all, Christians interpret the Hebrew Bible in light of the Christ (Messiah) who has already come, whereas Jews do not. Second, the Christian canon is closed in a way that the ancient Hebrew one was not. Prophecy had ceased in Israel about four hundred years before the coming of Christ, a fact borne out by the Old Testament as we now have it, but there was no settled decision in the time of Jesus as to whether divine revelation had come to a permanent end. There had been times of spiritual dearth in Israel before, but they had been followed by revival and the production of new Scripture. When John the Baptist appeared, he was not rejected as an imposter on the ground that a ministry like his was no longer possible.

Christians, on the other hand, received the Hebrew Bible as a closed canon that cannot be extended because it points to the Christ who has already come. The New Testament is also a closed canon and has been since the first generation of eyewitnesses to its contents passed from the scene. Its precise extent was not universally agreed on for some time, and debates continued about whether certain books were genuinely apostolic in origin, but these are secondary matters. The principle was that since the fullness of time had come, no new revelation was possible. God still speaks to and through the church, but he does so in a different way; no one today can claim the kind of authority that was given to Moses, the Old Testament prophets, or the apostles of Jesus.

More significantly, Judaism has generally stressed that the Hebrew Bible is law, whereas the Christian church has understood it more as prophecy. Of course, "the Law and the Prophets" belong together, and neither faith tradition has emphasized one to the exclusion of the other. But whereas Jews find it natural to ask how the law of Moses can be extended and applied in situations not originally envisaged by the ancient Israelites, Christians do not. In the church, the Mosaic precepts are regarded as spiritual principles whose practical application depends on the extent to which they have been fulfilled (and superseded) by the gospel of Christ. This may lead to abolishing them (as in the case of the food laws, which are believed to be no longer applicable) or to a deeper and more stringent application of their teaching—as with the Ten Commandments, where prohibitions on murder and adultery are extended to include evil thoughts and desires and not limited to external actions.[47] As for prophecy, Jews regard this as belonging to an eschatological future in which they may or may not believe—messianic Judaism is (and has always been) a minority pursuit in the Jewish world. But for Christians, prophecy has been fulfilled in Christ. There is an eschatological dimension to it, to be sure, but that too is bound up with him. The coming of the Messiah at the end of time can therefore only be the return of Christ, and not the appearance of some hitherto unknown figure.[48]

2. Ancient Israel (like its modern counterpart) was a secular, human nation with its own traditions, culture, language, and territory comparable to those of other nations around it. It was possible to join this nation, but that was not encouraged, and as time went on, external influences (such as foreign wives) were increasingly ruled out. In the early days, a woman like Ruth could marry into a Jewish family without difficulty, but that would have been much harder later on, especially after the exile.[49] As a corollary of this, physical heredity played a central part in Israelite life. The priestly caste was a tribe of its own that traced its lineage back to Aaron, the older brother of Moses. No one could choose to become (or refuse to be) a priest, because that was determined by birth. Similarly, Jesus inherited his kingly title from his ancestor David and could not have obtained it otherwise. A man like Herod might rule over the Jews as their king, but in theological terms he was a usurper and could never have been anything else.[50]

In sharp contrast to this, the Christian church was not a nation in the usual sense of the word, even if such language was sometimes used to describe it.[51] Membership was open to everyone, and the miracle of the first Pentecost was intended to demonstrate the universality of its message. The church did not fold in on itself in order to survive but reached out to embrace people of every tribe and tongue. Evangelism, a concept unknown before the coming of Christ, became the chief raison d'être of the church, which saw its primary task as the proclamation of the gospel to the ends of the earth. Offices in the church, such as they were, were never inherited, and measures were sometimes taken to make sure that this principle would be observed. One of the reasons that celibacy was imposed on the Western clergy in the Middle Ages was to ensure that they would not have legitimate children who could inherit

47. Matthew 5:21–30.
48. Acts 1:11; 1 Corinthians 15:20–28; 1 Thessalonians 4:13–17.
49. See Ezra 9–10.
50. See Matthew 2:1–12 and the pointed quotation from Micah 5:2 in v. 6.
51. See 1 Peter 2:9.

their positions. In the church, it was possible to become a minister (and to cease functioning as one) in a way that was inconceivable in ancient Israel. Likewise, kings and other rulers who became Christians were not entitled to a special status in the church, even though that was often granted to them in later centuries, nor did secular government come within the church's remit, though again there were exceptions in the Middle Ages and later.

There have certainly been many attempts to establish Christian states and governments, but none of these has ever enjoyed the kind of divine sanction that was accorded to the Davidic kingship in ancient Israel. It is not too much to say that the idea that civil government should be secular (in the sense of "nonreligious") is the product of Christian thinking and can be traced back to the command of Jesus, who told the Jews that while they should give Caesar his due, they should distinguish that from what they owed to God.[52]

3. Ancient Israel's spiritual life centered on the Jerusalem temple and especially on the great atoning sacrifice, which was made there once a year by the high priest. As the writer to the Hebrews pointed out, the high priest had to perform this and many lesser rituals on his own behalf as well as for the salvation of the people, because he was essentially no better than they were.[53]

By contrast, the Christian church's spiritual life centered on worship in gathered communities. Jesus was present among them wherever two or three assembled in his name; he was not tied to a temple or an earthly location of any kind. The high point of worship was not the atoning sacrifice but the memorial of that sacrifice, which had been made once for all by Jesus on the cross. It was the focus of Christian worship not for what it was in itself but for what it represented. Christian ministers were not priests in the Old Testament sense. They were preachers and evangelists who had been called to proclaim that Christ had put an end to the need for sacrifice and that the Jerusalem temple traditions were now redundant.

It was for that reason that the early church had nothing that could be compared with the Jerusalem temple. There has never been a central building or place where Christian worship has been concentrated or to which it ought to be restricted. Christians can (and do) worship anywhere without distinction. There have been times when they have given special prominence to Jerusalem and the so-called Holy Land; some people still make pilgrimages to various sites, among them Bethlehem and Nazareth, where Jesus was born and where he grew up, but this has never had the spiritual importance

52. Matthew 22:15–22.
53. Hebrews 5:2–3.

that attaches to worship in Jerusalem (and on the Temple Mount) in the Jewish mind.[54]

The church had no use for the temple because its purpose had been fulfilled in Christ, but it was a different story when it came to the synagogue. Synagogues did not exist in biblical Israel but developed at a later date, partly to serve the needs of the Diaspora communities and partly to cater to Jews who lived in Palestine. We know from the New Testament that there were several synagogue buildings in Galilee and elsewhere, some of them built and paid for by gentile admirers of Judaism, including Roman military officers like Cornelius. Even Jerusalem had synagogues, although the temple was near at hand and could easily have been visited at any time. The word "synagogue" originally referred to the congregation of people that met together, but as this normally happened in a designated building, it was soon extended to include the building as well. Synagogues were places where Jews met to pray, to hear the Bible being read, and to be instructed in their faith. They were informally organized, partly because there was no provision for them in the Mosaic law (as there was for the temple) and partly because they were still a relatively new phenomenon.

Exactly who controlled what happened in a synagogue is hard to determine. There must have been important local people who had a say in how it was maintained, and we know that there were people called *archisynagōgoi* who had a controlling interest in them. One of these, a man called Crispus, was converted when Paul preached at Corinth, an event that caused a major stir in the Jewish community because it deprived the synagogue of one of its leading backers.[55] Beyond that though, we are largely ignorant. Presumably the *archisynagōgoi* were expected to ensure that worship was conducted on a regular and orderly basis and that instruction would be provided for the youth, but that is a logical guess with little or no hard evidence to support it. No doubt the *archisynagōgoi* relied on the senior members of the congregation for support, but again, this is speculation, and the pattern probably varied considerably from one place to another. The whole system was run informally, which is one reason why Jesus and his disciples, including Paul on his later missionary journeys, found it so easy to gain acceptance in them—at least initially.

Whether synagogues had teachers who could instruct the people in the meaning of the law is unknown. A growing body of men, whom we call rabbis,

---

54. It may be noted in passing that Christianity differs from Islam in this respect also. For Muslims, there is a sacred duty to make the pilgrimage to Mecca, but nothing of that kind has ever obtained within the Christian world, even when pilgrimage has been encouraged and developed.

55. Acts 18:8.

were being trained for this purpose, but in the time of Jesus the pattern of later centuries had not yet been established. Jesus was called a rabbi by people who did not know how else to address him, but this did not mean that he had received any formal theological education or that he held an officially recognized post in Jewish society.[56] It was only after the destruction of the Jerusalem temple in AD 70 and the disappearance of the traditional priesthood that the synagogue acquired the importance that it has since maintained in the Jewish world. Judaism was able to survive the catastrophe because there was an already well-established network of institutions that functioned without much reference to the Jerusalem temple. We should therefore not be surprised to discover that it was the synagogues, and not the temple, that provided a model for the organization of the earliest Christian congregations.

In Hebrew the words "synagogue" and "church" are virtually the same— "synagogue" is *knesset* and "church" is *knesiyah*, both of which mean "assembly."[57] It is only in Greek that significantly different terms are found— *synagōgē* for the Jews and *ekklēsia* for the Christians, with no real distinction in meaning. *Ekklēsia* was a word used for the assembly of citizens in Greek cities such as Athens, but the Christian version was not really a kind of parliament, as that connection might suggest. Nor was there anything in Israelite tradition that could be compared with it. In the early days, Christians were not allowed to erect buildings for worship, so the natural extension of the word *ekklēsia* from the assembly to the building in which it met took time to develop.[58] But long before that happened, the word *ekklēsia* had acquired connotations that clearly set it apart from the synagogue, not only in terms of religious faith but in terms of practical organization and significance as well.

For a start, the word "church" included all professing Christians. It could be used in the singular as well as the plural, referring as it did to the sum total of believers as well as to particular gatherings of them. The church was described as "the body of Christ," into which every member was baptized, and

56. See Matthew 23:7–8.
57. *Knesset* in Modern Hebrew is the term used for the Israeli parliament.
58. This may explain why the word *ekklēsia* did not always catch on. In the Germanic countries of northern Europe, the preferred term was a variant of *kyriakē* (belonging to the Lord), from which the English words "church" and "kirk" both derive. The same word also penetrated the Eastern Orthodox world, where variant forms of the Russian *tserkov'* are often found. Exceptions often go to the opposite extreme and demonstrate how the word for the building could be applied to the congregation, and from there to the universal church—Romanian, for example, uses *biserică*, from the Latinized Greek *basilica*, and Polish has *kościoł* (Czech *kostel*), derived from *castellum* (castle). In Eastern Europe, many languages distinguish Roman Catholic churches from Eastern Orthodox and Protestant ones by using different words for them. Thus, a *kościoł* is always Roman Catholic, a *tserkov'* is Eastern Orthodox, and a Protestant church may be called something else—perhaps a *chram* (temple) or something similar.

in which each had a designated place.[59] This body was a unity that had to be preserved as such in order to demonstrate to the outside world that there was one Lord, one faith, and one baptism.[60] The universality of the Christian gospel demanded this, and any tendency to divide into sects that followed different leaders was strongly resisted by the leaders of the main apostolic churches.[61]

Second, and as a corollary to the need to maintain this overarching unity, the church had a highly centralized organizational structure that was quite alien to the synagogue. Overseeing them all were the apostles—the disciples of Jesus, along with Paul—to whom local congregations could appeal and who did not hesitate to "interfere" in them if necessary. Paul's Letter to the Romans, for example, was addressed to a congregation that he had never visited, but that in no way diminished his authority. No Jewish leader could have written to a synagogue like that. Internally, each congregation was structured to a degree that was unimaginable in the synagogue. We do not know precisely how this was worked out, and there may have been a number of variations across the Mediterranean world that later merged into a common pattern, but it is clear from the New Testament records that a pattern of governance and responsibility was in place. When Paul wrote to a local church, he expected to be obeyed, and that implied that there must have been local people who were able and willing to put his recommendations into practice. Who they were (and by what names they were called) have been matters of considerable dispute, but that they existed can scarcely be doubted.

Third, and perhaps most important of all, the church had a mission to convert the world. It was not a club of expatriates, as the Diaspora synagogue could so easily have appeared to be. There was no hierarchy of membership, with Jews occupying a special place, though no doubt that was part of the agenda being promoted by the so-called Judaizers. To enter the church was not to reinforce one's ethnic or social identity but to lose it. Christians did not spend their time cultivating a sacred language like biblical Hebrew, even though it was the medium in which the Scriptures had originally been revealed. They used Greek, mainly for practical reasons, because it was the common tongue of the Mediterranean world of their time. Unlike modern Christians, they showed no interest in translating the Bible into any other language, even though Paul occasionally found himself ministering to people who may not have understood what he was saying.[62] Class differences certainly existed within the church, but those who paid attention to them were severely

59. 1 Corinthians 12:27.
60. Ephesians 4:5.
61. See, for example, 1 Corinthians 1:11–17.
62. Acts 14:11.

criticized.[63] The church was open to all, and even practices that were in themselves unobjectionable could become problematic if they impeded the work of evangelism. Thus, for example, speaking in tongues was tolerated in the Corinthian church, but not if it gave outsiders the wrong impression, because that would have created a barrier to the work of mission.[64] No synagogue would have compromised its Judaism in order to attract others by giving them a good impression—the very idea of doing such a thing would have horrified its members. But Christians were not interested in esoteric exclusivity—as far as they were concerned, the door of the church was open to all who professed faith in Jesus Christ and who had been filled with his Spirit.

This brings us to the final and most theological of the differences between Judaism and Christianity. Both religions worshiped the same God, but whereas Jews saw him in all his majestic unity and sovereign majesty, Christians believed that they had penetrated into his inner life. They were seated in the heavenly places in Christ Jesus.[65] They had access to the Father, through the Son, in the Holy Spirit.[66] They were born again.[67] None of this made any sense to Jews, as the story of Nicodemus reminds us. When Jesus told him that he had to be born again, he thought that he was somehow supposed to go back into his mother's womb![68] That was an absurdity, of course (and to be fair, Nicodemus knew it), but it is symptomatic of the different ways in which Jews and Christians approached God. Jews were attached to physical and material things in a way that Christians were not. For Christians, the kingdom of God was not an eschatological hope but a present reality that they knew by their union with Christ in the Holy Spirit. To put it another way, Christians worshiped the one God in a Trinity that was not defined for some centuries but that was a reality in their experience. In the end, it was that experience that made it impossible for them to continue as Jews in the synagogue and that forced them to work out a theology for which Judaism had no need. Jews bore witness to their faith by being circumcised and living according to the myriad precepts of the Mosaic law, but Christians confessed Christ, and it was that confession that led them to give the church an intellectual structure quite different from anything to be found in the synagogue.

Another important sign of the differences between Israel and the church was that there seems to have been little or no carryover of leadership personnel

63. James 2:1–13.
64. 1 Corinthians 14:20–25.
65. Ephesians 2:6.
66. Ephesians 2:18; Galatians 4:6.
67. John 3:7.
68. John 3:4.

from one to the other. None of the disciples of Jesus had any previous standing in the Jewish world that they had to abandon when they followed Jesus, nor did they have a rabbinical education. Paul was exceptional in that respect, but he was also the most vocal in his denunciation of the old order and did not seek to press his advantage in order to gain greater acceptance in the church. There is also no sign that any Jewish priest or rabbi who became a Christian was given a comparable position in the church. It is hard to believe that when new churches were formed out of divided synagogues, none of the leaders passed from one system to the other, but if they did we are not told of it. The criteria for leadership in the church are spelled out on more than one occasion in the New Testament, but knowledge of Jewish learning or experience in running a synagogue are not included among them. In the church, God was doing a new thing, and while knowledge of the old pattern might have been useful at times, it was not essential in the new dispensation.

We must therefore conclude that Israel cannot really be regarded as the Old Testament church. The continuities between the Old and the New Testaments were refracted through the prism of Christ, who changed everything. The final word on the subject surely belongs to the apostle Paul, who wrote to the Philippians:

> If anyone else thinks he has reason for confidence in the flesh, I have more: circumcised on the eighth day, of the people of Israel, of the tribe of Benjamin, a Hebrew of Hebrews; as to the law, a Pharisee; as to zeal, a persecutor of the church; as to righteousness under the law, blameless. But whatever gain I had, I counted as loss for the sake of Christ.[69]

Such was the testimony of a devout Jew who became a Christian, and it would be hard to find a clearer statement of why Israel and the church were not just the same thing in a different guise.

Did Jesus Found the Church?

No one doubts that the Christian church grew out of the life and ministry of Jesus, whose teaching governs its practice and whose person is the object of its worship. Scholars dispute why this is so, and there is a great gulf fixed between those who believe that Jesus taught his disciples what they should do after his death and resurrection and those who claim that the first Christians

---

69. Philippians 3:4–7.

pieced together the wreckage of Jesus's failed ministry and relaunched his teaching (in a highly modified form) as the Christian church. Many observers prefer to adopt a position somewhere between what they perceive as these two extremes, but there can be no doubt that the fundamental divide is between those who believe that the church is the product of a divine revelation given in and through Jesus Christ and those who think that it emerged out of complex social factors that coalesced around him.

Either way, both sides in this debate agree that the intense Christian concentration on a single individual was unknown in Judaism and is rare among the world's major religions. Outsiders might think mistakenly that Islam grants a similar position to the prophet Muhammad, but Muslims respond by explaining that Muhammad is only a human being, not a divinity. Buddhists, too, would deny that the Buddha is the object of a cult, though he is certainly venerated in a way that would shock Muslims if anything similar were to surface in Islam. Hindus believe in the possibility of divine incarnations, but they do not focus on one individual god who became a human for a particular purpose. Jesus is unique, because only he claimed to be God and therefore deserving of the highest form of worship known to humankind. But if there is no doubt about that, many questions arise when we start to consider how this came about. Did Jesus himself intend for it to happen? Was he trying to establish a church that would preserve his memory and teaching, or did it grow up accidentally after his untimely death?

The answers to these questions are complicated by the fact that many modern scholars incline to the second of the views outlined above and therefore reject the traditional "orthodox" account, either in whole or in part. In particular, they believe that Jesus did not intend to found anything, and certainly not an institution that would grow into the Christian church as we know it. Broadly speaking, they are inclined to think that he was a revolutionary prophet who challenged the establishment of his time and was ultimately silenced by it. His disappointed followers then got together and decided to preserve his memory in what we now call the church. What motivated them to back such an obvious failure is the great unanswered mystery, and it is at this point that such theories tend to lose whatever credibility they might otherwise have. There were disciples who followed Adolf Hitler to the grave, but not beyond, and modern neo-Nazis do not worship him or claim that he is still alive. More worthy figures such as Mahatma Gandhi and Nelson Mandela have been widely admired, but they have left no organized following and have never inspired a religion dedicated to them. Only in cults such as Rastafarianism in the West Indies or the cargo cults of the South Pacific can we find anything remotely similar to the claims made for Jesus Christ, but they are so obviously false that no one, except members of these groups, takes them seriously.[70]

Jesus is unique in this respect, but why? Even if we accept everything that has been claimed for his divinity and his earthly mission, what evidence is there to suggest that he started a church? And what would the word "church" mean in this case? Those who doubt that Jesus ever intended to found a church can point to the fact that the word occurs only twice in Matthew and not at all in the other three Gospels, in sharp contrast to the idea of the "kingdom," which was one of the main themes of Jesus's teaching. At the very least, this suggests that the concept of the "church" was at best marginal to Jesus's mission and may even be an attempt to recycle his kingdom emphasis for the more prosaic (but also more realistic) limitations of the world in which his disciples had to minister. Those who assume (as many modern commentators do) that the word "church" in Matthew must be an interpolation by some later writer who was concerned to speak to the conditions of his time and does not reflect Jesus's teaching can use the fact of its rarity to support their position, though other interpretations are also possible. It may be asked, for instance, why Matthew has only two references to the church, only one of which has any real bearing on our subject, if he wanted to emphasize its importance. Would he not have peppered his Gospel with references to the "church" placed in the mouth of Jesus, if he was trying to claim Jesus's authority for the institution whose origins he was exalting?

There is also the problem that Jesus spoke Aramaic, not Greek, so Matthew (or the source from which Matthew received his information) must have been translating some other word in this way. Unfortunately, we can only guess what that word might have been, and it is possible that there are two different ones lying behind it. One of the passages in which Matthew refers to the "church" is concerned primarily with the disciplining of a wayward brother. According to the Gospel account, Jesus told his disciples: "If he [the erring brother] refuses to listen . . . tell it to the church. And if he refuses to listen even to the church, let him be to you as a Gentile and a tax collector."[71] In this instance Jesus could have used a number of words that might be roughly translated as "fellowship," "company," and so on. If the translation as "church" represents a later interpretation, it is hard to see why the author would have referred to gentiles (who by then would have been fully accepted

---

70. Rastafarianism is a cult dedicated to the memory of Ras Tafari, who became emperor of Ethiopia as Haile Selassie I. The cargo cults of Melanesia worship such "deities" as John Frum, a mythical American airman, and even the Duke of Edinburgh. They are interesting from a sociological point of view but theologically they are absurd.

71. Matthew 18:17.

as church members) or even to tax collectors, who do not appear as villains in later Christian literature.

We cannot answer these questions, but this text is of minor importance compared to the other one, which was to become and has remained one of the most controversial in the entire Bible. It is the climax to Peter's confession of Jesus as the Messiah, and in it Jesus says: "You are Peter, and on this rock I shall build my church, and the gates of hell will not prevail against it."[72] In later centuries this statement, which Matthew attributed directly to Jesus, would be used by Roman Catholics to justify the primacy and jurisdictional supremacy of the Roman see, of which Peter was supposed to have been the first occupant. This interpretation, which has few if any scholarly defenders nowadays, has caused all kinds of reactions in the course of history, not least from Protestants who have attacked the papacy's modern pretensions by denying its authenticity.

Polemic of this kind makes it difficult to come to a balanced conclusion about the verse itself, but one important fact may be noted. Jesus speaks of the "church" in the singular but in a way that clearly refers to the entire body of believers and not just to a single congregation. Elsewhere in the New Testament, a "church" is usually a specific gathering of believers in a particular place. In that sense it is frequently used in the plural. There are relatively few occurrences of the word in the singular, which would make us conclude that it must refer (at least in those instances) to the entire Christian world. Once again, we may legitimately wonder what the original Aramaic term was and whether "church" is the best translation for it. But whether it is or not, it is the term that has come down to us, and we must try to make sense of it as it stands.

One thing that can be said about this verse is that Jesus was talking about the future. He was not making plans for the immediate establishment of a church himself but thinking of something that would come into being later. We know that "later" means after his death and resurrection, in which case Jesus built his church at one remove—not directly but in and through his Holy Spirit, as the Acts of the Apostles attests. This interpretation is backed up by the so-called farewell discourses of Jesus in John 13–17, where he tells his disciples that he must go away, but that after his departure he will send them the Holy Spirit, who will guide them into all truth. Interestingly, Jesus never mentions the establishment of the church, but it is hard to see how the first readers of the Fourth Gospel could have interpreted his words in any other way—after all, they knew all about Pentecost!

72. Matthew 16:18.

If this interpretation is accepted, the question of whether Jesus should be called the church's "founder" becomes largely a matter of definition. As the earthly Jesus of Nazareth, he did not (and did not claim to) set up an organization that could conceivably have been called a "church." But as the risen, ascended, and glorified Christ, he was the church's founder, because it was in that context that he sent the Holy Spirit to put his intentions into effect. Given that the incarnate Jesus and the heavenly Christ are one and the same person, the question must be posed in a different light. It is not so much whether Jesus founded the church as it is when and in what circumstances he did so.

Jesus did not set up an evangelistic movement when he was still on earth, but he did train his disciples to preach and baptize and then sent them out to do so, which shows that he must have had some sense of organization, even if it was ad hoc and temporary. What happened to those who were baptized by the disciples? Did they simply fade away, as though their baptism meant nothing, or were they the seed that was being sown, so that when the Holy Spirit was poured out at Pentecost, they would be ready and willing to receive him? The fact that Jesus deliberately chose disciples—they were not merely fans attracted to his message—surely shows that he had some long-term purpose in mind. The disciples themselves certainly thought so, and they fought with one another over what place would be allocated to them in the coming "kingdom" that they believed Jesus was planning to set up.[73] They may have misunderstood his plans completely, but at least they knew that he was intending to use them for something.

Those who deny that Jesus had any desire to set up a church often have in mind the institutional structure that was to emerge in later centuries. They may be prepared to accept that he had some idea that his message would survive his death, but not that it would develop into a vast network that in some of its later manifestations would become very worldly and appear almost as a kind of spiritual tyranny. Jesus could hardly have intended that! But while we can agree with the skeptics on that point, it also seems to be the case that Jesus did have a vision of spreading his message to the ends of the earth, a vision that sooner or later would have required a structure that we could call a "church." Whether the form that structure eventually took was what Jesus originally envisaged is impossible to say and would have been meaningless to his disciples, who could not possibly have thought that far ahead. But to conclude that Jesus never intended to found a church at all is surely going too far. The evidence points to a different conclusion, and we must follow it where it leads.

73. Matthew 20:20–28.

Another factor that has influenced modern perceptions has been the Catholic tendency to connect the incarnation of Christ with the church, which the apostle Paul described as Christ's "body." Paul's imagery is clearly symbolic when it is used in 1 Corinthians 12, for example, where it follows hard on the breaking of bread in worship, which is described in detail in the preceding chapter. This connection has been picked up by liturgists who have made a neat link between the bread used in Holy Communion, the "body of Christ" imagery in the epistles, and the idea that the church is in some sense the ongoing incarnation of the Son of God. On that reading, the idea that Jesus came into the world and left behind the church becomes more plausible, and variations of that theme have been found in devotional literature of a Catholic tendency.

The difficulty with that interpretation is that it is clear from the New Testament that the physical body of the resurrected Christ ascended into heaven, leaving nothing—not even a relic or two—behind. The church as we know it did not exist at that point; it only came into being ten days later when the Holy Spirit descended on the disciples at Pentecost. It is true that Jesus predicted this, and that before his departure he promised that he would send his Spirit to them, but this was not the same as staying behind himself, albeit in another form. If this is the model that a theologian has in mind when asking whether Jesus founded the church, then it is understandable that the answer will be negative. Jesus did found the church, but he did so in and through his Holy Spirit and not by leaving his body behind on earth. Once that is understood, there should be no difficulty in allowing the claim that Jesus was indeed the founder of the society that worships in his name and propagates his teachings.

2

The New Testament Church

From Disciples to Apostles

That the Christian church began shortly after the death and resurrection of Jesus is generally accepted, even if some skeptics doubt whether the events described in the Acts of the Apostles occurred in the way that the text says they did. There is no evidence that would support an alternative history, and regardless of what actually happened on the day of Pentecost, it is certain that there was a church in Jerusalem only a few years after Jesus's death. Those who challenge the traditional account of its origins have to explain how it could have emerged as soon as it did. How likely is it that a discouraged group of disciples, scattered and diminished by the events of the crucifixion, would have rallied behind a man like Peter and established a movement that would quickly gain a large following?

Extraordinary as the events recounted in Acts are, any alternative scenario is more implausible still. The disciples of Jesus had all run away when it looked as if their teacher would be eliminated, and there is no reason to suppose that they would have come together again only a few days later. They were strangers in Jerusalem and would have had no reason to stay there; indeed, the Gospels tell us that they went home to Galilee as soon as they could.[1]

1. Matthew 28:7, 10.

Only a very powerful countervailing factor could have overcome their natural desire to get back to normal (as they would have seen it), and that factor was the bodily resurrection of Jesus from the dead. When the disciples saw the risen Christ, all doubt vanished, and from then on they were committed to the mission of spreading the gospel that Jesus had entrusted to them. During the forty days that Jesus remained on earth after his resurrection, he reminded them of what he had taught and explained the deeper meaning of his life and death. He commissioned them for their future mission and told them to wait patiently at Jerusalem until the Holy Spirit should come and give them the power to accomplish it.[2] They were to suffer persecution, and many of them would meet violent deaths, but as far as we know they never wavered again, however tempting that may have been at times.

The change that came over Peter and his companions in the wake of Pentecost is borne out by the way they were perceived at the time and are still perceived today. To put it simply, those who had been disciples now became apostles. From being students who sat at Jesus's feet they were transformed into messengers sent to proclaim what they had been taught. Those who had merely absorbed his teaching now became teachers of others, charged with spreading the word of salvation to the ends of the earth. It was a radical transformation, and its implications took time to be fully absorbed. Of the twelve men whom Jesus had chosen, Judas Iscariot was clearly out of the picture. He had betrayed Jesus to his enemies, and when he was overcome with remorse for his evil deed, he went out and hanged himself. He was replaced as one of the Twelve by a certain Matthias, chosen by lot, of whom we know nothing other than that he had been with Jesus from the beginning of his ministry and had also witnessed the resurrection, two qualifications apparently considered essential for anyone who might be called to fill the role of an apostle.[3]

In the stories of Jesus's earthly ministry, Peter, James, and John stand out as a kind of inner circle of disciples. They followed Jesus everywhere and were especially close to him at key moments, such as his transfiguration. Most of the other disciples remain fairly shadowy figures, the only partial exception being Thomas, who initially doubted whether the resurrection could have happened and was not convinced until he put his hand into Jesus's wounds.[4] Jesus criticized Thomas for his unbelief, however, and we hear no more about him in the New Testament. Nevertheless, from the evidence we have, we can

2. Luke 24:44–49; Acts 1:1–14. See also Matthew 28:19–20; John 21:15–23.
3. Acts 1:15–26.
4. John 20:24–29.

say that all eleven of the remaining disciples were present in Jerusalem when the Holy Spirit fell upon them, and there is no reason to suppose that they did not participate fully in the work of preaching and evangelism that had been entrusted to them.[5] But once the day of Pentecost was over, we have little or no evidence about what most of them actually did. Nathanael and Matthew, for example, fade into obscurity, even though the First Gospel was attributed to the latter. Perhaps the James who was the author of a New Testament epistle was the same man as the James who accompanied Peter and John during Jesus's earthly ministry, but that is doubtful. There were many Jameses about, including two among the disciples of Jesus, so it is hard to know which is which.[6] John the "beloved disciple" is also known from the corpus of writings attributed to him, though whether he was the author of the Gospel, the three epistles, and the book of Revelation that together constitute the Johannine literature is uncertain and has been widely doubted, in both ancient and modern times.

The one man who unambiguously connects the disciples with the apostles is Peter.[7] We know far more about him as a follower of Jesus than we know about any of the others, though it must be said that the portrait is by no means a flattering one. There can be no doubt that the Peter who denied Jesus during his trial was the same man who took the lead on the day of Pentecost, and his restoration to grace figures prominently in the Fourth Gospel, though it is not mentioned in the other three.[8] Peter was clearly the leading figure in the early days of the church, though he had no authority greater than that of his fellow disciples turned apostles. For example, when he was mistaken he was rebuked by his colleagues, and there is no sign that this response was out of place.[9] Even in the Jerusalem church, he was *one* of the pillars of the establishment, as Paul expressed it, not the only one.[10] If Peter was the leader, he was still only the first among equals, not a superior who commanded and expected unquestioning loyalty from everyone around him.

5. Acts 1:13; 2:4.

6. The most likely candidate for the authorship of the epistle is James the Just, who was a half-brother of Jesus and Peter's successor as the leader of the Jerusalem church, though this can only be a conjecture. See Acts 12:17; 15:13–21; 21:17–26.

7. See M. Bockmuehl, *Simon Peter in Scripture and Memory: The New Testament Apostle in the Early Church* (Grand Rapids: Baker Academic, 2012), for a recent survey of the evidence for Peter and his ministry.

8. John 21:15–19.

9. Galatians 2:11–14. Contrast Paul's willingness to contest Peter's attitude with the deference he felt he owed to the Jewish high priest (Acts 23:2–5). Ananias enjoyed a status that Peter did not have.

10. James and John shared this distinction with him. See Galatians 2:9.

Peter never lost his importance as a central figure in the church, but it seems that in later years he was overshadowed by Paul and faded somewhat into the background. His literary output was not great, being confined to two short epistles (though the authenticity of the second one has been widely questioned). Perhaps he was also the true author of the Second Gospel, which, according to the second-century church historian Papias, is an account of the memoirs that he dictated to Mark.[11] How and where he died is uncertain, though the last chapter of John's Gospel suggests that he was crucified (according to legend, upside down), and an ancient tradition locates his burial place in Rome.[12] Beyond that, we know nothing with any degree of certainty.

This has to be said because one of the most enduring and intractable controversies in the church concerns Peter and the nature of the commission he received from Jesus. Theologians argue over the exact meaning of Matthew 16:18—did Jesus mean that Peter was to be the foundation stone of the church, or was it Peter's confession of faith on which the believing community would be built? As we have already seen, scholars tend to look at the matter differently. For them the real question is whether Jesus said anything like this at all, and most of them incline to the view that it was a later interpolation designed to bolster a notion of the "Petrine primacy" of Rome that was gradually emerging in the early church. What can we legitimately say about this?

First of all, there can be no doubt that the Roman church, even if Peter was its first "bishop," did not enjoy the kind of primacy in the Christian world that later popes would claim for it, using Peter's confession as their justification for doing so. As the capital of the empire, Rome was always accorded a position of prominence, and after Christianity became the state religion it was granted the seniority among the churches of the Roman world that seemed appropriate for the old imperial capital, but there was never any suggestion that its bishops were the arbiters of Christian doctrine. Not one of the ancient councils summoned to resolve doctrinal conflicts met in Rome, nor was its bishop present at any of them. A case can be made for saying that at the Council of Chalcedon in AD 451 it was Pope Leo I's *Tome*, composed for the occasion and sent via messengers to be read out to the assembled delegates, that persuaded the bishops to accept his understanding of the person and natures of Christ. But if that is true, they did so on the strength of his argument, not because Leo was the head of the primary see in Christendom with a corresponding right to determine its doctrine on his own authority.

11. Eusebius of Caesarea, *Historia ecclesiastica* 3.39.15.
12. For the current state of scholarly opinion on this, see Bockmuehl, *Simon Peter*, 148–49, who concludes that while Peter *may* be buried under the Vatican, this cannot be regarded as certain.

The Roman church appears from time to time in the New Testament—in the famous epistle that Paul wrote to it around AD 57, in the closing chapters of Acts, and probably also in the oblique reference to "Babylon" that we find in 1 Peter 5:13. But apart from the last of these, which is obscure, there is no sign that Peter was in the city when the first church was founded there, and certainly no indication that he was ever its head. Particularly telling in this respect is the fact that when Paul wrote to the Roman church he made no mention of Peter at all, which seems strange if Peter were its head, especially as Paul sent greetings to a large number of less prominent people.[13]

In fact, scholars increasingly believe that the Roman church did not have a single head until well into the second century—the list of popes that is officially accepted is regarded by almost everyone today as legendary at best.[14] The notion that the current pope is Peter's successor and therefore entitled to all the honors and privileges that attached to the original head of the church is a myth that was elaborated in the Middle Ages and canonized in the nineteenth century with the proclamation of papal infallibility in 1870. It has had a powerful impact and remains an important factor in the life of the modern church, which cannot be reunited until the issue of Petrine primacy is resolved, but a myth it is nevertheless, and it is hard to see how real progress toward the reunion of the churches can be made unless and until that is recognized on all sides.

The question surrounding Peter is only the extreme example of something that affects the entire body of disciples turned apostles. Apart from legends and traditions that have been handed down with greater or lesser veracity, we know virtually nothing about which apostles led which churches. Was John the bishop of Smyrna or Ephesus at some point? Did Mark establish a Christian community in Alexandria, as was later believed? Did Thomas go to India, as legend has it? We do not know the answers to such questions. What we *can* say is that the first Christian churches were not spontaneous gatherings of believers who then formed an association to secure and perpetuate their convictions. On the contrary, they were established by particular individuals who were either apostles themselves or men acting as their delegates, as Titus did in Crete.[15] Rome is perhaps an exception to this, because people from all over the empire made their way there, and it is quite possible that individual Christians did so long before any apostle visited the city. But if that was the

---

13. See Romans 16:3–15.

14. It should be said that the term "pope," though now reserved in the West for the bishop of Rome, could be applied in ancient times to the head of any church and is still commonly used in the East to designate any parish priest.

15. Titus 1:5.

case, it is the exception that proves the rule, because nowhere else do we come across a church that emerged more or less spontaneously.

The planting of Christian congregations across the world started after Pentecost and seems to have had little to do with anything that had gone before. This is particularly striking when we consider what happened to people who appear in the Gospels but are seldom if ever mentioned in the early church. Jesus was friendly with Mary, Martha, and Lazarus in Bethany, but were they later leaders in the church? There is no mention of them in that capacity. The same must be said of everybody else Jesus came across, including his own mother, Mary. The thousands to whom he preached and ministered—what happened to them? We do not know. We tend to assume that most of them joined the church (the law of averages would suggest that at least some of them did), but there is no evidence to support this assumption—it is all speculation. There is certainly nothing to suggest that people who knew Jesus personally or who were related to him enjoyed a special status for that reason—rather the reverse.[16] This has some significance for debates in the modern church, because those who advocate the ordination of women sometimes point to Jesus as one who gave women special consideration. It has even been suggested that Mary Magdalene was an apostle who in some sense was senior to Peter and John, because after his resurrection, Jesus appeared first to her and asked her to communicate the good news to the disciples.

In this case, the bare facts are indisputable, but there is no reason to suppose that Mary acquired any special standing in the church as a result. There is no sign that she ever exercised any sort of apostolic ministry, and until very recently, no one ever suggested that she did. Unfortunately, claims of this kind must be regarded as special pleading in the interest of modern church politics and have nothing to do with the actual evidence. Another example of this kind of abuse comes from Romans 16. When Paul wrote to the Roman church, he mentioned Andronicus and Junia, his kin and fellow prisoners (as he describes them) who were well known to the apostles and had become Christians before him.[17] But this did not give them any seniority in the church; presumably they had to listen to Paul's preaching and accept his authority along with everyone else he wrote to. The notion that today a woman can be ordained and minister in the church because Junia was an apostle is an unwarranted interpretation of the evidence, propagated by those who want to believe it rather than by those who are persuaded by facts alone.

16. See Matthew 12:46–50.
17. Romans 16:7.

As far as the other apostles and the churches they founded are concerned, we know so little about them that it is impossible to draw any firm conclusions. There is a widespread belief today that there was a Johannine group of churches based in Ephesus, which was quite independent of the Pauline mission but later merged with it. Some people also believe that there was a Matthean community at Antioch to which the first Gospel was addressed. The truth is that there is no evidence to prove or disprove theories like these. We know that Paul did not want to preach the gospel in places where it had already been taken by someone else, which suggests that if a Pauline and a Johannine community coexisted in the same city (Ephesus?), the former had probably arrived first.[18] We also know that Paul was deeply opposed to rivalries based on adherence to particular apostles and teachers, because he insisted that there was only one head of the church—Jesus Christ.[19] Furthermore, experience suggests that once divisions occur they usually become wider and deeper as time goes on. There is very little evidence of competing groups coming together and burying the hatchet so completely that future generations are unaware that such differences ever existed. The weight of probability argues against such theories, but they remain firmly entrenched in New Testament scholarship and so far have proved impossible to dislodge. Perhaps the best conclusion here is to suggest that our ignorance of what the apostles did is such that we are not meant to look to them to provide authoritative models for church life today. They did what they did, but we are not expected to follow their pattern, of which we have little knowledge and no experience.

Having said that, the church has always claimed that it is built on the foundation of the prophets and apostles.[20] Apostolicity has traditionally been regarded as one of its hallmarks, and Paul felt obliged to defend his own qualifications to be an apostle. There were rival teachers who apparently claimed the title for themselves but whom the New Testament writers refer to only as "false apostles."[21] What is apostolicity, where (or in whom) is it located, and how do we recognize it?

In Paul's defense of his own apostolic ministry, we learn that there were two essential criteria for being an apostle. The first was that the individual must have been called by God; the second was that he must have seen the risen Christ. There were plenty of people who had seen Jesus after his resurrection

18. 2 Corinthians 10:16.
19. 1 Corinthians 1:10–17.
20. Ephesians 2:20.
21. 2 Corinthians 11:13. See also 2 Peter 2:1, which speaks of "false teachers" and "false prophets."

but who were not apostles, perhaps as many as six hundred in all.[22] It was therefore not enough merely to have seen Jesus after he came back from the dead. It was also necessary to have received a calling to that ministry, which was only given to people who met the other criterion as well. Paul knew that he was exceptional because he had not been a disciple of Jesus and had even persecuted the church before his conversion, but he attributed his apostolic calling to a special act of God's grace that he did not deserve and that had not been given to anyone else.[23] Following this logic, the apostles and their ministry died out in the first generation, and there can be none today, although the papacy and some small Protestant groups have claimed to preserve the office in their different ways. The pope is regarded by his followers as the living successor of Peter, complete with the prerogatives of his apostolic ministry, and some Protestant pastors have claimed the title for themselves, but this way of thinking was alien to the early church. Paul instructed Timothy and Titus about how they were to carry on his ministry once he was gone, but he did not suggest that they would become apostles in his place, and there is no sign of an apostolic succession anywhere else either.

The disappearance of the apostles and their active ministry does not mean that apostolicity has ceased to have a bearing on the life of the church, however. It was the duty of the apostles to transmit the teaching of Jesus to other believers, not just because they had been witnesses to his earthly ministry but because after his resurrection he gave them a special charge to that effect.[24] As long as they were alive, local churches could appeal to them for guidance, as we know the Corinthians did when they wrote to Paul about various matters that were troubling their church. After the apostles' deaths, their writings, along with the writings of others who worked closely with them and in some sense under their supervision, were collected together in what became the New Testament. Practically speaking, the authority of the apostles nowadays is the witness of the New Testament, which remains foundational for Christian doctrine.

No doubt there was a great deal going on in the early church that has not been recorded for us—John's Gospel tells us as much.[25] But what was not written down has no lasting authority for us today because its apostolicity cannot be demonstrated. For example, it has long been the tradition to sign a new Christian with the sign of the cross at his or her baptism, and that practice may go back to the apostles themselves. It is certainly very ancient,

22. See 1 Corinthians 15:5–8.
23. 1 Corinthians 15:8–11; 2 Corinthians 11:1–33; Galatians 1:11–17.
24. Matthew 28:19–20.
25. John 21:25.

and there is nothing wrong with it, but it cannot claim the authority that something specifically recorded in the Scriptures can. Admittedly, in some cases it can be difficult to decide what the New Testament actually records. For example, in 1 Corinthians 11 Paul explains in some detail how to conduct a Communion service but gives no indication of who should preside over it. There must have been somebody in charge, and logic would suggest that this person was the head of the local church. But we do not know for sure that it was he who presided at the celebration, still less that he was the only one who was allowed to do so. That development, however natural it may seem to us now, came later and therefore does not enjoy the authority that attaches to the words of institution themselves, which are found in the biblical text. In other words, the doctrine and structure of Holy Communion are clearly set out in Scripture, but the identity of its president (or celebrant) is left undetermined. Individual churches have to decide what to do about this, but whatever solution they adopt, they cannot claim that it has the same biblical warrant that the ceremony itself enjoys.

If we look at the New Testament, we can see that the books contained in it tend to be associated one way or another with Peter and John (among the disciples of Jesus) or with Paul. The breakdown is as follows:

Peter	John	Paul
1 Peter	John	13 signed epistles
2 Peter	1 John	Luke
Mark	2 John	Acts
(Jude)	3 John	(Hebrews)
(Matthew)	Revelation	
(James)		

Scholars debate the precise authorship of some of these books, but their arguments are speculative and secondary to the church's understanding of its tradition. When it came to deciding which books should be included in the New Testament canon and which should not, it was the above pattern that won the day and that we have inherited. Only three books, two of them of considerable importance, do not fit readily into the above scheme. Matthew has no obvious connection with Peter, but since it seems to be an elaboration of Mark and contains references to Peter that are not found elsewhere, it belongs most naturally with him. Jude was the brother of James, and modern scholarship has detected links with 2 Peter. Hebrews is anonymous, and even in ancient times there was considerable speculation about it. Apollos is perhaps the most likely author, but whoever it was, there are clear connections with the Pauline circle out of which it almost certainly emerged.[26] So likely is this that Paul was regarded as the author in later times, though this is no longer widely accepted today.

The formation of the canon took time, and there was some debate over certain books, but although some scholars make much of this, their hesitations can be greatly overdone. What we know for sure is that a substantial core of books was universally accepted as canonical. Differences of opinion were confined either to a recognized subset of letters (the four minor Catholic, or General, Epistles) or to books whose authorship was unknown or disputed (Hebrews, Revelation).[27] We can also say that there is no evidence to suggest that books that do not form part of the present canon were ever accepted as authoritative by any significant number of Christians. Even a work such as *The Shepherd of Hermas*, though it is appended to some important codices of the New Testament, never attained canonical status in the church. Whoever Hermas was, he was not an apostle, nor was he closely associated with one, so his book, however popular and useful it may have been, was decisively rejected.

One tricky aspect of apostolicity is that it is not altogether clear whether it was a gift given to individuals who could then exercise it on their own, or whether it was something that could only be applied collectively. That there were at least twelve apostles is clear, but did they have to act in concert for their decisions to be valid? What if one apostle differed from another?

In the very early days of the church there is no sign of any disagreement among the apostles, and the impression we get is that they acted together, even if Peter was usually their spokesman. Later on, Paul struck out on his own and felt no need to report back to the other apostles, because as he explained to the Galatians, he had received his commission not from them but directly from God himself.[28] His independence even extended to writing to churches that he had neither founded nor visited, Rome being the obvious example. Paul evidently took it for granted that his advice was appropriate and would be heeded, even though he had no personal connection with the church to which he was writing.

The only occasion on which we see the apostles conferring together in order to resolve a disagreement occurs in Acts 15, over the issue of admitting gentile converts to full membership in the church. In that case we find that a collective decision was made that allowed for some compromise in the

26. See G. L. Cockerill, *The Epistle to the Hebrews* (Grand Rapids: Eerdmans, 2012), 6–10, for a recent review of the question of its authorship, which comes down in favor of Apollos.

27. The standard authority for this subject is B. M. Metzger, *The Canon of the New Testament: Its Origin, Development, and Significance* (Oxford: Oxford University Press, 1987).

28. Galatians 1:11–17.

direction of soothing sensitive Jewish consciences; on the main issue, however, Paul's insistence on admitting gentiles was ratified, and his rebuke of Peter's anti-gentile behavior in Antioch was upheld (see Gal. 2:11–14). The consensus held, and the issue never again divided the church, though it would probably be true to say that the concessions to Jewish sensitivities were not widely applied and disappeared from view fairly quickly.

As far as applying the notion of apostolic consensus to the church today is concerned, the only way to do this consistently is to look for the common teaching of the New Testament. If we interpret one text in a way that makes it conflict with another, we are dividing the apostolic witness and creating division where there should be none. If that happens, we should conclude that we have either misunderstood the text or are misapplying it, and moderate our stance accordingly.

The Organization of the Church

Tied to the question of apostolicity, but even more controversial, is that of church organization. How did the first Christian congregations operate? Were they independent of one another, or did they belong to an umbrella structure to which they had to conform in matters of doctrine, if not always in questions of liturgical or pastoral practice? For over a thousand years, these questions were seldom (if ever) raised; it was simply taken for granted that the medieval church was the direct and legitimate offspring of the New Testament one. Painters of the time did not hesitate to clothe the apostles in medieval dress or to portray Peter as if he were the pope they themselves knew. There was only a very weak sense of historical development, and it was largely confined to the expansion of the Christian mission. But even there, horizons were limited. The British, for example, came to believe that Joseph of Arimathea had brought the gospel to them very soon after the resurrection of Christ, so that Britain heard the good news almost as quickly as the countries mentioned in the New Testament. In that way the medieval church in England could claim a direct link to the apostles and equality with the ancient churches of the Mediterranean world.

It was only during the sixteenth-century Reformation that this indifference to history was challenged, partly because Protestants could not accept the claims being made by the Roman papacy and partly because, when they looked to the New Testament to determine how a church should be governed, they realized that it was very different from the one they actually knew. However, they ascribed the changes not to natural developments over time but to the corruption of external influences and human sinfulness. They believed that if these were removed, a pure church, reflecting the New Testament pattern, could be restored. Unfortunately, in attempting to recover this lost ideal they came up with widely different conceptions of what it actually was. The end result was that the Protestant churches were permanently divided into different (and often hostile) camps that evolved into distinct denominational "traditions" that are often harder to overcome than the corruptions they were originally trying to correct. How is it possible that people who are equally committed to the scriptural evidence have emerged with such radically different and seemingly incompatible conclusions?

Various answers to this question can be given, but they are all based on one fundamental fact—the evidence of the New Testament is not sufficiently detailed to allow us to re-create an authentically "biblical" church to the exclusion of any alternative. It may have been the case that individual congregations were organized along different lines, but we do not have enough details to be able to compare one with another. It may also be that many of the churches lacked any fixed organization. Perhaps they operated on a fairly ad hoc basis, with little sense that there was only one right way of doing things. There may even have been, as some modern commentators have suggested, different (rival?) groups that operated independently and did not have much to do with one another.

The root of the problem we face in trying to assess the evidence is that the New Testament never gives us a detailed outline of the way any particular congregation was structured. We do not know how Christians in Corinth, for example, organized their common life, and Corinth is one of the better-documented churches. Paul tells us that "Chloe's people" have informed him that there are divisions in the church there, but who were these people?[29] Most likely, Chloe was like Lydia or Priscilla and Aquila, who had a congregation meeting in their house, but what conclusions can we draw from that?[30] Her people, whoever they were, were clearly not cut off from other Christians in Corinth, because if they were, they would presumably have been unconcerned with divisions in the church that did not affect them. They must have been participants in some wider network, but where that was based and who supervised it, we cannot say. Paul does not tell us to whom his letters were sent, but it is obvious that they must have gone to someone who could be trusted to make the right use of them.

In the case of Corinth, Paul tells us that three members of the church there—Stephanas, Fortunatus, and Achaicus—are visiting him in Ephesus at

29. 1 Corinthians 1:11.
30. For Lydia, see Acts 16:40; for Priscilla and Aquila, see 1 Corinthians 16:19.

the time and presumably staying with him in the house of Priscilla and Aquila (who came there from Corinth themselves), where a congregation also meets, and that Stephanas was the first convert in Achaia.[31] We can perhaps assume that the three visitors took Paul's letter back home with them, but we have no idea what standing they had in the Corinthian church, if any.

For most of the other churches, including the one in Rome, we know next to nothing. We can guess that Paul's Letter to the Romans was taken there by Phoebe, who is described as a deaconess of the church at Cenchreae (one of the ports of Corinth), but where did she deliver it when she arrived?[32] Priscilla and Aquila turn up again, this time in the city from which they were expelled in AD 49, and we may perhaps assume that they were Paul's immediate contacts there.[33] But as far as we know, neither they nor anyone else whom Paul names in the last chapter of his letter had any official standing in the local church, and there is no sign that Paul acknowledged any such structure of authority. Yet the letter's contents imply a functioning organization with which Paul wanted to connect in order to use Rome as a base for evangelizing Spain. He also knew that there were internal tensions in the congregation between Jewish and gentile Christians, but they had not split into separate groups. What prevented them from going their separate ways? Was there a leadership that was holding them together in spite of their differences and that Paul was trying to encourage? We do not know. We have his letter as evidence that there was a large Christian community in the imperial capital, but that is all.

In Rome as elsewhere, there must have been somebody who coordinated the church's meetings, but we do not know who that was or what exactly that person did. Given that most of the early churches met in houses, it would seem natural that the head of the house organized these gatherings, but what authority he or she may have had is unknown. This is an important question today, because we know that the head of the house could be a woman like Lydia or Chloe. Did this mean that the local church could be under female headship of some kind, or did these women merely offer their residences as a venue for the churches to meet? We do not know.

What the New Testament tells us is that originally the apostles governed the church in Jerusalem. They did the preaching and ran the daily administration. Soon, however, the church found itself having to minister to the poor, the elderly, widows, and others in social need who were members of the congregation. The apostles found it impossible to do that and to preach the gospel

31. 1 Corinthians 16:15–19.
32. Romans 16:1–2.
33. Romans 16:3–4; Acts 18:2.

at the same time, so when complaints about inefficiency started to surface, they decided to divide their responsibilities by asking church members to elect "seven men of good repute" to serve as *diakonoi* (deacons or ministers) who would take care of these administrative and charitable needs. Once elected, the *diakonoi* had hands laid on them in a ceremony analogous to what we would now call "ordination."[34] But although they were appointed to a specific task, the lines between them and the apostles were blurred at times. For example, Stephen, the first martyr, preached the gospel even though he was a deacon, and the same was true of Philip.[35] On the other hand, Paul spent much of his time coordinating a relief effort for the poor churches of Judaea, a task that would theoretically have fallen on the *diakonoi*, assuming that the Jerusalem pattern was copied elsewhere, which we do not know.[36] The evidence for a clearly defined diaconal ministry is therefore ambiguous and inconclusive, and the hard-and-fast distinctions that were made in later times were almost certainly unknown to the first generation of Christians.

It has long been assumed that the early churches had elders (*presbyteroi*) who exercised a collective leadership over them and that this system of government had been taken over from the practice of the synagogue. That is possible, but the evidence that the synagogues had an eldership comparable to the Christian one is unsatisfactory. No doubt a certain respect was accorded to older people in the synagogues, and they probably had a good deal of say in what went on, but this was not a formalized office.[37] On the other hand, we know that there were elders in Jerusalem who worked alongside the priests, though what they did is not entirely clear.[38] They were obviously part of the Jewish establishment and were neither priests nor scribes, so we are left to suppose that they exercised a judicial and administrative role, a conclusion that fits the contexts in which they are mentioned. Whether they served as a model for the early church is impossible to say, though their existence suggests that the first Christians would not have been surprised by the appearance of somewhat similar elders in the church. Who created them, however, and in what circumstances is not known.

34. Acts 6:6.
35. Both men were appointed together; see Acts 6:5. Stephen's ministry is mentioned in Acts 6:8, and Philip's in Acts 8:26–40.
36. 2 Corinthians 9:1–15.
37. For the nature of the evidence, see R. Beckwith, *Elders in Every City: The Origin and Role of the Ordained Ministry* (Carlisle: Paternoster, 2003), 28–41. The concept of a Jewish eldership as the prototype of its Christian equivalent has recently been examined and comprehensively rejected by A. C. Stewart, *The Original Bishops: Office and Order in the First Christian Communities* (Grand Rapids: Baker Academic, 2014), 121–34.
38. Acts 4:5, 8, 23; 6:12; 23:14; 24:1; 25:15.

The first mention of Christian elders occurs in the context of famine relief. The prophet Agabus had gone to Antioch to tell the Christians there about the sufferings of their brothers at Jerusalem, and in response to his pleas, they sent relief to the elders of the afflicted community.[39] We can assume from the context that these elders were the appropriate people to receive such funds, which suggests that they had an administrative role not unlike that of the deacons, but we know no more about them than that. Elders next appear in the course of Paul's first missionary journey to Galatia. After establishing congregations in Antioch, Iconium, and Lystra, Paul and Barnabas retraced their steps, encouraging the new converts and appointing "elders for them in every church."[40] There is nothing to suggest that this was a novelty, and we know nothing about who they were or what they did. Their theological education must have been very rudimentary, because we know that soon after Paul's departure the Galatian churches fell for the teaching of Judaizers who had come along to tell them that they had to be circumcised and keep the law of Moses in order to be true Christians.[41]

That the appointment of elders in Galatia was not a unique occurrence is clear from what is said elsewhere in Acts. After Paul went to Jerusalem to sort out the problems raised by the Galatian mission, we are told that the decisions reached were to be communicated to the churches by men appointed by the apostles and elders, along with the rest of the congregation at Jerusalem.[42] We do not know what the elders did, but it would seem from the way they are mentioned that they had a special place in the church. They were neither apostles nor deacons, but they exercised an authority associated with that of the apostles and apparently equal to theirs. Certainly when the letters were delivered, they were noted as coming from both the apostles and the elders at Jerusalem, a statement that apparently gave the decisions they contained added weight.[43] We also know what happened when Paul stopped over at Miletus, on his way to Jerusalem. While waiting for his ship to sail, he sent word to Ephesus, asking the elders of the church there to come to him, which they duly did.[44] That the elders of the church exercised a spiritual role is clear from what James says about the procedure to be followed in the anointing of the sick, which was to be performed by them.[45]

39. Acts 11:30.
40. Acts 14:23.
41. Galatians 1:6–7.
42. Acts 15:22.
43. Acts 16:4.
44. Acts 20:17.
45. James 5:14.

Who were these elders? Were they simply senior members of the congregation, who had no formal authority but whose views were treated with the respect normally accorded to older people in Jewish society? Or were they responsible leaders who had been chosen or appointed (how and by whom?) to lead the church? Quite possibly they were a combination of both. It would have made perfect sense for the apostles to have given formal recognition to people whose seniority would have made others defer to them anyway, though it seems unlikely that age could have been the only criterion for the eldership. Timothy was commissioned by Paul to fulfill a role that gave him authority over elders, despite his evident youth, though Paul realized that this might cause a problem in some circumstances.[46]

That local churches ought to have elders is made clear in the Pastoral Epistles, though many modern scholars take this as evidence that they are postapostolic in date. Paul sent Titus to Crete with a commission to appoint elders in every city, though once again, this directive raises as many questions as it answers.[47] Was Titus supposed to appoint one elder per congregation? How did the selection process operate? The Jerusalem church had elected its first deacons, but that does not seem to have been the case in Crete, even though the criteria for determining acceptable candidates seem to have been similar. The Jerusalem deacons had to be men of good repute, and what this meant was spelled out very clearly in the Pastorals.[48] An elder had to be above reproach, which in practical terms meant that he had to be monogamous and his children had to be believers who could not be accused of rebelliousness. As a man, he had to be humble, even-tempered, sober, peaceable, and generous. Hospitality and self-discipline were essential. Above all, he had to be able to teach sound doctrine and rebuke those who rejected it. This was a tall order, because it demanded a familiarity with Christian teachings that few villagers would have possessed. How realistic was it to expect Titus to find such men? In the circumstances, he would have done well to come across even one such person in any given church, and it may be that he often had little choice but to appoint whoever was available. In the smaller places especially, that may have led to putting one man in charge of the church, not by design but of necessity. Again, we do not know.

In historical terms, the biggest question about the elders is whether (or to what extent) they were also "overseers" (*episkopoi*). For many centuries it

46. 1 Timothy 4:12. A similar problem occurred later on in the Magnesian church. See Ignatius of Antioch, *Ad Magnesios* 3.

47. Titus 1:5.

48. Titus 1:5–9. See also 1 Timothy 3:1–7, which gives essentially the same qualifications for an "overseer" (*episkopos*).

was assumed that the New Testament *episkopoi* were identical to the bishops of later times and that the elders (*presbyteroi*) belonged to a lower order of "priests."[49] This interpretation was challenged at the time of the Reformation, on the ground that the words seemed to be interchangeable. Commenting on Titus 1:7, John Calvin wrote:

> This passage plainly shows that there is no difference between a presbyter and a bishop, for he [Paul] now freely applies the second title to those he has formally called presbyters, and in discussing this subject he uses both names indiscriminately with the same meaning, as Jerome has also noted in his commentary on this passage.[50]

This view became a hallmark of presbyterian polity and was rejected by traditionalists who preferred an episcopalian church structure, but in the nineteenth century Calvin's observation was confirmed by the Anglican scholar (and later bishop) J. B. Lightfoot, since which time it has become the established scholarly orthodoxy.[51] Lightfoot believed that the presbyterate and the episcopate became distinct offices at a later stage, when the presbyters chose one of their number as their leader. An alternative scenario was put forward by K. E. Kirk, who thought that presbyters were derived from the apostles and bishops, who appointed them as their assistants.[52] A third suggestion, made recently by Alistair Stewart, is that each congregation originally had an *episkopos* and that these *episkopoi* banded together to elect a *presbyteros* to oversee them.[53] That would explain why John could call himself an "elder" (*presbyteros*), when he was clearly an overseer with a commission that extended well beyond the limits of a single congregation.[54] Only later was the terminology reversed, and *presbyteroi* became bishops overseeing local *episkopoi*, who were then rebranded as *presbyteroi*. It is a conclusion that seems far-fetched

49. The word "bishop" is a corruption of *episkopos*, but the origin of the word "priest" is less clear. It may derive from *presbyteros*, but more likely it comes from the Latin *praepositus* (overseer), which confuses the issue still further. It should be noted that the use of "priest" to denote a person who offers a sacrifice is an extension of the word to translate the Greek *hiereus* (Latin: *sacerdos*), for which there is no true English equivalent.

50. J. Calvin, *Commentary on Titus*, trans. T. A. Smail, ed. D. W. Torrance and T. F. Torrance (Edinburgh: Oliver & Boyd, 1964), 359. Note that Calvin was merely repeating an observation made by Jerome but overlooked for more than a thousand years.

51. J. B. Lightfoot, *The Christian Ministry* (London: Macmillan, 1901), a reprint of a tract that originally appeared as part of his 1868 commentary on Philippians.

52. K. E. Kirk, *The Apostolic Ministry* (London: Hodder & Stoughton, 1946).

53. Stewart, *Original Bishops*, 144–85.

54. 2 John 1; 3 John 1.

and relies on special pleading, but the fact that it could be proposed at all shows how difficult it is to make sense of the data available to us.

Lightfoot's view has been challenged and modified to some extent, but it has not been overturned. If there was a difference between elders and bishops in the New Testament church, it was that an individual congregation might have had several *presbyteroi* but never more than one *episkopos*, whose duties of oversight would probably have made it necessary for only one person to be in charge. Whether that *episkopos* was also a *presbyteros* is probable but not certain, and there may have been exceptions. Certainly there is no sign that an *episkopos* was superior to a *presbyteros*; their duties overlapped, and they worked together as far as we can tell. On the other hand, all the indications are that the apostles identified themselves more readily with the *presbyteroi* than with anyone else. Not only did John use the designation of himself, but so did Peter.[55] As long as the apostles were alive there was no need to define other ministries too precisely, but after their departure someone had to take over the church's leadership. It was probably at that point that the *episkopoi* stepped into their shoes as far as they could and represented the interests of the church in different congregations and to the wider Christian world, but in the nature of the case, that was a postbiblical development.

As far as public worship was concerned, the first Christian churches appear to have allowed a lot of what we would now call "audience participation." Indeed, it was because this kind of spontaneity had got out of hand in the Corinthian church that Paul felt obliged to try to rein it in. He did not forbid it outright, which is important to note, but he laid down certain ground rules that someone would have had to administer.[56] Who? That we do not know. Paul also advised that women should not speak in the church, which suggests that it was happening and causing problems.[57] Many commentators have tried to maintain that the prohibition was not Pauline but came from a later time, while others have suggested that it was purely practical in nature—women who were educated and responsible would presumably have known how to behave in public and so would not have been subject to such restrictions. But these attempts to explain away the ban on women ignore the fact that the biblical text gives theological reasons for it: the priority of the male in the created order and the fact that it was the woman who led the man into sin, not the other way around. The practice of the early church was therefore determined not by prejudice but by principle, a

55. 1 Peter 5:1.
56. See 1 Corinthians 12, 14.
57. 1 Timothy 2:11–15.

fact that too many modern commentators, eager to promote the ministry of women, prefer to overlook.

How organized early Christian worship was is equally unclear. Christian congregations sang psalms, hymns, and spiritual songs, but did they do so a cappella or with musical accompaniment? Most likely it was a cappella, but as with so much else, we have no way of knowing for sure, and there was certainly no ban on the use of musical instruments. Presumably they also prayed, but apart from the Lord's Prayer, which may have been in regular use as early as the late first century, it is impossible to know what form their prayer took.[58] Was it liturgical in the later sense, or extempore, according to the inspiration of the individual praying, as the speaking in tongues of the Corinthian congregation would suggest? Or maybe both forms of prayer co-existed? Was there a sermon, and if so, what was it based on and how central was it to the worship service? Was it exegetical, thematic, evangelistic—or what? We know that congregations met to share the Lord's Supper together, but although Paul gave some fairly detailed instructions about how this should be conducted, there are still many questions.[59] We do not know who presided, how often it was celebrated, or even whether it formed part of a wider meal, as it obviously did at the Last Supper.

We do not even know at what times Christians gathered together for worship. They may have done so most regularly on the "Lord's day," which corresponds to Sunday, the day of Christ's resurrection.[60] But, of course, Sunday was not a public holiday, and many people may not have been free to join in then. In some places it appears that the church met daily and lived a semicommunal life, though that diminished fairly quickly as the problems it caused became evident. They probably met early in the morning or at night, partly because those were times of relative relaxation, and once persecution began, it would have been harder to detect Christians in the dark. But even here we are reduced to speculation—we simply do not know what happened on a regular basis. There must have been some consensus, since otherwise the church would not have met at all. There must also have been some way for believers to connect with one another—could a Christian have gone to Ephesus, for example, and lived there indefinitely without having any contact with (or even knowledge of the existence of) the local church? The evidence suggests that this was not the case: Paul knew to whom he was writing at Rome (though

58. Regular use of the Lord's Prayer is enjoined in the *Didache*, which can be dated to the late first century and is probably the oldest nonbiblical Christian text.

59. See 1 Corinthians 11:17–34.

60. This use of the term the "Lord's day" can be found in the New Testament; see Revelation 1:10.

he does not specifically tell us), and when he went there himself, somebody found out in advance and a delegation met him after he landed at Puteoli.[61] Who took responsibility for this?

Our ignorance of details like these must make us cautious. People in ancient times were not worried—they obviously had experience of such things and could guess what was happening in a way that we now find difficult to imagine. But that some kind of organization was in place, and that it was functioning with a high degree of efficiency, can hardly be doubted. We have to remember that Paul wrote most of his epistles to places where problems had arisen, and this fact may be distorting our perception of the church as a whole. There were many congregations that apparently did not have the kind of troubles that plagued Corinth. Does that mean that Corinth was exceptional? Or merely that we are ignorant of the difficulties that occurred elsewhere but have not been recorded?

The fact that we have no answers to such questions must make us pause when trying to use the New Testament church as a model for our common life today. There may be some things, such as the need for oversight and orderly worship, that can legitimately be deduced from the available sources, and we must try to make sure that they are applied to modern church life. But we should also have the humility to admit that it is impossible, on the basis of what we know, to build a complete church structure out of the evidence we have—at some point, even the most slavishly literalist interpreters of the New Testament are forced to supplement what it says if their church is going to function properly. It may be possible to have a church today that is faithful to the principles of the New Testament, but not one that reproduces an early Christian congregation with any degree of accuracy. The data needed to ensure that are simply not available.

The Mission of the Church

Whatever the pattern of its ministry may have been, and however its worship and organization were structured, there is general agreement that the church's primary goal was spreading the gospel to the ends of the earth. This was part of the Great Commission that Jesus gave to his disciples, and it very quickly established itself, not only as a major preoccupation in itself, but also as one of the most important ways in which the church was different from the synagogue. Modern research has shown that Jews were more open to proselytism

61. Acts 28:15.

in ancient times than they later became, but even so, it was hardly one of their top priorities. For Christians, however, preaching the gospel to those who had not heard it, but who were now being called by God to repent and enter into a new life, was an all-consuming interest. The word *apostolos* itself means "one who is sent," and the missionary impulse was central to the church from the start. Shortly before his ascension into heaven, Jesus had told his disciples to preach the gospel, beginning at Jerusalem and spreading out across Judaea and Samaria, and from there to the ends of the earth.[62] They were to baptize the nations in the name of the Father, Son, and Holy Spirit and teach them the way of salvation.[63]

Some scholars have regarded these last words of Jesus as a later reconstruction by Christians anxious to project their own activities back onto him, but such skepticism is belied by the facts. Peter's Pentecost sermon reached pilgrims from many parts of the world, and it must be assumed that at least some of them took the message, and their own new adherence to the church, back to where they had come from. If that was the case, then that first evangelistic outreach laid the foundation for the emergence of Christian communities in places that were far from Palestine, long before any apostle could have reached them. What is certain is that the mission to Judaea and Samaria got under way almost immediately. We also know that there was a Christian group in Damascus within a few years, because it was while he was on his way to persecute it that Saul of Tarsus was suddenly converted.[64]

Central to the church's mission was the act of baptism, which was given by the apostles to those who made a profession of faith.[65] Baptism had already figured in the preaching of John the Baptist and in the earthly ministry of Jesus, and there is no indication that those who had been baptized then had to be rebaptized after Pentecost, although the rebaptism of such people was practiced at a later stage.[66] It was expected that this baptism would be accompanied by the descent of the Holy Spirit, marked especially by an outbreak of speaking in tongues, though the two things were not necessarily connected.

---

62. Acts 1:8.

63. Matthew 28:19–20.

64. Acts 9:2.

65. The definitive work on this subject is now E. Ferguson, *Baptism in the Early Church: History, Theology, and Liturgy in the First Five Centuries* (Grand Rapids: Eerdmans, 2009). The book is written from a baptistic perspective, with a corresponding de-emphasis on household baptism as evidence for the rite being administered to infants.

66. Acts 19:2–5. But note that a few verses earlier on, Apollos (who only knew John's baptism) was given fuller instruction but was apparently not baptized a second time (Acts 18:25–26). The difficulties raised by these two examples are discussed in Ferguson, *Baptism*, 180–82, but he comes to no firm conclusion as to how they can be resolved.

When Peter preached to Cornelius and his household, we are told that the Spirit descended on them before they were baptized, and there were other examples of baptism (such as that of the Ethiopian eunuch) that were apparently not accompanied by any miraculous manifestations.

Before long, the "signs and wonders" that originally accompanied baptism faded out to such an extent that by the fourth century, when commentary writers tackled the question, they had to admit that they had no experience of such things and assumed that they had ceased after the first generation of converts. In modern times, Pentecostal and charismatic groups have attempted to restore this element to Christian experience and have even regarded it as fundamental, but they have not tied it to baptism in the way that the early church did. For most Christians today, there is no obvious connection between baptism and the manifestation of extraordinary spiritual gifts. Baptism remains a requirement for church membership, but the gifts are much less common and are never emphasized outside charismatic circles.

That the apostles and their colleagues administered baptism to those who made a profession of faith has never been disputed. Questions have arisen only over whether they also baptized believers' children who could not make such a profession for themselves, and over the mode by which the rite was administered—were baptismal candidates immersed in water, sprinkled with it, or a combination of both? Early Christian paintings show Jesus and others wading knee- or waist-deep into a river and then being baptized by having water poured over them—was this the standard method by which baptism was administered?

As with so many other things, there is no definitive answer to these questions. It is only since the sixteenth-century Reformation that they have been asked in any serious way; before that, no one seems to have raised these issues as a matter of theological principle. Immersion, either total or partial, was certainly practiced, but was it the norm or considered essential? It is hard to believe, for example, that it could have been applied to the Philippian jailer and his entire household when they were baptized in the middle of the night.[67] The important thing seems to have been that baptism should take place as soon as possible after a profession of faith, a principle that must have encouraged flexibility concerning how and where it was done. One thing is certain: there was no need to instruct baptismal candidates at any length, nor were they obliged to be baptized during a worship service, as would normally be the case today.

---

67. Acts 16:33. Ferguson, *Baptism*, 179–80, does his best to allow for the possibility that the jailer and his household were somehow immersed, but even he does not press the point.

Whether infants were baptized along with their believing parents is a highly controversial subject to which no definitive answer can be given. Those who reject the practice of infant baptism today naturally try to demonstrate that theirs was the practice of the early church, whereas those who practice it try to prove the opposite. The evidence is inadequate to decide the question either way, but it is only since the sixteenth century that differences over this have divided the church. Those who insist that only professing believers can be baptized have to assume that everyone in a given household made such a profession, even though that is not stated in the New Testament. There is also the problem that whereas a Jewish boy was circumcised without question when he was eight days old and Jewish children were included in the Passover meal celebrations, there is no suggestion that this did not apply to the children of Christians with respect to baptism or the Lord's Supper. Could women be admitted to the church as the equals of men, but not children? Did parents leave their offspring at home during church services or forbid them from partaking of the Supper? If not, could the children have consumed the consecrated bread and wine without having been baptized? Again, we have no answer.

All we know for sure is that by AD 200 infant baptisms were taking place, and that Tertullian (who tells us this) disapproved of the practice. The reason he gave, however, was not that the children had not made a profession of faith. He believed that baptism was effective, regardless of that, and thought that it removed the stain of original sin. For him, the problem was that children who had been unknowingly cleansed of sin might well sin again without realizing it and thereby lose their salvation.[68] We are operating here in a different mental universe from the one that informs modern debates on the subject, which is a further reminder that our concerns cannot be readily answered by an appeal to evidence that was not intended to address the questions we are most likely to ask.

What we can say, and the evidence of Tertullian confirms, is that the early Christians believed that baptism had the power to cleanse recipients from their sins. At times, it was even seen as a kind of exorcism, chasing away the devil and delivering the newly baptized person from his power.[69] Unlike circumcision, baptism did not leave a mark on the body, which made it much easier for someone to leave the Christian community, and we know that even in New Testament times there were a number of such backsliders, most of whom (it was thought) could not be brought back to the church later on. Once they had tasted the heavenly gift, as the writer to the Hebrews remarked, it was

68. Tertullian, *De baptismo* 18.5.
69. See Ferguson, *Baptism*, 522–24, 537–88, for examples of this.

impossible to restore them to repentance if they had fallen away.[70] Whether
this also meant that they would lose their salvation if they sinned again after
baptism was a question that was apparently not raised in the first generation,
though (by an extension of the above principle) it became an important issue
later and was capable of dividing the church, particularly in North Africa.[71]

A more important question in New Testament times, and one that actually did split the church to some extent, was that of Jewish-gentile relations.
From a very early stage, when almost all Christians would have been Jews,
the church's mission began to reach out to the gentile world. This happened
because Paul and others went to the synagogues in the Diaspora, most of which
contained a significant number of "God-fearers" who believed in the God of
Israel but who for whatever reason did not take on the full requirements of
the Jewish law. The pattern seems to have been that Paul would preach in a
Diaspora synagogue and win over a section of his hearers, who would then
leave and form a church. From the controversies that subsequently erupted
in these churches, we can deduce that the God-fearers formed a significant
proportion of these converts, who were then no longer outsiders in the way
that they had been in the synagogues.

The difficulty was trying to decide how to reconcile two different cultures
in a single community. The God-fearers had never submitted to Jewish laws
and thought that the gospel justified their refusal to be bound by such legalism. Jewish Christians were reluctant to abandon their traditions, and even
if they could be persuaded that the God-fearers were right in principle, they
remained susceptible to feelings of guilt that they were giving up something
that was of central importance to their identity. In hindsight, the remarkable
thing is that both sides managed to stay together in spite of their differences,
which did not last beyond the first few generations.

The importance of the synagogue as the birthplace of the gentile church
should not be underestimated. When Paul went to Athens, where he did not
preach in the local synagogue, there were very few converts to his message.[72]
The reason for that is made plain in the text itself. Gentiles who had not been
exposed to Judaism or to the Hebrew Scriptures had no mental framework
within which they could place the Christian gospel. Words like "resurrection" meant nothing to them, and it would have been pointless for Paul to
have argued his case by referring to the covenant promises made to Abraham
and his descendants, since his audience would not have known what he was

70. Hebrews 6:4–6.
71. It seems that the earliest reference to this is found in *The Shepherd of Hermas*. See
Ferguson, *Baptism*, 214–16, for a discussion of the relevant passages.
72. Acts 17:22–34.

talking about. For all its inadequacies, the Jewish law had been a schoolmaster pointing the way to Christ, and without it, that way was much harder to find.[73]

In practice, it was virtually impossible to start a church without people who had a deep knowledge of the Hebrew Scriptures and who were able to interpret them in the light of Christ. The first Christian churches did not have statements of faith in the way that we have today, but some beliefs were essential to membership, and the New Testament makes it clear what they were. First came complete acceptance of the Old Testament as the Word of God that had been fulfilled in Christ.[74] Next came the confession that the Son of God had become a man and had suffered and died for the sins of the whole world.[75] Finally, there was the conviction that he had risen from the dead, ascended into heaven, and sent his Holy Spirit to bring the community of the church into being.[76] Anyone who doubted or denied these basic principles was unacceptable as a member of the church.

There was also a strong social dimension to the early Christian communities that could not be ignored. After an early experiment with a form of primitive communism in which converts pooled their resources for the common good, a less ambitious (but more practical) form of social outreach was devised. Churches were expected to take care of their less fortunate members and to look out for their interests. This aspect of their common life was one that made a deep impression on outsiders, who noticed that Christians were different from other people in a way that impressed them.[77] (Jews were also different, but although they took care of their coreligionists in much the same way as Christians did, they practiced an exclusivity that tended to alienate outsiders, who were often made to feel unwelcome in their midst.) The churches turned this around, using their concern for one another as evidence that they really were one in the Spirit.

It was this dimension more than any other that kept the different churches in communion with one another. They all shared a common belief, at least in principle, though there were many deviations and problems in individual cases, as the New Testament epistles make clear. But the fact remains that the apostle Paul was able to go around the churches of Greece collecting money for the less fortunate Christians in Palestine, and he took this task so seriously that he went to Jerusalem, risking his own safety, in order to deliver the funds himself. That Christians were capable of demonstrating such charity to

---

73. Galatians 3:24.
74. Hebrews 1:1–2.
75. John 1:14; 1 John 2:2.
76. Acts 1:1–2:4.
77. Tertullian, *Apologeticum* 39.7.

people they did not know and who (in some cases at least) probably resented their presence as gentiles in the church showed more clearly than anything else that the bonds uniting believers in Christ were real. The church's mission was bearing fruit and creating a new kind of common life that the world had not known before.

In terms of practical organization, the mission work of the church was based on two main centers: Jerusalem, which was natural, given the church's origins, and Antioch. Antioch was the capital of Roman Syria, the province in which Judaea was located, and so it must have seemed obvious to many that sooner or later the church would establish itself there. It was in Antioch that believers were first called Christians, and from there that Paul undertook his missionary journeys.[78] Even Peter turned up in the city and appears to have lived there for some time, though we have no way of knowing how long he stayed or what he did when he was there.[79] What we do know is that the pattern thus established carried over into the wider mission, which was overwhelmingly urban-based. Even in Galatia, which was treated as a unit for missionary purposes, the Christian congregations were gathered in provincial cities such as Iconium and Lystra. Rural mission, at least outside Palestine, was virtually unknown.

This pattern reflected the nature of the Roman Empire, which was itself a league of cities, of which Rome was the chief. It was to leave its mark on later generations, so that even today a bishop in an episcopally ordered church will almost always be assigned to a city, not to a territory. Exceptions to the rule are few and largely confined to areas where there are no cities to speak of, such as in the Arctic or northwestern Australia. Otherwise, the urban footprint is visible down through the ages, even at times when at least 80 percent of the population lived in the countryside. Like it or not, this created a dynamic that spurred on further mission to unreached areas, ignoring the deeply conservative rural populations. Today, when urban Christianity seems to be in decline and churchgoing seems to be relatively healthier in rural areas, it is worth bearing in mind that this was not the thrust of the early church, which used the relative freedom that urban life allowed as an opportunity for spreading the gospel.

A Doctrine of the Church?

Did the apostles and their companions have a doctrine of the church? Most Christians have always assumed that they had, and apologists for particular

78. Acts 11:26.
79. Galatians 2:11.

denominational traditions have often tried to show that theirs was the right contemporary manifestation of it. Unfortunately, much of this argument has concentrated on matters of organization (or "polity," as it is formally called), which, as we have seen, cannot be fully worked out on the basis of the New Testament alone. At most, we may be able to argue that episcopalianism, presbyterianism, and congregationalism can all claim some biblical support but that the New Testament witness is not so precise as to make any one of these positions irrefutably the most orthodox. Also, the disappearance of the apostles ensures that it is impossible to re-create the early church now. Somehow or other, their absence has to be compensated for, and that in itself guarantees that the modern church will be different from the one we read about in the Bible.

A New Testament doctrine of the church, if there is one, cannot be found by looking at particular congregations, because too little is known about them for general conclusions to be drawn. But the fact that we cannot piece together a detailed picture of how the Christian communities were organized does not mean that the apostles had no understanding of the church as a distinct entity. They clearly did, and they believed that it had a claim on the loyalty and participation of everyone who owned the name of Christ.

The majority of references to the church in the New Testament apply to particular congregations, which evidently functioned as autonomous units. Paul wrote to the church in particular places, and the same emphasis on the local community appears in the letters to the seven churches of Asia in the book of Revelation.[80] What this tells us is that the church was present in particular contexts and was not just a theoretical construction that had no particular manifestation anywhere. In the ancient world, where the idealism of Platonic philosophy was a force to be reckoned with, this emphasis on concrete situations had an importance that may escape us today. It was not good enough for the apostles to have a paradigm of what the church ought to be like but that did not (and probably could not) actually exist in the material world.

The church was the creation of the Holy Spirit, as the Pentecostal outpouring testified, but it was worked out in the time-and-space communities into which Christians were gathered. People saw the Spirit at work, both in their own lives and in their relationships with others who shared their experience. The apostles were adamant that no one could control the work of the Spirit; all they could do was recognize it when they saw it and accept it, whether they wanted to or not. We see this, for example, in the way in which Peter and the Jerusalem church responded to the conversion of Cornelius. They

---

80. Revelation 2–3.

had not expected that the Spirit would descend on gentiles and were initially hesitant about it, but when they realized that that was what had happened, they submitted to what they saw as God's will and changed their perceptions accordingly.[81] This humility was characteristic of the apostolic church. When faced with the confusion that the abuse of spiritual gifts had caused at Corinth, Paul did not use his authority to clamp down on them, because he knew that the Holy Spirit was at work in the church and that he had no power to control or prevent that.

Paul saw his ministry as one of theological guidance to a congregation that had to think through how the different gifts could be exercised in a harmonious way. It was by setting out the basic principles of order and love that he taught the Corinthians how to think about their experience, and in that way he hoped that they would adjust their behavior so as to glorify God and avoid the apparent chaos the gifts were causing. In their relationship to the local churches, the apostles represented the wider Christian world. Sometimes this led them to issue policy guidelines for all the churches, as they did following the resolution of the Jewish-gentile conflict at the Council of Jerusalem.[82] At other times they wrote to offer spiritual counsel to churches that needed it, wherever they might be. Thus we find that Paul wrote to the Romans, even though he had never been to Rome and had no particular association with the church there. Peter wrote to the "elect exiles" of Anatolia, although he had no known connection with them.[83] James, who was probably the head of the Jerusalem church, addressed his letter "to the twelve tribes in the Dispersion" over whom he had no particular jurisdiction.[84] Such roving commissions were an integral part of the apostles' ministry, guided and directed by the Holy Spirit, and accepted as such by the recipients. The local churches were autonomous but not independent or cut off from one another, because the apostles kept a watching brief over them to ensure that they remained faithful to the gospel message that they had heard and were called to proclaim.

The local congregation of believers was distinguished by its social comprehensiveness. Male and female, Jew and gentile, slave and free—all were one in Christ Jesus.[85] But at the same time, human distinctions were respected. Jewish Christians did not cease to be Jews, and if they wished to continue observing the law of Moses, they could do so. At the same time, they had to respect the

---

81. Acts 11:1–18.
82. Acts 16:4–5.
83. 1 Peter 1:1. Anatolia is what we now call Turkey in Asia and included the provinces mentioned in the letter: Pontus, Galatia, Cappadocia, Asia (Minor), and Bithynia.
84. James 1:1.
85. Galatians 3:28.

freedom of gentile Christians, because the law was not an integral part of the gospel and could not be imposed as if observing it were necessary to salvation. Similarly, secular differences between slaves and masters were also respected. The apostles did not advocate slavery as an institution, but they did not claim that emancipation was an obligation enjoined by the gospel either. Instead, they sought to restructure the nature of slave-master relationships in a way that would make the fellowship of believers the determining factor in them. They were not blind to the injustices of slavery, but believed that submission to it was the right way to imitate the example of Christ and the one that was most likely to convict the oppressors of their evil behavior.[86] Above all, they did not seek to abolish the differences between men and women, which went back to the creation, but to transform them. Wives were to submit to their husbands, but husbands were to sacrifice themselves for their wives, and in that way they would achieve the equality of difference.[87]

These injunctions were not simply counsels for peace within the community but were directly tied to the overarching relationship of Christ to the church, which was his bride.[88] The reality of the church was to be manifested in the lives of its members, which were changed irrevocably by the coming of the Holy Spirit. People who had been deeply immoral had been washed clean, sanctified, and justified in the name of Jesus Christ.[89] This was fundamental. The church was a body of sinners who had been saved by grace, but that salvation produced a transformation in their lives that was proof that God had begun a new work in them and in the world. Not everybody in the church lived up to this standard, but those who did not had to be disciplined or even expelled, because the community could not tolerate their sinful behavior in its midst.[90]

The church was the body of Christ in the sense that he was the head and everyone else was part of him. Each member of a congregation had a place in it, which might be very different from that of others but which was equally necessary and valuable. There were no expendable church members; there was no one who did not count. God shows no partiality, so everyone who believed in Christ was accepted on equal terms.[91] What was required was a common confession of faith, without which there could be no unity.[92] However much the apostles believed in the necessity of baptism, it paled into insignificance in

86. Ephesians 6:5–9; Colossians 3:22–25; 1 Peter 2:18–25.
87. Ephesians 5:22–33.
88. Revelation 22:17.
89. 1 Corinthians 6:9–11.
90. 1 Corinthians 5:1–13.
91. Acts 10:34–35.
92. Galatians 1:8–9.

light of the gospel.[93] Likewise, the Lord's Supper bound the churches together, but not if it was abused.[94] The sacramentalism of a later age cannot be found in the New Testament, where faith and the indwelling presence of the Holy Spirit in the hearts of believers were the factors that determined who belonged to the church and who did not.

Local communities modeled the church, but they were part of a universal network. This was clear from the beginning, as Christians in different places showed solidarity with their fellow believers who were suffering in one way or another.[95] This was a reminder to everyone that although Christ was fully present in their midst when they gathered together, he was also bringing into being a community that stretched across the world. The apostles were the living witnesses of this reality. They had a roving commission that took them to different places and brought home to local congregations what God was doing in other parts of the world. It was their faith and their teaching that constituted the presence of the church. Paul knew that not all those who preached the gospel did so from the right motives. Some disliked him and tried to rival his activities. But instead of rebuking such people and demanding that they submit to his authority, Paul rejoiced as long as it was the true gospel that was being proclaimed.[96] It was not the messenger but the message that counted, because it was the message that founded the church, the pillar and ground of truth.[97]

Whether this constitutes a "doctrine" of the church largely depends on how we define our terms. The apostles did not have a worked-out theory of what the church should be, but they knew in their hearts what it was, and when the occasion arose, they expressed it. Later generations would try to read their minds, with varying degrees of success, but the words of Peter sum up their thinking:

> You yourselves like living stones are being built up as a spiritual house, to be a holy priesthood, to offer spiritual sacrifices acceptable to God through Jesus Christ. . . . You are a chosen race, a royal priesthood, a holy nation, a people for his own possession, that you may proclaim the excellencies of him who called you out of darkness into his marvelous light. Once you were not a people, but now you are God's people.[98]

It would be hard to put it any better than that.

93. 1 Corinthians 1:14–17.
94. 1 Corinthians 11:17–22.
95. See Acts 11:27–30 for an early example of this.
96. Philippians 1:15–18.
97. 1 Timothy 3:15.
98. 1 Peter 2:5, 9–10.

3

The Persecuted Church

The Disappearance of the Apostles

The New Testament tells the story of the church's origins in a way that can be summed up by the title of one of its major books, the Acts of the Apostles. What they did and where they went after the ascension of Jesus form the framework of everything else, and although there is much that we are not told, we get a fairly good idea of how the original community expanded and spread across the Roman world. But for all its importance as a source for the history of the early church, the New Testament does not tell us what happened once the apostles left the scene. Like the book of Acts, it leaves us suspended between two eras, the one in which there was still a direct connection with the life and ministry of Jesus, and the subsequent period when personal memory turned into historical tradition. It is difficult to date this transition, and to many it must have been imperceptible at the time. Polycarp of Smyrna, for example, was martyred in AD 156, having been a Christian for eighty-six years. We do not know whether that means that he was eighty-six years old at the time or whether he made a profession of faith as a child, but either way, he was a man who had been in personal contact with the apostles and the churches they had founded. As far as we can tell, when he died he believed that nothing of any substance had changed during his lifetime. At the time of his martyrdom, he was one of the last remaining links with a bygone era, but whatever developments had occurred in the previous century, they seem to have made little impact on him.

No doubt many Christians at that time would have felt the same way. Life evolved more slowly in ancient times than it does today, and in most towns and villages little would have been different. People's memories would doubtless have grown vague in some respects, but they were used to recounting great events, and the oral traditions that handed them down would have been known and shared by Christians everywhere. If extraneous material had crept in, somebody would have noticed, if only because it would probably not have spread across the entire Roman Empire. Local variations would most likely have remained just that, and they could have been corrected by those with a wider knowledge and perspective. Something like this seems to have happened with the Gospels. Matthew, Mark, and Luke, the so-called Synoptic Gospels, all tell the same story, and the variations among them are relatively few. Matthew and Luke may have copied Mark (and each other), but perhaps they wrote down the oral tradition independently, in which case the degree to which they correspond is truly impressive. John's Gospel is an independent witness, which many scholars have thought postdates the synoptic tradition, but perhaps not. It contains features that appear to be very ancient and in some respects may be more "historical" than the others.[1]

What is certain is that by the time the Gospels were written down, the apostles were fast disappearing from the scene. John may still have been alive in the last decade of the first century, but the others had already died or ceased to be active. What significance did this have for the church? Lack of evidence makes it difficult to say for sure, but there seems to have been some debate about the nature and extent of the apostles' legacy. In particular, there were people who started claiming that the apostles had received secret instructions from Jesus that they had not revealed to their churches.[2] As if by magic, these hidden teachings now resurfaced, when their authenticity could no longer be directly verified. One of the persistent themes of this arcane literature is asceticism; it seems that the apostles were thought to have advocated things such as celibacy and fasting to a much greater degree than they had ever stated publicly. There was a certain plausibility in this, of course, since it was known that Paul preferred the celibate state, but as he explicitly stated that celibacy was not meant for everyone, the claim of apostolic authority for this position seems implausible and was quickly rejected by most.[3]

1. See J. A. T. Robinson, *The Priority of John* (London: SCM, 1985).
2. Irenaeus of Lyons, *Adversus omnes haereses* 3.1–2; Tertullian, *De praescriptione haereticorum* 27.1.
3. See 1 Corinthians 7:1–40.

Another possibility was that divine revelation continued through the ministry of prophets who had no connection with Jesus or the apostles but whose words were just as authoritative as theirs. This was the claim made by Montanus, who appeared in Asia Minor sometime in the mid-second century and attracted a considerable following. The issue quickly became one of principle: Was divine revelation binding on the church still being given, or had the apostolic commission come to an end? The general consensus was that it had ceased, and that what we call the canon of the New Testament was in principle closed. There would still be debate about some of the books included in it, but only those with a recognized apostolic pedigree would be accepted as authoritative.

That in turn forced the church to consider who had the right to interpret the canonical texts. Initially, it was claimed that the larger churches of genuine apostolic origin, such as Antioch, Ephesus, and Rome, were more likely to have preserved the authentic message intact. Partly this was because the apostles themselves had taught those churches, and partly it was because these churches were so big that any attempt to hijack them in the interests of one particular interpretation would be less likely to succeed. Too many people knew the truth, and that would serve as a check on eccentric behavior of that kind.

It was perhaps inevitable that the void left by the disappearance of the apostles would be filled by the *episkopoi*, or bishops of the local churches. Paul seems to have intended Timothy and Titus to fulfill such a role, but whether this was a widespread policy is unknown. We know that Ignatius of Antioch, writing in AD 118, told the people of Smyrna that they should respect the bishop as they would Christ himself and listen to the presbyters as they would listen to the apostles.[4] Ignatius was afraid of heretics and was trying to protect the church against false teaching, which he thought could best be done by adhering to what the bishop had to say. But whether he thought that the bishop was a direct successor of the apostles is not clear; for him, as for everyone at this period, it was the content of their teaching rather than the bishops' personal connections with the apostles that was most important. Probably the reason was that few bishops had such links; like everyone else, they depended on the inherited tradition, which was increasingly being codified in the New Testament.

Whatever the truth of the matter, there can be no doubt that once the apostles were gone, the danger of false teaching was greatly increased and had to be dealt with. False teachers multiplied, some of whom took considerable liberties with the emerging canonical tradition. Tatian, for example, writing

4. Ignatius of Antioch, *Ad Smyrnaeos* 8.

about AD 150, tried to harmonize the four Gospels because he thought there should be only one narrative, and Marcion, at a slightly earlier date, wanted to drop the Old Testament and purge the New of anything that sounded too Jewish. They were both eventually rejected, but there was a growing sense in the church that it had to protect itself against this kind of danger. The more the memory of the apostles faded into the background, the more urgent that need became, and we must not be surprised to discover that a large proportion of the Christian writing that has come down to us from the second century is concerned with the problem of defending the church's teaching against heresies of one kind or another.

Orthodoxy and Heresy

The question of continuity between the apostolic and the postapostolic churches has been made more complicated for us today by the fact that since the early nineteenth century there has been a strong tendency in critical scholarship to claim that there were significant differences between the two. These have supposedly been glossed over in the official record and can only be detected now by a critical reading of the primary documents and the use of external source material, such as papyri and inscriptions, that has come to light in modern times. The main thrust in this direction came from the work of Ferdinand Christian Baur (1792–1860) and the scholars he gathered around him at Tübingen. The thesis of the Tübingen School, as the work of these men is collectively known, was that the apostolic church was a community of the free spirit, in which many different theological views coexisted and church membership requirements were minimal. But according to them, before long there was a hardening of positions, and in the second generation there emerged a powerful trend toward institutionalization. This took the form of increasingly inflexible structures, codified doctrines, and the denunciation of dissenters as "heretics." Baur labeled this tendency "early Catholicism" and claimed that it could be found in the New Testament as well as in the writings of the so-called apostolic fathers of the second century. In particular, "early Catholicism" was present in Luke, Acts, and the Pastoral Epistles, which in his view meant that these books had to be postapostolic in origin and therefore were not the work of their professed authors.

Once this thesis took hold, it was not long before scholars were finding a more developed theology in other New Testament books as well. That extended the scope of Baur's original criticisms even farther, so that it came to be accepted that the Johannine literature, some Pauline epistles such as

Ephesians and Colossians, 2 Peter, and the Epistle to the Hebrews were all written in postapostolic times, perhaps as late as the mid-second century in some cases. In other words, the New Testament represented more than the first flush of Christianity; it also contained texts that testified to later developments that took the church away from its primitive roots.

Baur and his colleagues were not disinterested scholars. They were liberal Protestants who wanted to attack the increasingly conservative pretensions of the Roman Catholic Church of their own time, as well as the narrow confessionalism of the German Lutheran and Reformed traditions. They were the inheritors of eighteenth-century Pietism, which in their eyes had downgraded the importance of religious dogma in favor of a greater emphasis on personal holiness and morality. They were also disinclined to believe in the miraculous and thought that Roman Catholicism was a medieval blend of myth and superstition rightly condemned by Martin Luther. As they saw it, their task was to carry on the Reformation by removing the remaining detritus of premodern irrationalism from the Protestant mind in order to create a purified, nondogmatic Christianity that could serve as a spiritual foundation for the scientific age in which they thought they were living. Their scholarly activities were thus geared toward providing a space for liberal thought to enter the German Protestant churches, and in this they were largely successful.

Of course there were plenty of people who rejected the Tübingen thesis and the liberalism that accompanied it. They believed that what appeared to Baur to be "early Catholicism" was part and parcel of the apostolic deposit of faith. In some cases, people who reacted against Baur became more sympathetic to the claims of Rome, and a few intellectual Protestants even became Roman Catholics because of it. The most famous of these, in the English-speaking world, was John Henry Newman (1801–90), who before his conversion spearheaded a revival of what we now call Anglo-Catholicism within the Church of England. His kind of conservatism was reactionary and had a limited appeal, but it did spur scholars to take a fresh look at the early church, with consequences for our understanding of it that are with us to this day. On the one side are those who believe that the records of the early church are generally trustworthy and give a good account of how it developed and matured. On the other side are those who insist that the mainline tradition is mainly propaganda for what became the dominant group and that it is only by reading the long-suppressed works of so-called heretics that we can get a balanced picture of what was really going on.

The Tübingen approach became more or less standard among German Protestants in the late nineteenth century and was represented by such men as Adolf von Harnack (1851–1930), who questioned the place of dogmatic confessional statements in the early church, and Walter Bauer (1877–1960), who tried to show that "orthodoxy" and "heresy" were labels applied by the victorious Catholic party to themselves and their opponents, respectively, sometime in the late second century.[5] The thesis has been challenged a number of times by the detailed scholarly work of men such as J. N. D. Kelly (1909–97) and H. E. W. Turner (1907–95), but it keeps coming back in somewhat different forms and has established itself as the mainline approach taken in popular textbooks and so on.[6] One of the reasons for this is that in the twentieth century a number of new manuscript discoveries appeared to substantiate the Tübingen claims. In particular, an important find at Nag Hammadi, Egypt, in 1946 revealed a mass of documents that presented forms of Christianity that had been denounced in ancient times by men such as Irenaeus and labeled by the Tübingen School as "gnosticism."

Gnosticism was not so much the doctrine of one individual or small group of people as it was a tendency present in many writers who were clearly influenced by the philosophical currents of their day. Broadly speaking, a gnostic was someone who believed in a dualistic separation between matter and spirit and who created mythological explanations for the creation of the world. The Creator God was inferior to the Father of Jesus Christ, because the former dealt with matter (which was intrinsically evil) whereas the latter had sent his Son to deliver us from matter's grip. Bauer had detected this tendency but lacked the mass of evidence to document it and had to rely on the reports of those who were opposed to it, even if the thought of some of them, such as Clement of Alexandria, was not all that different. Clement is thought of as "orthodox," but he spoke out in favor of *gnosis* (knowledge) and so apparently breathed the same philosophical atmosphere as men such as Basilides and Valentinus, who have not escaped the condemnation of later generations that have regarded them as "heretics." Was it therefore possible to believe that such men were victims of a political takeover of the church by a group that proclaimed itself to be "orthodox" at the expense of everyone else?

5. A. von Harnack, *A History of Dogma*, trans. Neil Buchanan (London: Williams & Norgate, 1894–99), originally published as *Lehrbuch der Dogmengeschichte* (Freiburg-im-Breisgau: J. C. B. Mohr, 1893); *What Is Christianity?*, trans. T. Bailey Saunders (London: Williams & Norgate, 1901), originally published as *Das Wesen des Christentums* (Leipzig: Hinrichs, 1900); W. Bauer, *Orthodoxy and Heresy in Earliest Christianity*, ed. Robert Kraft and Gerhard Krodel (Philadelphia: Fortress, 1971), originally published as *Rechtgläubigkeit und Ketzerei im ältesten Christentum* (Tübingen: Mohr, 1934).
6. J. N. D. Kelly, *Early Christian Creeds*, 3rd ed. (London: Longman, 1972); Kelly, *Early Christian Doctrines*, 5th ed. (London: A. & C. Black, 1977); H. E. W. Turner, *The Pattern of Christian Truth* (London: Mowbray, 1954).

What all sides in this debate agreed on is that by the third century (at the latest) there was a conscious difference between the "orthodox" and the rest, and that the former were in control of the levers of the worldwide church. Orthodoxy might not have been precisely defined at this stage, but there were already signs that candidates for baptism had to answer a number of questions that were designed to root out beliefs regarded as deviant, and the enforcers of such discipline kept in touch with one another by means of periodic councils that met to decide common doctrinal policy. Concomitant with this development was the emergence of the monarchical episcopate in individual congregations, which was a necessity if the system so conceived was ever going to work. Each church had to have a recognized leader and spokesman who could articulate the orthodox line and impose it on his congregation.

The details of this picture have frequently been challenged and modified, but the broad outline has proved to be remarkably resilient. How fair a presentation of the early church is it? As with everything else to do with this period, evidence is scarce and much of it can be interpreted in different ways. Irenaeus attacked "heretics" right, left, and center, but what exactly was his relationship to these people and his motive in seeking to condemn them? Was he trying to protect the purity of the church (as he claimed) by narrowing it down to include only those who agreed with him?

How plausible is the Tübingen reconstruction of early Christianity? At the most basic level, it is hard to deny that the first Christians had a basic sense that there was a right way to believe about Jesus and a wrong way, even if they sometimes disagreed about what those ways were. Even if they did not use terms such as "orthodoxy" and "heresy," the concepts were clearly there, and it was only a matter of time before various forms of right and wrong belief would be labeled as such. To some extent, this kind of distinction went back to Judaism, though in Jewish circles the range of permissible opinions was always much broader than it would be in Christianity. For example, there were Jews who denied the resurrection of the flesh, which was obviously not a viable option for Christians. From the beginning, therefore, the church could only accept a range of views narrower than what the synagogue had been used to, because otherwise its basic message would have been hopelessly compromised.

On the other hand, many (if not most) of the false teachers whom Paul complained about were men who were trying to make the church too narrow in a different way: by imposing various Jewish practices on its members. Christians had greater freedom than Jews in practical matters such as eating and drinking, but not in terms of belief. This was inevitable, because once attention was focused on the person and work of Jesus Christ, what was (or could be) said about him became of central importance. If Christians did not agree about who Jesus was and what he did, or if their opinions were so vague as to be virtually meaningless when put to the test, then their faith would lack all content and no gospel could have been preached at all. Belief in a divine incarnation was anathema to Jews and incomprehensible to those gentiles for whom matter was evil and fundamentally opposed to the goodness of God.

Yet if Christians did not believe in the incarnation, they would have no Savior to proclaim. The various halfway houses devised in attempts to reconcile these incompatible positions may have been well intentioned, at least in some cases, but they were dangerous and had to be countered. Jesus could not have been a half-man, nor a phantom, nor an angelic being in human form. He had to be sinless but not incapable of becoming sin for us. Somehow or other, humanity and divinity had to be reconciled in him. It took many centuries to devise a formula that most Christians could agree on, and even then there were dissenters, but the need to find a clear and unambiguous statement of faith in the incarnate Son of God was an ever-present priority. So too with the Holy Spirit, whose activity and presence were fundamental to Christian experience and whose relationship to the Father and the Son had to be properly understood. Once again, finding a formula to express this was not easy, and even today no universally satisfactory one has been found, but Christians knew they had to say something in order to explain their faith as clearly and accurately as possible. Inevitably there would be false starts, and some attempts would have to be rejected. Whether those who propounded such solutions should have been condemned as wicked betrayers of the faith may be questioned, and no doubt some heretics suffered unfairly for their mistakes, but objectively speaking, the church had little choice but to warn its members not to succumb to ways of thinking that would destroy the gospel and lead them astray.

The apostle Paul was particularly sensitive to the possibility that his message might be corrupted by others, and the fact that his mission was dogged by false apostles who sought to undo his teaching, as well as by church members who contested his authority, only sharpened his sensitivity on this point. Writing to the Galatians, for example, he declared: "If we or an angel from heaven should preach to you a gospel contrary to the one we preached to you, let him be accursed."[7]

Paul knew that that was happening, but he was not primarily interested in the details of the errors that had seduced the Galatians. As far as he was concerned, *any* deviation from his teaching was to be condemned, whatever form it might take. Precise labels could be assigned to these errors at a later date, but

7. Galatians 1:8–9.

the important thing was that the problem should be recognized and dealt with, which is why he wrote his letter in the first place. Orthodoxy was a matter of the heart before it became a textbook definition of the faith. That it should appear in Galatians is of special significance, because this is one of Paul's earliest epistles and has always been regarded as authentic. If he could speak this way so early in his missionary career, how can we doubt that the condemnations found in other New Testament epistles may be equally ancient in origin?

The exact nature of the heresies that sprang up in the New Testament church is unknown, though many scholars have detected early forms of gnosticism from the language used to combat them. That would not be surprising, given that the pagan world was dominated by dualistic philosophies that taught that spirit was good and matter was evil, a division that orthodox Christians could not accept because it was incompatible with the biblical account of creation and with the incarnation of the Son of God. In the course of combatting views of this kind, Christian leaders came to understand that the church had to restructure the mental universe of the ancient world if its message of salvation was to have any meaning. But before it could address the pagan establishment, it had to achieve unity within its own ranks, and that meant enforcing a stronger discipline than had been necessary at the beginning.

The nature of the heresies that the church had to face and the extent of their influence can be gauged from the writings of Irenaeus (d. 200?), a native of Smyrna who later became the bishop of Lyons in what is now southern France. Irenaeus made an encyclopedic catalog of all the deviant forms of the faith that were known to him and countered each one with a defense of whatever Christian truth they opposed.[8] His work was not a systematic theology in the later sense of the word, but it was comprehensive, and Irenaeus was the first Christian writer to have left enough material for us to be able to reconstruct a complete belief system.[9] The fact that he was also a bishop is telling, because by his time it was becoming increasingly clear that it was the duty of the bishops to protect and defend the church's faith. By no means every theologian was in episcopal office—Tertullian and Origen, to name but the two greatest in the next generation, were both laymen—but it was the bishops, acting as the heads of their local churches, who had to decide what would and would not be accepted as orthodox Christian teaching.

This orthodoxy was also taking the form of a confession of faith that was imposed on candidates for baptism. The New Testament practice of baptizing

8. Irenaeus of Lyons, *Adversus omnes haereses.*
9. See E. Osborn, *Irenaeus of Lyons* (Cambridge: Cambridge University Press, 2001); D. Minns, *Irenaeus: An Introduction* (London: T&T Clark, 2010).

a person immediately on profession of faith was abandoned in favor of a period of instruction, or catechesis as it was called, during which new converts would be instructed in the rudiments of Christianity. When they came for baptism, which was now regularly performed during a worship service in the church, they would be asked questions relating to this instruction and be expected to recite approved answers.[10] There was no fixed form of words, and a number of formulas have survived that give us some idea of the variety that was tolerated. What is striking about them is not how they differ from one another but how much alike they are. To the modern reader, they all sound remarkably like what we call the Apostles' Creed and are instantly recognizable when we come across them embedded in some other text.[11]

The standard pattern of confession was trinitarian, even before the doctrine of the Trinity was elaborated. There were three parts, devoted respectively to the Father, the Son, and the Holy Spirit. The Father was acknowledged as the Creator—a gesture that should probably be interpreted as primarily anti-gnostic and anti-Marcionite in its emphasis. The Son's incarnate life was set out in detail, with the points of theological importance being especially emphasized. Finally there was a line about the Holy Spirit, occasionally supplemented by other things that did not fit elsewhere—the church, baptism, the forgiveness of sins, eternal life, and so on. From the evidence that has survived, it seems that it was the *pattern* of Christian truth, not the exact *form* of the words used to express it, that mattered. The text of the Apostles' Creed that we use today appears for the first time in the writings of Priminius (or Pirminius) of Reichenau, sometime between 710 and 724. It owes its fame to the fact that it was picked up more than half a century later by Charlemagne and made the standard form in the liturgies composed by the churchmen of his court.[12] But the basic idea can be traced back to the second century and shows that the church had already become a society that demanded a confession of orthodox belief from anyone who wanted to belong to it.

The Spread of the Gospel

Who wanted to join the church and why? According to the New Testament, the message of the gospel was taken primarily to Jews and only secondarily

10. Descriptions of the procedure occur in the second century. See Justin Martyr, *Apologia I* 61; Tertullian, *De corona* 3.2–3. There is even a short notice about it in *Didache* 7, which may date from before AD 100.

11. Kelly, *Early Christian Creeds*, 30–61.

12. Kelly, *Early Christian Creeds*, 398–434.

to gentiles, many of whom had already come within the Jewish orbit, but by the time of Irenaeus, Jewish Christianity had virtually disappeared. Very few Jews were still being converted, relations with the synagogue were distant and frequently hostile, and there was relatively little attempt to reach out to them. The church, which a century earlier was debating whether to admit gentiles, had become an essentially gentile organization and has remained so ever since. What happened to produce such a momentous change of direction?

The hostility of the Jewish establishment to the early Christians is well documented and completely understandable. Had all Jews become Christians, Judaism would have ceased to exist, and few people welcome their own imminent extinction. That those Jewish leaders who felt it was their duty to maintain their national and religious identity should have done everything in their power to crush the nascent Christian movement is therefore hardly surprising. What is perhaps harder to understand is that many Jews in the Diaspora seem not to have heard of Christians for many years after the death and resurrection of Jesus. It was not until AD 49 that the Roman synagogue was disrupted by the kind of dispute over his claims that we are familiar with from Paul's missionary journeys. Paul himself was frequently allowed to preach in synagogues because no one knew who he was, and that was twenty years or more after the first Pentecost. It is easy for us to be impressed by the large numbers of converts recorded in Acts and forget that the Jewish world was much bigger than that. One of the main centers of Judaism was Alexandria, and there is not a word about any Christian church there before the second century. It was therefore possible for many Jews to grow up in the synagogue without encountering Christians at all, even in the days when most Christians were Jews themselves.

Another factor at work was the tragic fate of the Jews in the Roman Empire. Palestine rose in revolt in AD 66, and when it was finally over, the temple at Jerusalem had been destroyed. The world in which Jesus and Paul had ministered disappeared, and Judaism had to reinvent itself. It did so remarkably quickly, but in the process it became much more conscious of its vulnerability. Nor was the destruction of the temple the end of Jewish suffering. There was a further revolt in Alexandria in AD 116–17, which decimated the community there, and yet another uprising in Palestine in AD 132–35, after which Jerusalem was razed to the ground and rebuilt as Aelia Capitolina, a gentile colony from which Jews were excluded. Christians had no interest in revolting against Rome, and in AD 66 they left Jerusalem in order to escape its inevitable fate. To be associated too closely with Jews was not in their interest, and self-preservation played a part in their growing separation from Jewish politics and culture.

Yet another problem was the different legal status that Jews and Christians enjoyed. For all their rebelliousness, Jews practiced a legal religion (*religio licita*) that the Romans tolerated because of its great antiquity. Christians did not benefit in the same way. From the Roman point of view, they were an unregistered cult that was a novelty and therefore had no right to claim recognition. A religion was supposed to be something that went back to time immemorial, but Christianity traced its roots back to recent events, and events, moreover, in which agents of the Roman state had played an inglorious part. For Rome to have allowed people to worship a man it had crucified as a criminal would have been to undermine its own legitimacy, which it could hardly do. The ironic result, however, was that potentially disloyal Jewish subjects were allowed to practice their faith openly whereas loyal Christians were not. As time went on, the latter came to see this anomaly as an absurd injustice, but in the meantime the different ways in which Jews and Christians were treated by the state was bound to sow dissension among the latter.

Finally, the family ties that had kept the first generation of Jewish Christians in contact with Jews who had not accepted Christ weakened over time. Christians were advised not to marry outside the faith, which meant that the children of converts were just as likely to wed gentiles as other Jews. As the younger generation mixed in this way, the emotional and cultural links to Judaism that their elders still felt faded away. The drift apart was gradual, but by the time of Ignatius of Antioch, Jews and Christians had gone their separate ways, and the church could no longer be considered "Jewish" in any real sense.[13]

The effects of this shift can be seen in the writings of a man such as Tertullian. When defending the bravery and convictions of Christians who would rather die than surrender their faith, Tertullian chose his examples, not from the Hebrew Bible, which was largely unknown outside Jewish and Christian circles, but from ancient Roman history. Christians were called to behave like the legendary heroes of the old Roman Republic (of whom they had heard), whose ideals had been so cruelly undermined by the moral corruption of the later empire.[14] The idea developed that the church could be the salvation of that empire because of the moral and spiritual fiber of its members. When writing to the emperor and the aristocracy of Rome, men such as Tertullian and his Greek predecessors—for example, Justin Martyr and Athenagoras of Athens—liked to emphasize this point. Their argument was that Christians

13. For a study of this process, see T. A. Robinson, *Ignatius of Antioch and the Parting of the Ways: Early Jewish-Christian Relations* (Peabody, MA: Hendrickson, 2009).

14. See Tertullian, *Ad martyras*, which was written in the late second century, and his *Apologeticum* 50.5–7.

were the empire's best citizens and the state was foolish to alienate them. They were potentially its most loyal defenders, but instead of embracing them and their ideals, the Roman authorities preferred to attack them.

As the empire weakened because of infighting over who should occupy the imperial throne, and as corruption in high places became increasingly blatant and intolerable, this message seems to have exerted a growing appeal. The Romans knew that something had to be done to save their empire, which everyone valued for the peace and prosperity it brought to the Mediterranean world, and increasingly it seemed that the church was the only organization with the will and the ability to do it. There was something about Christians that gave them an inner strength that was sadly lacking in wider Roman society. They were prepared to endure suffering and even death for their beliefs, and they stuck together. People who came into contact with them sensed that they were dealing with a spiritual power that they could oppose but not overcome. Gradually more and more were persuaded of its truth, and the church began to win converts as a result.

In addition to its inner strength and growing network of congregations, the church had something else to offer the Greco-Roman world: the intellectual coherence of its doctrines. Ancient pagan society was split between the mass of the people who practiced a religion scarcely distinguishable from superstition and an intellectual elite that despised popular beliefs and looked to various kinds of philosophy for comfort. It would not have been so bad if the philosophies they adopted all agreed on the essentials, but they did not. Stoicism, for example, taught that everything that existed was material. Even spirits were just very refined forms of matter, a belief that seems odd to us but that was at least an attempt to overcome the dualism so prevalent in other philosophical systems. Sharply opposed to the Stoics were the Platonists, who were slowly turning their master's teachings into a pseudoreligion of its own. They believed that reality was spiritual—material things were merely corruptions of the ideal. And so it went—Epicureans, Cynics, Aristotelians, and others all offered variant forms of philosophical thinking, none of which proved to be very satisfactory when examined in any depth, and none of which could dislodge the superstition of the masses.

It was here that Christian evangelists saw their opportunity and took it. They mercilessly pilloried the inconsistencies and inadequacies of the various pagan belief systems that they encountered. In their place they offered a faith that embraced reason but was not bound by it. They maintained not only that the universe was an internally consistent whole but that its Creator could be known in a personal way. In fact, it was the Christians who introduced into serious intellectual discourse the notion of a personal relationship with God as the foundation of human life. The philosophers had talked of friendship, but this was only between equals and was reserved for the intellectual elite. It also tended to have a strong homoerotic dimension that ensured that it would never catch on widely. The church, by contrast, had a coherent view of a world guided and governed by love, in which each element had its proper place. Conflict was not the inevitable clash between abstract forces of nature but rather the result of disobedience and rebellion against the Creator, which he himself had put right by sending his Son to bridge the divide created by sin and open up the possibility for human beings to recover the harmony that had been lost.

This message had considerable appeal, and from about AD 150 on, and certainly after AD 200, Christians were very much in the intellectual running in the Roman world. This was particularly evident from the attempts that pagans made to counter their growing influence. One of them, a man called Celsus, writing around AD 180–90, was refuted point by point by Origen in a massive defense of Christianity that can still be read with profit today.[15] The most interesting thing about Celsus is that he had already accepted the basic premises of Christian thought. He agreed with his opponents that the world was an orderly universe and that it was possible to live in harmony with it. The difference was that he thought a philosopher could do that just as easily as a Christian—in fact, more easily, because he could abstract the underlying principles and make them the core of his belief system, without having to get bogged down in the material details or be tied to a historical figure like Jesus.

By demonstrating the impossibility of separating out the material from the spiritual and proclaiming that in Christ the universal ideal had become a particular human being, Origen showed that Christianity was superior to anything the pagans had to offer, which inevitably made it more attractive to a growing number of the educated. The underlying strategy was clear; once pagans started thinking along Christian lines, men such as Origen could argue that the Christian solution to the questions they were asking was better than anything they could devise themselves, and so conversion to Christ came to seem the best answer available.

There were critics of Christianity who thought it was just another Eastern mystery religion that dabbled in superstition and philosophy and drew its strength from imposing strict rules on its members, who formed what amounted to a secret society. That this was not true is most obviously shown by Christians' willingness to defend their faith publicly whenever they were

15. Origen, *Contra Celsum*, trans. and ed. H. Chadwick (Cambridge: Cambridge University Press, 1953).

given the opportunity. Unbelievers were invited to try it and see for themselves, something no mystery cult would ever have done. At the same time, Christian belief had specific content that had to be accepted—it was not a case of worshiping some superior power about which little or nothing could be known for certain. Jesus Christ had come into the world to reveal the God unknown to the pagan world, and to understand the meaning of the universe it was necessary first to know and relate to him.

That the church was making inroads into the intellectual elite by working out a form of systematic theology and imposing it as orthodox belief is clear. What is less well known, because it is virtually undocumented, is the progress that it was also making lower down the social and intellectual scale. The urban nature of the first churches makes it hard to say how far the gospel message spread into the countryside, which was certainly far less evangelized than the cities when Christianity was finally given legal status. But we hear of villagers in North Africa who had become Christians well before AD 200, and there is no reason to suppose that they were unique. By AD 300 there were even buildings dedicated to Christian worship, though whether they had been built for that purpose is unknown. It is remarkable, for instance, that in the persecution of AD 303, the first thing that happened was that the church building across the street from the imperial palace at Nicomedia was torn down. What surprises us most about this, of course, is that there was a Christian structure there to begin with.

It was around AD 250 that a turning point was reached. Before that time, the church had been a small minority that suffered intermittent persecution by the authorities but that the majority of people could ignore, at least most of the time. After AD 250 the church was a more formidable presence, especially in the eastern provinces of the Roman Empire, and it could no longer be overlooked. Evidence for this comes from a surprising quarter. In AD 260, Queen Zenobia of Palmyra, a city in the Syrian desert that had long been a Roman client state, revolted against a decaying empire and managed to capture the city of Antioch, which she held for the next twelve years. She did not live there herself but appointed a governor to act in her name. This was Paul of Samosata, the Christian bishop of the city.

Paul of Samosata thus became the first Christian bishop to occupy secular office—an intriguing portent of what was to come later on. But why did Zenobia choose him? No doubt she thought that she could count on his loyalty, since he would have had little desire to return to Rome, under whose rule he would have been persecuted. However, Christians were generally loyal to the Roman state in spite of the difficulties under which they labored, and a number of leaders in the Antiochene church were not happy with Paul's position. In

AD 268 they called a council together and deposed him for heresy. Perhaps Paul really was a heretic, but the obscure nature of the proceedings, combined with the obvious political implications, must make us wonder whether that was their real motive. It seems just as likely that there were many loyal Romans in the church who did not want anything to do with Zenobia, and it is a fact that after her defeat, the church was treated quite leniently in Antioch. By that time, Paul had either fled or died—we hear no more about him. Nevertheless, it seems reasonable to conclude that the real reason he appealed to Zenobia as a potential leader was that he commanded an impressive support base. With Paul on her side, she could probably count on the backing of a sufficiently large number of people to be able to maintain her grip on the city. If that was how she thought, then it is evidence, admittedly somewhat tenuous, that the church was the dominant social force in the city at that time.

A more objective way of judging this phenomenon is based on the papyri discovered in Egypt. These all come from rural areas—they would not have survived otherwise. Here again, we can see that AD 250 represents a kind of watershed. Before that time, Christian papyri were relatively uncommon, but afterward their volume increased dramatically. Given that literacy was never a majority accomplishment in the ancient world, it is hard to correlate this finding with the spread of the gospel to the lower and rural classes, but that there was a substantial increase in the number of nonintellectual Christians in the second part of the third century is undeniable. The church had become a social institution in a way that it had not been before; as its impact increased, so did its attractiveness to outsiders. Something it had was working, and slowly a whole society was being transformed. By the time it was legalized, it was already so well established that it could not be eradicated. Unable to beat the Christians, the empire joined them, and a new phase in the history of the church began.

Another indication that points to a deeper social penetration from about AD 250 onward is the language used in public worship. Until about AD 200 the majority of Christians were Greek-speaking, even if they spoke Greek as a second language. But works in other languages, especially in Latin, were starting to appear. When the Greek-speaking Irenaeus went to Lyons in AD 178, he could minister there in his mother tongue, presumably because the church was still largely a Greek-speaking import. But Latin was already being used in North Africa, where it was completely dominant by the end of the century. Rome, which in many ways straddled the linguistic divide, had both Greek- and Latin-speaking elements as late as the mid-third century, when Hippolytus wrote in Greek and his contemporary Novatian in Latin. But soon after that the Roman liturgy was latinized, and before long the use of Greek had been virtually eliminated. What we now call indigenization had taken place—a sure sign that the church was putting down roots at a deeper social level than had previously been the case.

A similar phenomenon can be observed in the eastern Mediterranean. From the time of Alexander the Great, Greek had been the common administrative language there, and it remained so. But in the third century, Christian writings in Coptic, the native language of Egypt, and in Syriac started to make their appearance. The use of Greek was not discontinued in the way that it was in the West, but the emergence of a polyglot church testifies to the same phenomenon of increasing indigenization. Admittedly, there were limits to this process; no one thought to translate the Bible into languages such as Gaulish, Basque, or Berber (in the West), or into Lycaonian, Illyrian, or Thracian (in the East). Nevertheless, in the course of its evangelization efforts in the third century, the church became multilingual in a way that it had not been before—the promise of Pentecost was becoming a reality.

Geographically speaking, archaeological evidence confirms that during the third century the church spread to every corner of the Roman Empire. By the end of the New Testament period such a network had been established only sporadically—in Palestine, for example, as well as in Asia Minor and Galatia. However, it was still not possible to go anywhere in the empire and find a church; large tracts of the West, in particular, remained virtually untouched. After AD 150, though, that was no longer the case. Soldiers in the Roman army and traders who had been converted took the gospel with them, establishing new churches as they went. By the time Christianity was legalized there were at least three bishops in Roman Britain, for example, which means that there must have been a considerable evangelistic effort there well before 313, though we have no idea where it came from or when. The same was true everywhere else, so that by the early fourth century there could hardly have been any major Roman town that did not have a church, even if the percentage of the population that adhered to it was still very small in many places.

The Baptism of Fire

We have little way of knowing how the gospel spread across the Roman world in the days before the church was legalized. Public preaching of the kind found in the New Testament was illegal and presumably rare, but perhaps it occurred in out-of-the-way places. Word of mouth must have been an important factor, but by its nature it is impossible to track or document. People in ancient times lived more public lives than most of us do now, and if someone in the neighborhood became a Christian, word of the conversion would have spread fairly quickly. How much effect it would have had on others, though, is hard to say. What we do know is that one of the most effective forms of evangelism was the public witness of Christians, which in the centuries of persecution meant giving one's life for the sake of Christ and the gospel. The Greek word for "witness" is *martyr*, a name that speaks for itself. As Tertullian put it: "The blood of martyrs is the seed of the church"; his observation is borne out by the place that martyrdom came to occupy in Christian self-understanding.[16]

Dying for one's beliefs was a rare occurrence in the ancient world. Wars and political murders were commonplace, and sometimes prominent people suffered as a result. The Roman philosopher Seneca (4 BC?–AD 65), for example, whose views as a Stoic were close to those of many Christians, was forced to commit suicide by the emperor Nero, not for his philosophy but because he was too close to the imperial throne and was felt by the paranoid emperor to be a threat to his position.[17] A century earlier, the great statesman and philosopher Cicero (106–43 BC) was proscribed and assassinated, again for political, not ideological, reasons. The main example of someone who was put to death by anti-intellectual bigots was Socrates, who in 399 BC was forced to drink hemlock because he had supposedly corrupted the youth of Athens and denied the city's gods. But the reaction to that was so fierce and long-lasting that nothing similar was ever again attempted. The Romans left philosophers alone as long as they stayed out of politics, and the same went for religious leaders. Jesus was put to death not because of his theological teachings but because Pontius Pilate realized that those teachings were a threat to the peace. Pilate did not care what Jesus thought, and he knew that in Roman terms Jesus was quite innocent, but he also understood that the Jewish establishment was baying for his blood, and that rioting would almost certainly have ensued if they had not had their way.[18]

Of course, Jesus knew that he had come into the world in order to die, and he sought to prepare his disciples for that. His death had a theological purpose that was necessary for accomplishing his mission, because without the shedding of his blood there could have been no forgiveness of sins. In that sense, it was a unique occurrence and could not be imitated or repeated by anyone else. But at the same time, Jesus also taught his disciples that they would have to take up their cross, too, if they wanted to follow him. Being his disciple was not easy, and he predicted that some of them, at least, would

16. Tertullian, *Apologeticum* 50.13.
17. For Tertullian's favorable view of Seneca, see his *De anima* 20.1.
18. Matthew 27:15–26.

die a death not dissimilar to his. As he told them, he had a baptism of fire that they were unable to appreciate while he was still among them, but it was not long before the reality would strike home.[19] To follow Christ to the end was to give up one's life for him, even before it was forcibly taken. The apostle Paul expressed it well when he told the Galatians that he had been crucified with Christ, and he clearly expected that experience to be the norm for every Christian.[20]

Those who had died and been born again spiritually were better prepared for physical suffering and death, because they knew that it would make no difference to their eternal destiny other than to hasten their full enjoyment of its blessings.[21] To that extent it was almost worth waiting for death, though the church never encouraged anyone to sacrifice himself voluntarily. Christians were meant to live life on earth to the full but to be ready to give it up if required to do so, not to go courting martyrdom for its own sake. In the event, seeking death turned out to be pointless, because before long martyrdom came to the church. The first instance of it is recorded in the Acts of the Apostles. Stephen the deacon was arrested for his preaching and condemned to death for blasphemy, the same charge that the Jewish high priests had tried to bring against Jesus.[22] Stephen's martyrdom is recounted at great length, but it was exceptional—and illegal. There was no general massacre of Christians by the Jewish leadership, even though the temple priests dearly wanted to stamp them out.

One of the onlookers at Stephen's stoning was Saul of Tarsus.[23] Saul volunteered to flush out Christians wherever he could find them and in later years accused himself of having been a persecutor of the church, but he was spectacularly unsuccessful and got nowhere. Nevertheless, Saul (or Paul, as we usually call him) was obviously more aware of the danger he faced from his opponents, and it seems that he was often close to death.[24] Both he and Peter are believed to have been martyred for their faith, though it is not certain when or where that happened. Most likely it was in Rome sometime after the great fire of AD 64, which Nero blamed on the Christians. The charge was fatuous of course, as everyone at the time recognized, but once Christians came under suspicion it was very difficult for the authorities to change course.

19. Luke 12:49–53.
20. Galatians 2:19–20.
21. Philippians 1:21–23.
22. Acts 6:8–7:60.
23. Acts 7:58.
24. 2 Corinthians 11:23–27.

We do not know how long the first persecution lasted or how far it extended, but after it Christians were no longer safe. Death, however, was not the only option open to the authorities. John was exiled to Patmos, but as far as we know, he survived the experience.[25] There was no settled policy or procedure for dealing with Christians, a problem that led to uncertainty and increased the possibility that they would suffer arbitrarily. In AD 111 we hear of the situation in Bithynia, where they were being denounced to the authorities, who did not know how to punish them. Pliny the Younger, the governor of the province in that year, wrote to the emperor Trajan about the problem, but his main concern was to know what he should do about the accusations, many of which were anonymous. It never occurred to him, or to the emperor, that being a Christian ought not to be a crime; they both agreed that it was and did not question it. Pliny assumed that there were laws against Christianity and only wondered how they should be enforced. Trajan advised him to ignore anonymous denunciations, because they were unworthy of the high standards of Roman justice, but he did not pursue matters any further than that.

This curious situation continued for another two hundred years. Christian apologists constantly pointed out that they were not guilty of anything and that persecuting them was irrational. However, although the case they made was unanswerable, it did not stop the government from pursuing its aims. But if Christianity was outlawed, it would be wrong to suggest that the persecution of it was constant or universal. There were long periods when nothing much was done to suppress it, and some parts of the empire were little affected. The Roman authorities lacked the means of enforcing their laws in the way that a modern state can, and usually they had better things to occupy their minds. But the threat of persecution was always there, and if there was a natural disaster that required a victim to appease the wrath of the gods, the Christians were natural sacrifices. Still, modern scholars agree that the traditional picture of them being thrown to the lions in the Coliseum is inaccurate. There is no evidence that that ever happened—the legend rests entirely on a rhetorical flourish of Tertullian, who claimed that every time something went wrong the people would cry out: "Christians to the lions."[26]

But although the legends are certainly exaggerated, intermittent and localized attacks on Christians were always a danger, and periodically the state tried to deal with the problem once and for all. Two great persecutions, one under the emperor Decius in AD 251 and the other under Diocletian in 303–5,

25. Revelation 1:9.
26. Tertullian, *Apologeticum* 40.2.

stand out as especially significant, and the second of these provoked a crisis that ultimately led to the official recognition of Christianity as a legal religion.

The Decian persecution came after a relatively long period of peace and seems to have been provoked by a growing realization that Christians were turning up everywhere. One of the people who suffered at this time was the great theologian Origen (185?–254), who was so savagely beaten that he never recovered from his wounds. Cyprian of Carthage (200?–258) was beheaded a few years later, during a second wave of persecution, but the details are obscure. What is clear is that educated and prominent church members were being targeted in a way that had not been true for almost a century, and that inevitably aggravated an already difficult situation.

It was the great persecution of Diocletian, however, that caused the real crisis. Diocletian was an energetic and reforming emperor, who was determined to put the empire straight once and for all. Getting rid of the Christian menace was part and parcel of that overall plan. He decided that only a root-and-branch persecution would have any effect, so he launched what today would be described as a reign of terror. Christians were seized and ordered to hand over any books or other treasures they might have. A person who complied was a *traditor* (hander over), a word that has come down to us as "traitor." The great persecution had a devastating effect, because by 300 a significant number of prominent people were Christians. Many of them tried to flee, and others abjured their faith in order to save their lives. But others went bravely to their deaths, and there were probably more martyrs in the two years that the persecution lasted than in all the others put together.

Diocletian's persecution ended in 305, when he resigned as emperor, and it became clear that it had failed. Too many Christians had survived the onslaught, and those who perished became heroes overnight. Somehow or other, the empire would have to make peace with the church, and that is what happened within a decade. Diocletian actually lived to see it—he did not die until 316—but he was in retirement and could do nothing about it. The cross of Christ had at last triumphed over the eagle of Rome.

In the church it was taken for granted that martyrs went straight to heaven when they died. There might be doubts about the spiritual state of those who committed sins after being baptized, but the baptism of fire wiped away any debt that they owed to God. The martyrs stood around the throne of Jesus, the Lamb who was slain, and they cried out for justice for God's people on earth.[27] Of all the links the church had between this world and the next, the pleas of the martyrs in heaven were among the most powerful. It was also

27. Revelation 6:9–11.

generally believed that the martyrs bore the wounds of their sufferings for eternity as badges of honor. Suffering became something to glory in—as long as it came uninvited. Those who sought to live for Christ would suffer persecution, it was believed, so it was by doing the right thing that God's people would be fulfilling the Lord's command to take up their cross and follow him. Martyrdom thus became a guaranteed form of sanctification for which there was objective proof. Good works might be done in secret, but a martyr was obvious to everyone, and honored accordingly. The burial places of martyrs became centers of pilgrimage, and some people believed that their relics had healing powers.

That superstition was never approved by any church council, but it was widely held, especially in North Africa, and proved to be very difficult to deal with once the official persecution of the church ceased. Some even wondered whether the persecutions had stopped because the church had lost its cutting edge and compromised with the surrounding world. In Carthage a schism in the church broke out when a woman called Lucilla wanted her bishop to bless the bones of a martyr as she received Communion from him. The bishop refused, whereupon Lucilla and her supporters accused him of collaborating with the enemies of the church who had so recently persecuted it. Lucilla seems to have been an inveterate troublemaker. When the bishop in question, a man called Caecilianus, was elected in 305, she and her friends rejected him on the ground that the man who consecrated him, Felix of Aptunga, had turned over the Scriptures to the authorities during the great persecution. They therefore proceeded to elect a rival bishop, a certain Majorinus, and did all they could to get him accepted in place of Caecilianus. They even sought the assistance of the emperor Constantine, shortly after he legalized Christianity in 313, but they failed to impress him with the justice of their case.

The result was that they broke away from the mainline church, which they accused of compromise and impurity, and established congregations of true believers. They came to be known as Donatists, from a man named Donatus, who was one of their early leaders and by all accounts a bishop of exceptional quality and character. Donatism had a powerful emotional appeal to people who had suffered persecution and felt betrayed by a church that in their eyes was more interested in currying favor with their erstwhile persecutors than in imitating those who had laid down their lives for Christ. It would be a century before its power was broken, and even then, it survived as long as there was a Christian church in North Africa.[28]

28. On Donatism, see W. H. C. Frend, *The Donatist Church: A Movement of Protest in Roman North Africa* (Oxford: Oxford University Press, 1952).

As long as persecution lasted, martyrdom was a powerful reminder that the church was at war with the forces that govern this world. Its mission could never be one of assimilating to wider society but had always to be in some sense confrontational. Christians could not live happily alongside pagans, because their worldviews were incompatible. Paganism was irrational and immoral, and Christians believed that it had to be suppressed if at all possible. It would be too much to claim that when the church came to power in the Roman world, it persecuted pagans in the same way as it had previously been persecuted, although there were certainly some cases of barbarous behavior by so-called Christians, most notably the dreadful murder of the pagan philosopher Hypatia in Alexandria in AD 415. It is true that Christians did all they could to persuade pagans to convert to Christianity, but they usually stopped short of killing them, if only because unconverted pagans would have gone to hell, which was not what the Christians wanted. Hard as it may be for modern minds to accept, the church's aim was to win others for Christ so that they might be saved. If the means used sometimes violated the free will of the victims, this should be compared to modern campaigns for vaccination and so on, which are occasionally forced on those who object. The general consensus was that salvation was good for the recipient, whether he knew it or not, and the church proceeded along those lines. If the church appeared to be tyrannical, it was in a good cause, an attitude that in some places persisted for centuries, though it seems to have died out now.

The Development of the Episcopate

As the church spread across the Roman world and faced new challenges, one of its most pressing concerns became the need to preserve its inner unity. This had never been easy, as we can see from the quarrels that erupted in the New Testament period. If it was possible for new believers to object to the teaching of the apostle Paul, whom they knew and had heard in the flesh, how much easier would it be for people who had not known the apostles to object to their teachings? Who had the authority to decide what was right and impose it on the church as a whole?

It was in this climate and against this background that the so-called monarchical episcopate emerged. Local churches often continued to have a form of collective leadership, but as time went on, more and more authority devolved to the bishop (*episkopos*), who was elected by the congregation and served for life.[29] In modern times great emphasis has been laid, especially in the

---

29. As he was probably already a senior figure when elected and people did not usually live as long then as they do now, it was unusual for a bishop to serve for a long time.

Catholic tradition, on the so-called apostolic succession, which is supposedly conveyed from one generation to another by the laying on of hands. But what mattered to people in the early church was not who had laid hands on whom but whether the bishop who was elected met the strict criteria laid down for the office in the Pastoral Epistles. A man could be consecrated by all the right people yet be unacceptable if his life and doctrine did not measure up to these requirements, and the early Christians had no qualms about deposing him if that were the case. As early as the *Didache* we read: "Appoint for yourselves bishops and deacons who are worthy of the Lord; men who are humble, not lovers of money, truthful and experienced, for they also serve you as your prophets and teachers."[30]

Similar thoughts were expressed by Clement of Rome, who was probably writing sometime around AD 95. Clement was aware that there was competition for the episcopal office and warned the churches not to terminate an episcopal appointment unless there was good reason to do so.[31]

A few years later, Ignatius of Antioch enjoined the churches to submit to the bishops and presbyters, though he was careful to insist that he could not tell them what to do, because he did not have the same authority as an apostle.[32] But although he saw himself as occupying a position subordinate to theirs, he did not hesitate to compare the relationship of a bishop to his presbyters to that between Christ (or God) and his apostles.[33] As far as Ignatius was concerned, there was a divine harmony in heaven and earth that was reflected in a hierarchy of authority, stemming from the Father to the Son, and through him to the bishops and presbyters of the church on earth. The duties of the bishop were primarily two. First, he was called to preach the Word of God in the congregation, and Ignatius warned people that those who did not accept his teaching were heretics.[34] Second, it was his duty to preside at the Eucharist, which had no validity otherwise.[35]

The testimony of these early witnesses is confirmed by Irenaeus, Clement of Alexandria (d. 215?), and Tertullian, all of whom were writing about two generations later. It was Cyprian, bishop of Carthage a generation after Tertullian, who developed the thinking of the church in greater detail and is today regarded as one of the most important early sources for what has

---

30. *Didache* 15.

31. *1 Clement* 44. The same warning was given by Cyprian of Carthage, writing about 150 years later. See *Epistulae* 40.2; 43.1.

32. Ignatius of Antioch, *Ad Romanos* 4.3; *Ad Ephesios* 3; *Ad Trallianos* 3.

33. Ignatius of Antioch, *Ad Magnesios* 6; *Ad Smyrnaeos* 8.

34. Ignatius of Antioch, *Ad Philadelphianos* 1–2.

35. Ignatius of Antioch, *Ad Philadelphianos* 4; *Ad Smyrnaeos* 8.

become known as "Catholic" teaching about the episcopal office. Cyprian was the first person to make specific reference to Jesus's statement to Peter in Matthew 16:18 as the basis for the episcopal ordering of the church later on. In his words:

> From there [Matthew 16:18], the ordering of bishops and the organization of the church flow outward over time, so that the church is founded on the bishops, and every act of the church is controlled by these same governors. Since this is founded on the law of God, I am amazed that some people have dared to write to me as if they represented the church. The church is established in the bishop, the clergy and all who stand fast in the faith.[36]

Cyprian acknowledged that the bishop derived his authority from Christ's charge to Peter, but he did not connect that with the bishop of Rome, whose claims to primacy over the church on the basis that he was Peter's successor he flatly denied.[37] Cyprian was quite prepared to write to the Romans urging them to sort out the affairs of their church, and did so on several occasions.[38] He even wrote a letter to Pope Lucius I (r. 253–54) congratulating him on his return from banishment and showing not the slightest sign of any deference due him as the successor of Peter and head of the church.[39] On the contrary, as this correspondence shows, it was more often than not the Romans who wrote to Cyprian asking for his advice, something that would be almost impossible to imagine in later centuries. At the very end of his life he presided over a council of eighty-seven African bishops, which rejected Pope Stephen I's condemnation of an earlier decree of theirs about baptism administered by heretics and reaffirmed their right to decide the matter for themselves.[40]

As far as the status and jurisdiction of bishops was concerned, Cyprian was aware that different standards of discipline were applied in different churches, but he insisted that each bishop was free to act as he chose in such matters, as long as he maintained unity of faith and worship with the other bishops and their churches.[41] The bishop was the focus of unity for the church, even to the point of being identified with it.[42] His office had

---

36. Cyprian of Carthage, *Epistulae* 26.1.
37. Cyprian of Carthage, *Epistulae* 70.3.
38. Cyprian of Carthage, *Epistulae* 3; 14; 22–23; 28; 40; 43; 47; 51.
39. Cyprian of Carthage, *Epistulae* 57.
40. *Decree of the Seventh Council of Carthage Held under Cyprian*, in *The Ante-Nicene Fathers*, ed. A. Roberts et al. (Grand Rapids: Eerdmans, 1951–53), 5:565. Stephen had died the previous year, so the condemnation was posthumous, but such freedom to reject papal authority would become inconceivable in later times.
41. Cyprian of Carthage, *Epistulae* 51.21; 71.3.
42. Cyprian of Carthage, *Epistulae* 54.14; 68.8.

been established by Christ in the form of the apostleship, but the other orders of ministry were human creations and therefore inferior in origin and authority.[43]

What emerges from all this is that Cyprian envisaged a church in which the bishops of every local congregation were both autonomous within their own jurisdiction and bound to one another by a collegiality grounded in their common adherence to, and responsibility for, apostolic teaching and practice. Problems, as and when they arose, were to be sorted out by councils to which bishops would be summoned. In North Africa this pattern was well established by the time Cyprian died, and there is evidence (from the deposition of Paul of Samosata, for example) that a similar procedure was in operation elsewhere. Continuing persecution of the church made it impossible to establish this on a regular basis, but the structure was in place, and when the church was finally legalized, it could (and did) come out into the open. The First Council of Nicaea in 325, which has gone down as epoch-making in the history of the church, was possible only because the groundwork for it had been laid in the centuries of persecution that had just come to an end.

An Evolving Doctrine of the Church

It was during those centuries of persecution that the church arrived at a level of self-understanding that makes it possible for us to say that ecclesiology was a definite part of Christian doctrine. Formal statements to that effect had to await a later time, but that was true of everything else as well—the great doctrines of the Trinity and Christology were not worked out until the church was free to operate as a legal corporation, and its own self-definition was part and parcel of that.

In the first phase of its development, the doctrine of the church was closely tied to the office of the bishop, as we have just seen. This was because the bishop represented Christ, and Christ was the shepherd of the universal church.[44] The body was constituted by the head, which was the basic principle of its existence. That in turn meant that the church existed only where Christ's teaching was maintained in its original purity.[45] Irenaeus was adamant about this and insisted that every faithful church preserved the truth handed down to it in common with its sisters throughout the world:

43. Cyprian of Carthage, *Epistulae* 64.3.
44. *Martyrdom of Polycarp* 19.
45. Theophilus of Antioch, *Ad Autolycum* 2.14.

The church received this preaching and this faith. Although she is scattered throughout the world, she carefully preserves it, as if she were living in a single house. She believes these doctrines just as if she had only one soul and one heart. She proclaims these truths, teaches them and hands them on in perfect harmony, as if she possessed only one mouth.[46]

Irenaeus was well aware that there were false teachers in the church, but he believed that they could be detected by their false doctrines and ungodly manner of life; the two errors often went together, in his view.[47] The gift of teaching came from the Holy Spirit, and where the Spirit was present, the church would also be found.[48] This view was echoed by his Eastern contemporary Clement of Alexandria and may be regarded as standard around AD 200.[49] Tertullian was equally insistent on the primacy of doctrine and of the unity of the apostolic tradition across the world.[50] Tertullian was more critical of the church's ministers than most of his contemporaries, but that was because he thought they were unfaithful to the teachings they were meant to profess, not because he disagreed with what they taught.[51] Origen, writing slightly later, had the same opinion.[52] But as with the office of the bishop, so with the doctrine of the church in general, it would be Cyprian who would crystallize the teaching of the fathers in the mind of later ages, and it is to him, more than to anyone else in the ancient world, that modern theologians most readily refer when they discuss the doctrine of the church.

Cyprian agreed with his predecessors about the importance of maintaining pure apostolic doctrine, and he believed that the bishops and presbyters were especially chosen and equipped for that task. However, he also recognized that there were impure elements in the church, and that as Jesus had said, the wheat and the tares would grow together until the harvest.[53] To his mind, that was a reality that Christians had to accept and was not an excuse for leaving the church. Those who set up their own worshiping communities on the ground that the church was imperfect were deluding themselves, not least by falsely assuming that they would be corrupted by the sins of others if they

46. Irenaeus of Lyons, *Adversus omnes haereses* 1.10.1.
47. Irenaeus of Lyons, *Adversus omnes haereses* 4.26.2–4.
48. Irenaeus of Lyons, *Adversus omnes haereses* 3.24.1.
49. Clement of Alexandria, *Paedagogus* 6.
50. Tertullian, *De praescriptione haereticorum* 20–21.
51. In *De exhortatione castitatis* 7, Tertullian argues that since the clergy are chosen from among the laity, they are not necessary to the constitution of the church, which can happily exist without them.
52. Origen, *Contra Celsum* 6.45.
53. Cyprian of Carthage, *Epistulae* 50.3. See Matthew 13:24–29.

continued to associate with them.[54] Aberrations had to be understood for
what they were and did not define the church as a whole. The forgiveness of
sins through baptism and repentance was a divine gift to the church, which
administered it in the name of Christ and according to his promises.[55] It was
for that reason that there was no salvation outside the church.[56]

Probably no statement about the church has caused more controversy than
this one. Cyprian was talking about baptism, which had been entrusted to
the church as a sign of the saving faith revealed in Christ. He was not saying
that its efficacy depended on the spiritual standing of the minister. As long as
it was administered according to apostolic teaching, it was valid, and those
properly baptized would naturally seek the fellowship of the church that confessed the apostolic faith. Cyprian did not have to decide which church that
was, because in his day there was only one body that could reasonably claim
the name. In later centuries his saying would be used to say that Protestants
were not saved because they had left the Roman Catholic Church, but that was
far from Cyprian's mind. Had he been alive in the sixteenth century, there is
every chance that he would have sided with Martin Luther against the pope.
We obviously do not know what he would have thought about Luther, but we
have plenty of evidence that he would have been prepared to reject the papal
claims that were advanced against Luther.

Cyprian also made an interesting distinction between water baptism
and the reception of the Holy Spirit. According to him, the Spirit can be
given only to someone who already exists, just as God breathed his Spirit
into Adam only after he had formed him from the ground.[57] The church's
baptism was the spiritual equivalent of this divine act of creation because
it prepared the recipient for the coming of the Holy Spirit. Only after baptism, therefore, could the Spirit come into someone, since before that he or
she was not alive in a way that would make the Spirit's operation possible.
To the modern mind, this opens up the possibility that water baptism may
be administered with no accompanying work of the Spirit, but that does
not seem to have occurred to Cyprian, except perhaps in cases where the
water was administered by a heretic. As far as he was concerned, the water
prepared the way for the Spirit, who came to honor its promise with the
fulfillment that can be had only by union with Christ. It was for that reason,
and in that context, that he uttered his other famous saying: who can have
God as his Father before he has the church as his mother? The church came

---

54. Cyprian of Carthage, *Epistulae* 51.25–27.
55. Cyprian of Carthage, *Epistulae* 72.10.
56. Cyprian of Carthage, *Epistulae* 72.21.
57. Cyprian of Carthage, *Epistulae* 73.7. See Genesis 2:7.

first and prepared the way, but it was God who gave the increase, as Paul had told the Corinthians.[58]

With that we have the fullest and deepest understanding of the church to appear before it was legalized in the fourth century. Cyprian's church was far from perfect, as he himself recognized, but it had not yet been swollen by the influx of large numbers of nominal believers, nor had it come under pressure from the state to modify its doctrine or its practices in any way. It was still a body that was in conscious and often open opposition to the surrounding world, that offered nothing to its adherents other than blood, toil, sweat, and tears—and, of course, eternal salvation. In such a situation, believers could be fairly confident that on the whole, the local congregations to which they belonged were faithful reflections of what the apostles had intended them to be. Only in the next stage of the church's life would that confidence be seriously tested, and it is to that story that we must now turn.

58. See 1 Corinthians 3:6–7.

4

The Imperial Church

Church and State

The legalization of Christianity in February 313 was an event that was to have profound implications for the church and for world history. In purely theological terms, there was no reason why it should have made any difference to the church at all. The church did not suddenly acquire a new doctrine, nor did it have to alter its structure or pattern of worship. The same beliefs, the same bishops, and the same patterns of devotion continued as before. The changes were of a different order altogether, but their cumulative effect was transforming. By the time they took root, the public face of Christianity had been altered beyond recognition, and whether we like it or not, the consequences of that transformation are with us to this day.

In the short term, the legalization of the church put an end to the hostility between the Roman government and its Christian citizens, for which there had never been any real justification, and gave the church a chance to breathe normally and stretch its wings. It is important to bear in mind that the events of 313 did not make Christianity the state religion. That did not happen until February 28, 380, when the emperor Theodosius I (r. 378–95) issued a decree to that effect. It was only after that that pagan cults and temples were officially suppressed, including the Olympic Games. In the interim, there were two generations in which Christianity coexisted with other religious systems.

The imperial family tended to belong to the church and to favor it whenever possible, but most of the emperors had pro-Arian sympathies, which set them on a collision course with the orthodox leaders of the church and led to a series of confrontations that Constantine probably never imagined. It certainly cannot be said that the state took over the church and bent it to its will, though many people today mistakenly think that.

To understand what happened it is necessary to go back to the late third century, when the Roman Empire found itself in a semipermanent crisis caused by the inability to secure a recognized line of succession to the imperial throne. Every time an emperor died or was removed, there were several rival candidates, and a form of civil war almost invariably ensued. The institutions of the state were strong enough to survive these upheavals, but the age was one of growing insecurity, and it was probably no accident that the church made its greatest strides forward at that time.[1] When Diocletian became emperor in 285, he decided that there would henceforth be four emperors, two senior and two junior ones. The senior ones would divide the empire into its eastern and western halves, and the older of the two would enjoy precedence over the other. After twenty years, the senior emperors would retire and be succeeded by the junior ones, who would in turn appoint others to fill the places they had vacated.

On May 1, 305, Diocletian duly resigned and compelled his Western counterpart, Maximian, to do the same. Maximian was succeeded by his erstwhile deputy, Constantius, who was then commanding the Roman armies in Britain. Unfortunately Constantius died after only a year in office, and the army stationed at York promptly elected his son Constantine to succeed him. This was a breach of the system set up by Diocletian, though it was understandable in the circumstances, and Constantine's irregular election was not recognized by the other emperors. To complicate matters still further, Maximian's son Maxentius had claimed his father's throne, and Constantine had to fight him in order to secure his position. Over the next several years he gradually marched on Rome, which he needed to capture in order to make good his claim to rule the empire.

On October 28, 312, Constantine's army was camped outside the capital, and he saw a vision in the night sky. The Christian *chi-rho* symbol appeared to him, with the words "In this sign thou shalt conquer" underneath it. Being a superstitious man, Constantine immediately ordered the *chi-rho* symbol to be painted onto his soldiers' shields, and the next day he won the Battle of the

1. See E. R. Dodds, *Pagan and Christian in an Age of Anxiety* (Cambridge: Cambridge University Press, 1968).

Milvian Bridge, which opened the capital to him. How much of this legendary story is true is impossible to say, but there is no doubt that Constantine
was so impressed by his victory that the following February he issued an edict
from his headquarters at Milan, granting legal recognition to the church. It
was a decree that could be applied only in the area he actually ruled, which
by then encompassed the entire western half of the empire. In the East, reactions varied from acceptance to outright rejection, and the Edict of Milan did
not take full effect there until Constantine finally subdued the whole empire,
which he did by 324.

Attitudes toward Constantine have varied enormously over the centuries.
In the Eastern church he was (and still is) venerated as a saint who was the
equal of the apostles, and for a long time similar views were held in Western
Christianity also. But in the past century or so this reputation has given way
to something quite different, as the church has entered what some have called
the "post-Constantinian" era. By this is meant that the alliance between throne
and altar that underpinned European civilization for centuries has given way
to a period of confrontation, in which the church now finds itself on the losing
end of social change. Many modern theologians have deeply disliked what
they have seen as complicity between church and state and have rejoiced in
this development, regarding the whole "Constantinian" experiment as a huge
mistake. Ignoring the fact that Constantine did not make Christianity the
state religion, they have blamed him for corrupting the gospel by establishing
a political connection that should never have come into being. As a result,
today Constantine has a bad press in academic circles, and his achievements
tend to be discounted.[2]

Is it possible to come to a balanced opinion on this controversial subject?
First of all, it may be readily admitted that Constantine's own faith was
rudimentary and in many respects inadequate. He was undoubtedly more
superstitious than pious and had little time for theological niceties. He was
not even baptized until he lay on his deathbed, perhaps because he did not
want to give the impression that he was favoring the church unduly or making himself subject to its discipline. In AD 321 he decreed that Sunday would
become a public holiday, but this was two-edged. On the one hand, it allowed
Christians to worship God on their chosen day, but it also honored the sun
god, who was a popular pagan deity at the time. People could take it either
way, and no one suffered discrimination for holding non-Christian beliefs.

As far as the church was concerned, it was free to regulate its own affairs
by a system of synods and councils that had gradually emerged during the

2. See A. Kee, *Constantine versus Christ: The Triumph of Ideology* (London: SCM, 1982).

centuries of persecution and that could now function in the open. In order to promote the unity of the worldwide church, the bishops of a given area would meet periodically and determine what their policy would be on whatever disputed subjects were causing problems at the time. For obvious reasons, they had to keep a low profile until 313, with the result that most of the synods (or councils) that met did so on a provincial basis, like the ones that Cyprian presided over in North Africa. Originally the words "council" and "synod" were synonymous and interchangeable—a *synodos* in Greek was a *concilium* in Latin, and this remains the official position to this day. But popular usage, at least in the English-speaking world, has tended to think of synods as more local and councils as more universal. Thus, for example, the Church of England is governed by its General Synod, whereas the World Council of Churches includes member churches drawn from all over the world.[3] In practice, the two words are no longer completely synonymous, but modern distinctions are arbitrary as far as the early church is concerned and may be ignored when its history is being discussed.

As we have already seen, the earliest synod/council was held at Jerusalem in order to determine how Jews and gentiles would live together in a single church. Its decisions are recorded in Acts 15, but how widely they were applied is unknown. It seems that the whole controversy blew over fairly quickly and that after a few years the provisions made at the synod were no longer needed. Nevertheless, a precedent had been set for resolving disputes by synodical procedures, and if a similar problem were to recur, a solution was readily available.

For the most part, the main function of the early synods was to establish a common discipline for all the churches. This may seem to us to have been unnecessary, as long as there was an underlying unity of principle, but our modern willingness to be flexible in nonessential matters is a luxury that the early Christians could not so easily afford. In a world where literacy was a minority accomplishment, where few individuals possessed a Bible, and where travel was much less common than it is today, differences of practice, however minor they might seem to us, could lead to the suspicion that underlying them were differences of doctrine—and therefore heresy. For example, it does not matter to us whether the bread used at the Lord's Supper is leavened or unleavened, and we are not disturbed by the fact that both customs were followed in the early church. But this difference was perceived by many as having special significance because Jews insisted on using unleavened bread for the Passover meal. Some Christians thought that they should therefore

---

3. In this context, Greek uses the word *symboulion* for "council" instead of *synodos*.

do the same, since that is what Jesus must have done at the Last Supper, but others thought that the use of unleavened bread was a Judaizing practice that ought to be avoided.

Similarly, some thought that Easter, the feast of the resurrection of Christ, should be celebrated on 14 Nisan, according to the Jewish calendar, and others argued that it should always fall on a Sunday, because that is the day on which the resurrection occurred. Again, we can see the pattern of Judaizing and non-Judaizing tendencies coming into play. The Easter controversy (which turned out to be the first of many) was resolved at the First Council of Nicaea in favor of a Sunday celebration, though it was decreed that it should always be after Passover.[4] The unleavened bread (*azymes*) controversy rumbled on for centuries and was not finally disposed of until 1439, when the sensible decision—that it did not matter one way or the other—was finally reached.

Synods might also be called upon to adjudicate the status and/or orthodoxy of a particular bishop, as happened with Paul of Samosata, and they would be expected to take whatever action was deemed necessary in the circumstances. This inevitably led to doctrinal decisions, which were assumed to be in accordance with the universal "rule of faith," though this could not often be proved. A church that had no means of enforcing its decisions had to walk by faith and assume that what it said would be respected, and for the most part, this seems to have worked. Certainly, when the church was legalized it emerged as a single worldwide body, not as a series of local organizations that were somehow in competition with one another. Given the difficulties of communication in the ancient world and the natural tendency of religious bodies to split over their differences rather than reach agreement, this was a remarkable achievement. It must make us skeptical of the widespread belief among scholars that the New Testament church was an uneasy coalition of different groups that were forcibly welded together at a later stage.

Not only does that idea go against common experience, but there was no force capable of producing the kind of unity so described. Had this sense of belonging together not been present in the churches themselves, it is hard to see how the Christian world would have held together once differences began to surface. Councils and synods may not have been universally popular, but their decisions were taken seriously and generally obeyed because most people were persuaded that their expression of a common mind was the work of the Holy Spirit. Later there would be synods that would attempt to overturn established orthodoxy, but these were soon spotted and ruled out as invalid—for example, the famous "robber synod" of Ephesus in AD 449,

4. This rule is still observed in the East but was abandoned in the West as early as 457.

whose one-sided "resolution" of the christological controversy was quickly repudiated. Maintaining order may have been difficult but was not impossible, and given the conditions in which it had to work, the early church was remarkably successful at it.

When Constantine legalized the church, he knew that it had become a powerful social institution, and he obviously wanted it on his side, but he was probably unaware of the tensions that were simmering inside it. No sooner had he issued his decree of toleration than the North African church erupted in the Donatist schism, and he found himself sponsoring a council of the Western church that met in 314 at Arles in an attempt to resolve it.[5] Before long, and ironically, Roman soldiers were being deployed to compel Donatists to accept Catholic ownership of the disputed churches—something that both the leaders of the church and Constantine must have wondered at. Only a few years after it was legalized, the church was already using the state to enforce its discipline.

In the East, Constantine came up against an even more serious problem. In 318, an Alexandrian presbyter named Arius had been condemned for preaching that Christ was a creature and not the Creator. Scholars debate the accuracy of this condemnation, and there can be no doubt that Arianism was much broader and more complex than anything Arius himself could have devised. But if the label was inaccurate, the phenomenon itself presented the church with a real challenge. Arianism forced it to define its doctrine of the person and natures of Christ much more precisely than it had ever done before. In the process a number of people came up with solutions that turned out to be inadequate and were eventually rejected. What happened to those people varied from case to case, but usually they were deposed from whatever church office they occupied (especially if they were bishops). Beyond that they were seldom persecuted or put to death; Arius himself lived to a good age, and so did many others. The popular image of a triumphant church that ruthlessly suppressed dissidents with state assistance is inaccurate, at least for the fourth and fifth centuries, and must be rejected.

At the same time, the legalization of the church had practical implications that could not be ignored. If there was division among Christians, which side was going to receive official state recognition? Donatism presented no problem on this score because it usually rejected the state and was rejected by it in turn. But Arianism was more difficult. Some leading Arians, or "semi-Arians," were close associates of the emperors and enjoyed their favor, while staunch

5. Arles was then the capital of Gaul (now France). The council also tried to resolve the Easter question, but without success.

defenders of orthodoxy were discriminated against. The most famous example of this was the case of Athanasius, bishop of Alexandria from 328 to 373, who was exiled no fewer than five times because imperial policy was against him. In the end, he triumphed because his theological convictions were more persuasive than those of his Arian opponents, but it cannot be said that he owed his victory to state intervention. Rather the reverse!

The complexity of the Arian issue was revealed almost immediately after Constantine's conquest of the East. By then Arianism was causing such dissension in the church that it was necessary to summon a council to sort the problem out. Constantine duly did so and appointed one of his supporters, Hosius of Cordoba (in Spain) as its president. The council met at Nicaea in 325 and took decisions that future generations would regard as of epochal significance. But before the bishops could get to Nicaea, some of them convened another council at Antioch, which met about six months beforehand and hammered out the policy that they would defend in front of the emperor. They did this because they felt that doctrinal decisions should be taken by the bishops without any participation from the state. Constantine was not even baptized at this stage, so it seemed more than a little incongruous that he should be sponsoring a church council whose purpose was to settle its internal affairs.

But in spite of that, the First Council of Nicaea set a precedent that was to endure for centuries. The Council of Arles in 314 had met with the emperor's permission, but Nicaea I assembled at his command. For more than a thousand years afterward, the Eastern churches would insist that all church councils should be summoned by the emperor and that if he (or his representative) were not present, its decisions would not be valid. No one said anything about the bishop of Rome; his absence from both Arles and Nicaea I was a matter of complete indifference. At the time of the Reformation, some Protestants adopted this Eastern view as part of their overall opposition to the claims of the papacy. Article 21 of the Church of England, for example, which was adopted in its present form in 1563, states quite clearly: "General councils may not be gathered together without the commandment and will of princes." Not until the secularization of Europe in the course of the French Revolution would that principle be called into question and abandoned, not least because there were no longer any princes (i.e., emperors and kings) willing or able to call one.

A sign of this imperial interest can be seen in the fact that the First Council of Nicaea has gone down in history as "ecumenical," a word that is normally translated as "universal" today but which had a somewhat different (and very specific) meaning in the ancient world. The *oikoumenē* was the Roman Empire, the extent of civilization as most people knew it.[6] An ecumenical council was therefore not so much "universal" as "imperial," requiring the consent of the emperor if its decisions were to become law. In spiritual matters, the bishops claimed the right to legislate for the church, and they expected the state to enforce their decisions. Imperial interference in church affairs must be understood in light of this. Emperors obviously wanted the church to make decisions they could live with, but the only way to ensure this was to try to influence episcopal elections. In later centuries this was to lead to open arguments between the emperor and the pope over who had the right to appoint the church's bishops. In theory this should have been a decision left to the church, but in practice the emperors (and other secular rulers) seldom had to stomach somebody they could not live with. At the time of the Reformation, the rulers often took over episcopal appointments, which in some countries they continue to make to this day.[7]

That, however, was still far in the future. When Christianity became the official religion, the church did not become a department of state but remained an independent power in its own right. Bishops could, and sometimes did, object to imperial policy, even to the point of calling emperors to repent of their sins. This happened in 388, for example, when Ambrose of Milan forced Theodosius I to do penance for the massacre of Thessalonica, which he had perpetrated for political reasons. Theodosius may have regretted making the church the state religion only eight years before, but such was the effect on popular opinion that he complied with Ambrose's wishes and set a precedent that would be admired (and sometimes followed) for centuries thereafter.

The main impact of state recognition on the church came in the way its internal affairs were governed. There had long been a tendency to group churches together along provincial lines, mainly for convenience, and this habit now became official policy. Local churches with a bishop were recognized as having a territory that was called a "diocese," borrowing another Roman term but using it in a different way. In Diocletian's empire there had been four dioceses, one for each of the four emperors, and each diocese contained several provinces. In the church it was to be the other way round: each province contained several bishoprics and therefore several dioceses. The vocabulary was borrowed from the secular administration, but as this example demonstrates,

6. The word is used in this sense in Luke 2:1.
7. Denmark and Norway are obvious examples of this. It was also the case in England until recently, and still is in theory. In practice the church nominates the candidate it wants, and the prime minister is expected, but not required, to agree, and there have been cases where such confirmation has been denied, presumably for political reasons.

the church operated according to its own needs and agenda, adapting what lay at hand as the occasion arose.

At the First Council of Nicaea it was decided that for jurisdictional (i.e., disciplinary) purposes the bishops and churches of the three largest imperial cities should enjoy regional precedence over all the others. This special position was accorded to Rome, Alexandria, and Antioch in that order, with Rome being responsible for the West, Alexandria for Egypt, and Antioch for eastern Europe and Asia. It was a division of labor that made sense and might have worked quite well, but before it could be implemented properly Constantine (perhaps unwittingly) made it inoperable. This was because on May 11, 330, he chose Byzantium, a Greek city on the Bosporus, as the future capital of the empire. He intended it to become the New Rome, but from the beginning everyone knew it as Constantinople, a name that did not give way to "Istanbul" until 1928.[8] In Constantine's scheme of things, Rome retained the prestige of the old capital, but real power was transferred to the East. Later on, when a separate Western empire was reestablished, the emperors usually resided not at Rome but at Milan or Ravenna, where they were closer to the frontiers that needed guarding against the ever-present barbarian threat. In political terms, Rome declined and became a shadow of its former self, though it continued to be the spiritual center of the empire, especially in the Latin-speaking West.

The creation of Constantinople posed a dilemma for the church. Before 330, Byzantium did not have its own bishop but was dependent on the neighboring town of Heraclea. That obviously could not continue, and before long Constantinople acquired both a bishop and an ecclesiastical establishment. But where were they to be fitted into the overall scheme of things? The bishop of the capital city could hardly be regarded as subordinate to Antioch (in whose jurisdiction Constantinople lay). As New Rome, it deserved a place in the sun—as it thought, immediately behind Old Rome. That, however, was easier said than done. To put Constantinople in second place meant demoting Alexandria, which was the leading city of the Greek world at that time. It was also a potential threat to Rome itself, since if the day ever came when Rome's prestige no longer counted, its church might be demoted just as its secular status had been.

This delicate situation was broached at the First Council of Constantinople in 381, which decided that there should be an order of precedence that put Rome first, Constantinople second, Alexandria third, Antioch fourth, and Jerusalem fifth. Before this time Jerusalem, by then a provincial backwater,

---

8. The modern Turkish name is a corruption of the Greek *eis tēn polin* (in the city), because Constantinople has always been known as just "the city" in Greek.

had not figured at all in the hierarchy, and its sudden appearance reflects an ideological shift. Whereas the order of precedence at Nicaea I had been established on the basis of the secular importance of the cities concerned, that of Constantinople I had a spiritual component. Rome was placed first, not just because it was the capital but because it was also the place where Peter had been martyred. This naturally led to the inclusion of Jerusalem because it had been the site of the first church, over which Peter had also presided. This pentarchy of bishoprics, whose heads came to be styled as "patriarchs," gradually imposed itself in the Eastern church, especially after the Council *in Trullo* held in 691–92, but it was slower to catch on in the West, and Rome did not formally ratify it until 1215.

By then, of course, the situation that had produced the original pentarchy had changed beyond all recognition. Alexandria, Antioch, and Jerusalem all fell under Muslim domination between 632 and 641, and apart from a brief period during the Crusades, they have remained in Islamic territory ever since. This left Rome and Constantinople, the former clinging to its ancient status and continually developing its Petrine claims in order to buttress it, the latter insisting that because the senior patriarch had overstepped the limits of his authority and fallen into schism, the Christian world had to look to Constantinople for guidance instead.

As time went on, the Roman see paid less and less attention to the claims of the other four patriarchates. It was the only major city in the West, and as the West grew increasingly detached from the empire, it came to be seen there as the natural center of the whole church. As a result, the term "pope" came to be restricted to the Roman bishop. He is also called the "pontiff," which derives from *pontifex maximus* (chief bridge builder), a title that originally belonged to a pagan official in ancient Rome and was later taken over by the emperor to designate his position as head of the traditional religion. When Rome was Christianized the emperors dropped it, only to see it transferred to the city's bishop instead.

This curious history is a reminder that the Roman emperors derived their authority from ancient traditions that had nothing to do with Christianity. When the new religion was adopted, practices that were incompatible with it were abandoned, but the state itself continued to function as it had always done, as the expression of the "democratic" will of the people, or as the official title had it, the "senate and people of Rome." With the advent of barbarian kingdoms in the West and their progressive conversion to Christianity, new forms of legitimacy had to be devised. In pagan times, their kings had been religious officials, but in the Christian world they had to give up their semi-priestly character. In return, they were consecrated in a coronation ceremony, which legitimized them in the eyes of the church and gave them the right to rule "by the grace of God." This pattern continued down through the centuries and still exists in the United Kingdom, at least in outward form. When King Edward VIII sought to marry a twice-divorced woman in 1936, the church refused to crown him because he was in breach of its marriage laws, and he was forced to abdicate—an example of how, even in recent times, approval by the church has continued to play a part in the selection of a monarch.

The development of the coronation ceremony as the way in which a monarch was given legitimacy reached its pinnacle on December 25, 800, when Pope Leo III crowned Charlemagne as emperor of the newly invented Holy Roman Empire. In theory it was a revival of the ancient empire of the West, which had disappeared with the deposition of the last emperor in 476, but this time it expressed the union of church and state in a way that clearly indicated that it was the church that set the rules. The Holy Roman Empire lasted until 1806, and although it was never as powerful as it was originally meant to be, its importance should not be underestimated. Throughout the Middle Ages, emperors and popes vied for supremacy in Western Christendom, while the other secular rulers—the kings of England and France, for example—looked on. Even in the sixteenth century, it was before the emperor Charles V that Martin Luther had to plead his case, and imperial domination of the papacy, which Henry VIII of England thought was illegitimate, was one of the factors that propelled him to detach his kingdom and its church from Roman authority.

In effect, the coronation of Charlemagne consecrated a division of Europe that had been in the making for four centuries, ever since Theodosius I divided the Roman Empire on his deathbed in 395. After 800 there were not merely two halves of a single empire but two different state systems that claimed the legacy of Rome. The Eastern empire, shorn of its Middle Eastern and African provinces (which had fallen to the Muslim Arabs), was a highly centralized state in which the emperor and the head of the church (the patriarch of Constantinople) lived in the same city and ruled the empire together. Both emperors and patriarchs were frequently deposed with the connivance of the other, and neither could claim absolute dominance. In the West, on the other hand, the emperor and the pope never lived in the same place. The empire was decentralized and even divided among the heirs of Charlemagne, and the papacy had to fend for itself. That proved to be a disaster, and for more than two hundred years popes were elected and deposed, sometimes with distressing frequency, by the street mobs of Rome. It was a scandal, but no one seemed to know what to do about it until a group of reforming monks, based at the Burgundian monastery of Cluny, determined to rescue it. They were more successful than they could have imagined, and in their hands the papacy was transformed into the most powerful European institution of its time.

The Rise of the Papacy

The growth and development of the Roman see has been one of the most important events—many would say *the* most important event—in church history. From playing a significant but by no means dominant role in the first five centuries, the bishop of Rome rose to occupy a position of such dominance that membership in the church came to be defined by whether a particular person or local congregation was in communion with him. For Roman Catholics, who now make up about two-thirds of professed Christians, this is still the case, though in recent years there has been a softening of attitudes toward other believers and a greater willingness to cooperate with them at many levels. For others, both in the historic Eastern churches and in the Protestant West, the papacy continues to be a benchmark against which they measure themselves. There are many things they dislike about the Roman church, but its demand for submission to the pope and his authority remains at the top of the list of things they cannot contemplate. Whatever else may divide them, some bishops of the Russian Orthodox Church and fundamentalist American preachers have this in common—to them the pope is the antichrist. How has an institution that was supposedly designed to express and defend the unity of the worldwide church managed to become such an instrument of division and even hatred?

When the last Western Roman emperor was deposed in 476, the empire did not officially dissolve. Instead, the imperial regalia were sent to Constantinople, and the fiction was maintained that the Western provinces had rejoined the East. This belief was popular with the masses of the people, who were loyal Romans and (for the most part) members of the same church as the Easterners were. But the reality was that their lands were ruled by barbarian tribesmen, who were not Romans in any sense. Most of them were either pagans or Arians, having been converted to that form of Christianity in the fourth century, thanks to the missionary work of one of their number, a Goth called Wulfila (Ulfilas), who had even translated the Bible into their language. Arianism was important to the barbarians, not because of its theology, which few of them could have grasped, but because it allowed them to practice a kind of segregation that kept their identity intact in a sea of potentially hostile Romans.

When the Eastern Empire attempted to reconquer the West in the sixth century, it had the support of the Roman church; the Arian kingdoms of Italy and North Africa were quickly overthrown. The imperial troops also invaded Spain but were unable to occupy more than a small portion of the southeast. Even so, the pressure was on the Arian Visigothic rulers of the rest of the peninsula, who in 589 submitted to Rome and renounced Arianism for good.

Further afield, the Frankish kingdom in Gaul had been pagan until its king, Clovis, was baptized into the Roman church in 496, the first important barbarian king to submit to the papacy. Clovis forced his warriors to follow suit, and France became "the eldest daughter of the church," a position that its kings were to cherish for the next thirteen hundred years. In the British Isles, pagan Anglo-Saxons had pushed the native Britons to the western fringes, where they maintained the Christianity they had received from Rome in the days of the empire. One of their number, Patrick, went to Ireland as a missionary; although he was not the first Christian in that country, its conversion was later attributed to his work.[9]

The Celtic church, as this amalgam of British and Irish Christians is generally known, has been the object of much romanticizing, with a whole mini-industry devoted to so-called Celtic spirituality. In fact, it was not very different from what existed in the rest of the Christian world at that time, and its special features, such as they were, were mostly due to a time lag that developed because they were increasingly cut off from other countries. The most significant element of this was that the Celts continued to celebrate Easter according to the rules laid down at the First Council of Nicaea in 325, although these had been modified at Rome in 457. Nobody bothered about this until a Roman mission was sent to the Anglo-Saxons in 597, with instructions to link up with the Celtic churches. At that point, the differences that had grown up between them became a barrier to cooperation, and the Celts were unwilling to submit to the Romans. Both sides then competed to evangelize the Anglo-Saxons, a task that was largely completed by 664, when a synod at Whitby was summoned to decide which form of Christianity the new church would adopt. The decision went in favor of Rome, and after that the Celtic churches gradually surrendered their independence, a process that was complete by 716.[10]

Long before then, however, the Roman church was undergoing a profound transformation. During the time when Italy was under barbarian (Arian) rule, the emperors in Constantinople cultivated the city's bishop as their representative in the West. In 519 the emperor Justin I granted him jurisdiction over the

9. See T. M. Charles-Edwards, *Early Christian Ireland* (Cambridge: Cambridge University Press, 2000), for the details.

10. The classic account, and our main source for the details, is Bede, *Ecclesiastical History of the English People*, trans. Leo Sherley-Price (London: Penguin, 1955). See also J. Blair, *The Church in Anglo-Saxon Society* (Oxford: Oxford University Press, 2005).

entire Western church, but this pro-Western stance went considerably farther. At a time when Egypt and Syria were increasingly falling under the influence of the so-called monophysite opponents of the Council of Chalcedon (451), which at Roman insistence had canonized the christological formula of "one divine person in two natures," Constantinople tried to impose that decision on its own eastern provinces, a move that alienated them and was not resolved until the Islamic conquests of the next century, when the monophysite areas passed out of Constantinople's control.[11]

After Italy was reconquered, Rome returned to the emperor's direct rule, and less deference was shown to it by the imperial authorities. In 595 the patriarch of Constantinople assumed the title "ecumenical"; Pope Gregory I (r. 590–604) protested, insisting that only he and his church had any right to such a designation, but his protest was ignored. Gregory is often regarded as the last of the ancient fathers of the church and the first of the medieval popes, and there is some truth to that. He tried to impose a monastic discipline on his clergy but failed because resistance was too strong. But he did have a vision for evangelism, as his famous mission to the English reminds us, and it was in his time that the church began to expand beyond the frontiers of the old Roman world in a significant way.[12]

For a century after Gregory's death, Rome's fortunes followed those of the Byzantine Empire, as the Eastern Roman world may now appropriately be called. The theological controversies that continued to dominate politics there spilled over to the West, but they were felt to be increasingly alien there. At one point, a pope was actually arrested and deported to the Crimea for apparently subscribing to a heresy of which neither he nor anyone else at Rome had much knowledge. The two parts of the Christian world were becoming strangers to one another, a fact that was confirmed after the Council *in Trullo* (691–92), when the Eastern churches sorted out the rules by which they were to be governed. Some of these—such as the enforced use of leavened bread in Holy Communion—conflicted with Roman practice, whether deliberately or not, and Rome never ratified the synod's decisions. It continued to abide by its own rules and to make new ones independently of the East, which in time gave it quite a different feel.[13]

---

11. The monophysites—or as they are now often called, "miaphysites"—held that the incarnate Christ had only one nature, in which the human element had been united to the divine.

12. See J. Richards, *The Popes and the Papacy in the Early Middle Ages, 476–752* (London: Routledge & Kegan Paul, 1979); R. B. Eno, *The Rise of the Papacy* (Wilmington, DE: Michael Glazier, 1990).

13. The importance of the Council *in Trullo* for understanding the later differences between the Eastern and the Western churches is not sufficiently appreciated. See G. Nedungatt and M. Featherstone, eds., *The Council* in Trullo *Revisited* (Rome: Pontificio Istituto Orientale, 1995).

In the eighth century the Byzantine emperor Leo III (r. 717–41) provoked a controversy over the use of icons in worship, which continued in one form or another until 843.[14] Leo wanted to eradicate them, but the defenders of orthodoxy insisted that to abolish pictures of Christ would be to deny the incarnation. Rome sympathized with the "orthodox" on this, but of course it could only do so because the emperor's effective power no longer stretched that far west. In 751 the last Byzantine garrisons in northern Italy were overwhelmed by the pagan Lombards, and Rome was suddenly exposed to their domination. In desperation, the pope turned to the king of the Franks, Pepin (Pippin) I, who, as it happened, had just deposed the last legitimate ruler of the Franks and installed himself in his place. Pepin and the pope needed each other, and an alliance was struck. In return for crushing the Lombards, the pope recognized Pepin's rule; in 754 the pope was granted legal title to the area around Rome. This was the origin of the Papal States, which would later stretch across central Italy and remain in the hands of successive popes until the whole of Italy was forcibly unified in 1870.

Once the papacy had established an alliance with the Franks, the creation of the Holy Roman Empire was probably only a matter of time. In that empire, and more generally across Western Europe, the church came to occupy a special place. It was a society within a society, operating according to its own laws and maintaining jurisdictional rights over its clergy and other "spiritual persons" such as monks and nuns. At the same time, many bishops also became secular rulers in what developed into a patchwork quilt of semi-independent states that owed an increasingly nominal allegiance to the emperor. The emperor himself was elected by the main princes, who included three archbishops—Cologne, Mainz, and Trier—and was then crowned either by the pope (if he happened to be in Rome) or by his representative. By the late Middle Ages the imperial office had become virtually hereditary in the House of Habsburg, which was headquartered in Vienna and ruled most of southeastern Germany. When the empire was finally dissolved by Napoleon, the Austrian emperor continued to enjoy the privileges of his ancestors, including the right to veto papal elections, which was not abolished until 1904. It can truly be said therefore that the creation of this "holy" empire was an event of long-lasting importance in European affairs.

At first, however, that destiny was far from assured. The original Holy Roman Empire collapsed as the dynasty that had created it fell apart. It was

---

14. On the iconoclastic controversy, see E. J. Martin, *A History of the Iconoclastic Controversy* (London: SPCK, 1930); L. Brubaker, *Inventing Byzantine Iconoclasm* (Bristol: Bristol Classical Press, 2012).

subsequently reconstituted on a narrower base, with what is now France forming a separate kingdom to its west. But it was still by far the largest European state and continued to claim the legacy of ancient Rome. Emperors interfered in papal elections, and for a time it seemed as though an arrangement similar to that which obtained in the Byzantine Empire would prevail in the West as well.

That did not happen. Instead, the monks of Cluny determined that the papacy should be reformed and made central to the life of the whole Western church. The key to this was seizing control of papal elections and taking them out of secular hands altogether. By a series of deft political moves, the monks managed to get their own candidate elected pope in 1049 as Leo IX. Leo promptly set about trying to impose the prestige of his office on the church as a whole, including Constantinople. In 1054 he sent a delegation there, demanding submission from the patriarch, which (of course) was refused. The legates then promptly excommunicated the patriarch and were duly excommunicated in return. When they returned to Italy they discovered that Leo IX had died, so the excommunications were officially null and void, but the incident came to be seen in later times as the point at which East and West broke definitively with each other.

After a short period of confusion, when it looked as though the Cluniac reforms might fail, they were reinstated with a vengeance, and in 1059 a college of supporting clergy was created to ensure that future papal elections would be conducted by them—in secret. These clergy were the cardinals, so called because they were the hinges (*cardines*) on which the door of St. Peter turned. To this day, the College of Cardinals continues to elect the pope, which gives it a key role in the Roman Catholic Church. From this point on, reform of church-state relations began in earnest. When William, duke of Normandy, sought papal approval for his proposed invasion of England in 1066, he was granted it on condition that he would allow the new papal reforms to take effect in his dominions. More dramatically, the papacy entered a conflict with the Holy Roman emperor over the same principle, which it won in 1077, when the emperor was forced to make a humiliating recantation at Canossa, in northern Italy. In fact, as later events were to prove, the papal victory was not as impressive as it looked at the time, but there could be no doubt that the popes were now independent actors on the political stage and that their voice and prestige counted for a great deal.[15]

Just how much the papacy mattered became clear only a few years later. In 1071 Byzantine forces in Asia Minor suffered a catastrophic defeat at

15. See W. Ullmann, *A Short History of the Papacy in the Middle Ages* (London: Methuen, 1972).

the hands of the invading Muslim Turks. Within a few years the invaders had reached the gates of Constantinople; the Eastern Empire seemed to be on the point of disintegrating. The emperor Alexius I (r. 1081–1118) made a desperate plea for help to the pope, who he thought was the best person to rally the West to come to his aid. Urban II took up the challenge and in 1095 preached the First Crusade—a holy war designed to repel the infidel and win back lands that had been lost to Christendom. Unfortunately for Alexius, very few soldiers in Western Europe were interested in relieving Constantinople. What lured them was the prospect of reconquering the Holy Land, which had been lost to the Arabs as far back as 638. Nevertheless, the crusaders made their way to Constantinople and began their campaign by besieging the ancient city of Nicaea, where a Turkish sultan had established himself. Fearing the wrath of the Westerners, the sultan secretly surrendered to the Byzantines, who let him retreat unharmed. This was seen by the crusaders as treachery, and relations between them and the Byzantines quickly deteriorated.

When they reached Antioch and captured it, the crusaders refused to hand it over to Alexius. Instead, they set up their own crusader state there and appointed a Western bishop as patriarch. This was tantamount to schism, since they refused to recognize the legitimate rights of the Greek incumbent. The same pattern continued as the crusaders marched south. By 1100 they had established a number of small states in Syria and Palestine under the theoretical overlordship of a king they set up in Jerusalem. The Eastern churches to which the majority of the local population still belonged were simply taken over and given Western bishops and clergy. Theological differences aside, the cultural gap between West and East was now visible for all to see, and it probably did more than anything else to ensure that the two great churches would remain separate from each other.[16]

There were, however, numerous attempts to bridge the divide, and perhaps they would have succeeded eventually had not politics intervened. The crusader victories had been possible because of a temporary weakness in the Islamic world, but in 1187 the Muslims were able to retake Jerusalem, and the crusader states were on the verge of extinction. This led to further attempts to shore them up, of which the Fourth Crusade was by far the most disastrous. Frustrated by their inability to get enough money to pay the Venetians to take them to Palestine, the crusaders turned on Constantinople instead. The

---

16. On the Crusades, see S. Runciman, *A History of the Crusades*, 3 vols. (Cambridge: Cambridge University Press, 1951–54); J. Richard, *The Crusades* (Cambridge: Cambridge University Press, 1999).

Byzantine throne was in dispute at the time, and one of the claimants promised that if they helped him take the city, he would reward them accordingly. They did so, but when the new emperor came to power, he found that the treasury was empty. The crusaders revolted and put Constantinople to the sack—the greatest crime that one group of Christians has ever inflicted on another. The Byzantine Empire temporarily collapsed into a series of ministates, some ruled by Greeks and others by crusaders who decided to stay on in the East. Constantinople itself became the capital of a Latin empire, which lasted until the Greeks retook the city in 1261.

Initially Pope Innocent III (r. 1198–1216) was horrified to hear what had happened, but he could not resist taking advantage of the situation. The papacy was now at the height of its power.[17] Innocent accepted the fall of the city as God's will and promptly set about establishing his own authority in the lands the crusaders controlled. Whatever the nature of the schism between East and West before, it was now permanent. The Eastern churches have never forgotten their humiliation, and even today there is often a feeling of distrust, amounting at times to hatred, between Eastern Orthodox and Roman Catholics that has been fueled by many subsequent outrages on both sides.

In the West, of course, this was scarcely noticed at the time. Innocent III managed to bring King John of England to heel by slapping an interdict on his kingdom—in effect, the clergy went on strike and refused to offer services until the king knuckled under. John did so in the end, and in the famous Magna Carta of 1215, he was forced to recognize the "liberties of the church"—one of the three provisions of that document still in force today.[18] In the same year, Innocent convened the Fourth Lateran Council in Rome, which set the seal on the reforms of the church that had begun 150 years earlier.

It looked as if the papacy was about to take over Western Europe, with civil rulers having to do its bidding whenever they were asked. But things did not work out that way. A series of premature papal deaths weakened the institution during the course of the thirteenth century, and it became clogged with bureaucracy. Gradually the secular rulers realized that they would have to establish civil services of their own if they were to compete with the papal administration and if they were to create effective centralized

17. See I. S. Robinson, *The Papacy, 1073–1198: Continuity and Innovation* (Cambridge: Cambridge University Press, 1990); A. Papadakis, *The Christian East and the Rise of the Papacy* (Crestwood, NY: St. Vladimir's Seminary Press, 1994); J. Sayers, *Innocent III: Leader of Europe, 1198–1216* (London: Longman, 1994).

18. See J. C. Holt, *Magna Carta* (Cambridge: Cambridge University Press, 1992).

governments, and they began to do so. Universities sprang up in Paris and Oxford, which turned out men capable of serving either the church or the state. Above all, the Crusades, which the papacy foolishly continued to promote, were a colossal failure. By 1291 there were no crusader states left in Palestine, and the Western knights who had gone there to defend them were homeless refugees. One group managed to set itself up in Rhodes, where it remained until 1522, when Turkish conquest forced it to find a new base in Malta. It was driven out of there by the French revolutionary armies in 1798, but the Sovereign Military Order of Malta continues to exist as a charitable organization, as does the Order of St. John, a Protestant equivalent set up in nineteenth-century England and now present across the Commonwealth.

The Order of the Templars was less fortunate. Unable to find a secure base, the Templars were at the mercy of any European ruler prepared to have them. King Philip IV of France envied their great wealth and decided to seize it by accusing them of heresy and occult practices that they had supposedly brought back from the East. The charges were fabricated, of course, but no one dared challenge the king of France, and the Templars were suppressed. The authority of the papacy, which had established the order in the first place, was dealt a blow from which its prestige never fully recovered.[19]

This tragic outcome was possible because a few years before, the popes themselves had been forced to leave Rome and settle in Avignon, a city in the south of France. This happened because Pope Boniface VIII decided to attack the French king (and by extension the other kings of Europe) over the issue of clerical taxation. The king thought he had a right to tax the church, but the pope insisted that he was robbing God of what belonged to him. The pope threatened the king with excommunication and issued a famous bull, *Unam sanctam*, in which he stated that only those who were in full communion with him would go to heaven. When Boniface died, the archbishop of Bordeaux was elected as his successor, but Philip IV refused to let him go to Rome. The papal government was forced to transfer to Avignon, where it was to remain until 1377, a period that came to be known as the "Babylonian captivity" of the church. Outwardly everything continued as before, but the popes could no longer dictate to the kings of Europe as they had done in the past, and, worse still, the papacy came to be seen as the tool of the French, with fatal consequences for its authority.

19. M. Haag, *The Templars: History and Myth* (London: Profile Books, 2008); M. Barber, *The Trial of the Templars* (Cambridge: Cambridge University Press, 1978).

Canon Law

The rise of the papacy was possible because it commanded an effective civil service that provided much of the secular administration required in Western Europe after the fall of the Roman Empire.[20] The early church had not performed weddings, but the absence of any reliable civil authority forced the church to step in and create "holy matrimony." In the process it revised ancient Roman procedures in light of the New Testament. Divorce, for example, was abolished and replaced by separation and annulment. Separation "from bed and board" was granted in cases of incompatibility, but it was not divorce. The parties were not free to remarry, and their children continued to inherit their goods and property. An annulment, on the other hand, declared that the marriage had never existed, and any children born from it were bastardized and disinherited. The parties themselves were then free to marry again. In theory, annulments could be granted only in cases of nonconsummation or of marriage within the prohibited degrees of affinity and consanguinity, but the pressure applied by wealthy people, especially kings and aristocrats who wanted to divorce and remarry, was often such that the rules were bent in their favor. At village level, almost everyone was related, and so if necessary the prohibited degrees could often be invoked as justification when needed. In theory, disputes could be resolved at the local level, but the parties always had the right to appeal to the highest court, which was the papal curia. The result was that the papacy found itself deluged with judicial cases that it had to resolve, often with little real information and sometimes years after an appeal was first launched.

Another area where the church took control was the making of wills. Priests were often the only people who could read and write, and they were entrusted with this task more often than not. Of course, those who made a will were encouraged to give something to the church, which ended up with a lot of property it could not dispose of. As time went on, more and more arable land was taken off the market in this way—an intolerable situation that was bound to cause trouble sooner or later.

But this was only the beginning. In order to govern itself more effectively, the church was subdivided into parishes, each of which had an incumbent priest who was supposed to know everyone in it. The parishioners were subject to a tithe of one-tenth of their income, which was assessed by officials appointed by the church and was collected by tax farmers, who got a commission on

20. On canon law, see J. A. Brundage, *Medieval Canon Law* (London: Longman, 1995); R. H. Helmholz, *The Spirit of Classical Canon Law* (Athens: University of Georgia Press, 1996).

whatever they managed to collect.[21] In some places the tithe revenue was meager and barely able to support a priest, but elsewhere it was enormous. The surplus was creamed off to the bishops and their cathedrals, which were built or rebuilt in sumptuous style. Nothing testifies to the renewed confidence and prestige of the medieval church more than the magnificent cathedrals that still dot the landscape and take away the breath of those who visit them. Wealthy parishes also erected enormous parish churches, most of which still survive and continue to bear witness to both the faith and the riches of a bygone age.

Tithing was a form of taxation, derived from the provisions made for priests and Levites in ancient Israel, which was designed to support the ministry of the church. Every productive member of the parish was expected to give 10 percent of his or her income to the church, which would then pay the clergy out of it. Tithe money could also be used for poor relief and for the needs of the wider church. The organization of a parish was complex, but it has to be understood if we are to appreciate what most Europeans of a later time imagined the church to be. The person who received the tithe was called the "rector," and normally he would be the parish priest. It was also possible for one man to be the rector of several parishes (an abuse later known as "pluralism"), and quite often the rectorship would devolve on the abbot of a monastery, which would "appropriate" the parish to itself and use the tithe revenue to support its own establishment. When this happened, the rector appointed a substitute, or "vicar," to reside in the parish and officiate at the services of the church. The vicar was paid by the rector out of the tithe revenue, but over time this came to be formalized. The tithes were subdivided into the "greater" and "lesser" ones. The greater tithes were those on wheat, hay, and wool: wheat, the food of humans; hay, the food of animals (very important in a rural economy); wool, the greatest cash crop. Everything else—the tithe on milk, sheep, and so on—belonged to the category of "lesser" tithes, and these were claimed by the vicar, who also came to be known as the "curate" because he had the "cure (care) of souls" in the parish.

Many vicars were wealthy enough to be able to hire substitutes of their own, and over time these came to be known as "(assistant) curates," as they still are today. This pattern was common all over Western Europe, though the terminology can sometimes be confusing. In France, for example, the resident clergyman was called the *curé*, and his substitute was the *vicaire*, with the result that these terms now mean the opposite in French of what they mean in

---

21. Tax farmers worked on contracts, which were known as "signatures" (*firmae*) because they had to sign them. In time, the word *firma* was extended to mean the plot of land assigned to the tax collector, which thus became his "farm."

English. But this is a difference of terminology, not of substance. The system was the same everywhere, and so it remained for centuries.

Being centers of learning, monasteries often housed monks who were skilled in the art of tax evasion, with the result that monasteries grew rich at the expense of the wider church and society. As the kings of Western Europe made good their claim to tax the clergy, this evasion grew steadily worse, fueled as it often was by a genuine conviction that the state was not entitled to revenue that had been dedicated to the service of God and his church.

The truth was that the church had become a state of its own, and in the process it had acquired an identity that it had not previously had. Although virtually everyone was baptized and therefore a church member of some kind, the "church" came to be understood as a corporation in society with its own personnel (the clergy) and way of operating. People used its services rather in the way that we now use schools, public libraries, and hospitals. However much we may feel that such institutions "belong" to us as social services, we are nevertheless aware that they are distinct bodies that function according to their own rules, and we do not regard ourselves as part of their staff, even if we use them regularly, take out membership subscriptions, and even sit on their governing bodies. Similarly, in the medieval church there were laypeople who helped out, not least as churchwardens in every local parish, whose duty it was to look after the fabric of the church and report ungodly behavior among the parishioners, so that the authorities could discipline them accordingly. But such people, important as they were, were not part of the corporation of the "church" and did not enjoy the benefits that belonging to it entailed.

To operate its vast network, the church required a functioning legal system, and this is what the papacy set out to construct. It had inherited ancient Roman law, which after the empire's conversion to Christianity had been expanded to include statutes relating to the church. These had been codified by Justinian I (r. 527–65), the Eastern emperor who spent most of his life trying to reconquer the West. Where he and his successors could impose their will, the written law of Rome prevailed and the church had little to do other than adapt it to its needs. But in the barbarian kingdoms of the West, a different situation prevailed. The barbarians had laws of their own, developed out of tribal custom, and they applied them as the need arose. In some cases they incorporated bits and pieces of Roman law, but on the whole theirs was an oral tradition that grew by precedent. Initially, there were no written codes, and when they began to appear, they were invariably far less sophisticated and comprehensive than Roman law. As a universal institution, the church could not be bound by local customs that might vary enormously from one place to another, so it preferred to work with Roman law—albeit modified by the specific needs of the church itself.

This was the origin of what we now call "canon law," which defined the church as a social institution and whose legacy is still with us today. Canon law was a mishmash of decisions taken by various councils of the church, sayings of the main church fathers, and Roman imperial legislation. At first there was no systematic ordering, and some of the sources could be read as contradicting one another. To bring order out of this chaos was the goal of a jurist called Gratian, who worked at Bologna in the mid-twelfth century. Around 1140 he produced his *Concordantia discordantium canonum* (Concordance of discordant canons), which rapidly established itself as the chief handbook for canon lawyers across the Western church. Popularly known as the *Decretum*, it never had any official status, but it was of such a high standard that no one questioned its authority. Additions were made to it in the thirteenth and fourteenth centuries, but these were of a different character. They were mainly the canons of the ecumenical councils held between 1173 and 1313, along with various papal decretals. Four separate collections were issued, one by the authority of Pope Gregory IX (1234), one by that of Pope Boniface VIII (1298), one by that of Pope Clement V (1313), and one by that of Pope John XXII (1328). A final collection was made by canon lawyers around the year 1500, and the whole work was then published as the *Corpus iuris canonici*. It remained the standard source for canon law in the Roman Catholic Church until 1917, when it was replaced by a more modern code (which was in turn replaced in 1983). The Protestant churches usually abolished it, though not without incorporating parts of it into their own legal systems. The Church of England tried but failed to replace it with a code of its own. Although the Church of England has subsequently developed its own canon law tradition, the ancient canons retain a residual authority in the Anglican world, making it different in this respect from either the Roman Catholic or the other Protestant churches.

To be effective, canon law required a system of courts, lawyers to staff them, and a body of commentary literature to explain how its principles ought to be applied in practice. An enormous legal edifice grew up as a result, with courts operating at several different levels. The pope had one, of course, but so did every archbishop, bishop, and archdeacon. In theory, a plea for the dissolution of a marriage could be taken to the archidiaconal court and then appealed to the bishop, the archbishop, and the pope, but it was also possible to go straight to the top, bypassing the intermediate rungs of the hierarchy. That is essentially what happened when Henry VIII wanted to have his marriage to Catherine of Aragon annulled. The disadvantage of that procedure was that it took many years, because of the need to assemble documents and then travel across Europe to present them to the papal tribunal, and the pope was not always as neutral as he was supposed to be. In Henry VIII's case, for example, the pope was the prisoner of the emperor Charles V, who was Catherine's nephew and deeply opposed to the annulment because he saw it as an insult to his family.[22]

Canon law was important because the church saw it as a means of extending Christian principles to aspects of everyday life that were not covered in the Bible. For example, it laid down the age of consent for marriage (twelve for a girl and fourteen for a boy) and specified how church officials should be appointed and disciplined. It also determined a number of liturgical questions concerning the celebration of the Lord's Supper. Its proponents saw it as a God-given supplement to Holy Scripture, even when it went against the sacred text, as in the imposition of clerical celibacy, for instance. In practice, because the Bible was a fixed text that could not be altered, whereas the canon law was a body of legislation and practice that grew and developed over time in order to meet the needs of the moment, canon law—rather than the principles laid down in the New Testament—came to dominate the life of the church. When Martin Luther (1483–1546) raised the standard of revolt, it was primarily canon law that he attacked as the "tradition" that the papacy had imposed on a church that was meant to be governed by Scripture alone.

Schism and Heresy

One important aspect of church life that the canon law had to deal with was schism and heresy. In theory, the distinction between these two was straightforward. A schism was a division in the administrative structure of the church that did not involve its doctrine. The Donatists in North Africa were schismatics because they rejected the authority of the bishops recognized by the mainline church, but they were not heretics because they did not deny any Christian doctrine. The Arians, on the other hand, were heretics because they did not accept the full deity of Christ, but they were not schismatics, because they did not want to leave the mainline church. Many of them tried to remain within it but were rejected because of their deficient doctrine. They could not be reintegrated into the church by administrative means but had to be reconciled by repentance and confession of the orthodox faith. This was particularly clear in those parts of the Western Roman Empire where

---

22. See H. A. Kelly, *The Matrimonial Trials of Henry VIII* (Stanford: Stanford University Press, 1976).

Arian tribes took over from the imperial authorities. The nature of the situation meant that orthodox Christians could not persecute the Arians who governed them, and since the Arians were such a small minority, they could not do much to harm the mainline church either, even though they sometimes persecuted its members.

By its nature, schism was often difficult to define because so much depended on the standpoint of the speaker. When East and West split apart, for example, the Western Church spoke of the "Eastern schism," but to the Eastern church it was the "Western (papal) schism"—as it still is today. Modern scholarship has done much to take the bitterness out of this difference of perspective, but Western writers still find themselves forced to use the traditional terminology, if only to make themselves understood.[23] Almost inevitably, schisms were more likely to be caused by nontheological factors such as overlapping claims to jurisdiction, but they were often just as difficult to sort out as any heresy and, as the division between East and West demonstrates, could be just as long-lasting.

Heresy was a matter of doctrinal error and was defined by that criterion. Isidore of Seville did that in the early sixth century, and his classification remained standard throughout the Middle Ages. It was incorporated into the canon law, with the result that aberrations that had disappeared in ancient times could be artificially revived if or when similar doctrines appeared in later times. For example, Arianism had died out by AD 600, but anyone who believed (or who was thought to believe) that Jesus Christ was a divine creature and not fully God could be called an "Arian," whether or not that individual had ever heard of Arius. Thus we find at the time of the Reformation, a man such as Luther was accused by his opponents of "Nestorianism" because he denied the doctrine of transubstantiation, an accusation that was anachronistic in every sense.[24]

The elevation of the church to the status of the official religion made schism an important political issue, because to split from the church was also to revolt against the state. Schismatics were therefore often persecuted by the emperors and kings as rebels, a practice that continued into the sixteenth century, when Protestants were frequently treated in this way. Heresy was a more complex

23. See S. Runciman, *The Eastern Schism* (Oxford: Oxford University Press, 1955); F. Dvornik, *The Photian Schism* (Cambridge: Cambridge University Press, 1948). Both books are by Western scholars who are sympathetic to the Eastern position.

24. Nestorianism held that the incarnate Christ had two natures, one divine and the other human, that were conjoined in the person of Christ but maintained their independent identities, making it possible for a purely human Jesus to exist. Transubstantiation, by contrast, taught that in the Eucharist, bread and wine became the substance of Christ's body and blood, something that Nestorians would have found inconceivable.

matter, because although it was an attack on the doctrine of the church, it was not so clear that it was also a crime against the state. It was also something that only theologians could adjudicate, not least because often the questions at stake were extremely subtle and hard for ordinary people to understand. Here the medieval church had to struggle to impose its will. Because heresy destroyed the soul, it was deserving of death, but the church had no power to execute the sentence it imposed on heretics. In this, it resembled the Sanhedrin that condemned Jesus to death. For the sentence to be carried out, Jesus had to be turned over to Pontius Pilate, who was reluctant to execute a man who in his eyes was innocent of any crime. The kings of Western Europe faced a similar dilemma when they were confronted with condemned heretics. They had no power to determine whether the charge was justified or not, but the church expected them to do its bidding without asking any questions.

A further complication was that the church preferred a novel method of execution—burning at the stake. In England, a nobleman had the right to be beheaded, whereas a peasant was hanged, but heresy crossed class boundaries, and it was felt that the punishment meted out for it ought to be classless too. There was also the theory that fire would purge the soul of its sin and allow the unfortunate victims to go to purgatory instead of hell, which, of course, was to their eternal benefit. Unfortunately, the state's executioners had no experience of burning people at the stake, and many of them thought that it was a procedure beneath their professional dignity. This led to resistance, which in the case of England meant that heresy did not become a crime until 1401, and it was almost another decade before anyone was put to death in the canonically approved way. Burning at the stake was never popular and was seldom practiced before the Reformation. It was only when Queen Mary I started burning Protestants publicly (and in significant numbers) that the full horror of the procedure was revealed, and public opinion turned against it. In later years it was reserved for those accused of witchcraft, and in the seventeenth century it fell into disuse.[25]

Deciding what constituted a heresy was the other problem the church had to face. Not every case could be assimilated to the classical heresies listed by Isidore of Seville, but there were still plenty of people who objected to some aspect of the church's teaching. Some, such as the Albigensians of southern France, were definitely unorthodox, and their doctrines, which were dualistic like those of the ancient Manichaeans, could easily be condemned as heretical.[26]

25. The last burning at the stake in England occurred in 1612. The practice was formally abolished in 1677.
26. S. Runciman, *The Medieval Manichee* (Cambridge: Cambridge University Press, 1947).

But the trouble was that almost anyone who complained about malpractice in the church could be accused of heresy, even if his or her only purpose was to put right something that had clearly gone wrong. This actually happened in a number of cases, and the founders of new religious movements, men such as Francis of Assisi, for example, were not above suspicion to begin with.[27]

The case that brought matters to a head was that of John Wyclif (ca. 1330–84). Wyclif was an Oxford professor who preached against the church of his day, which he accused of having fallen into error. According to him, it had drifted away from acknowledging the sole authority of Scripture in matters of doctrine and in its adoption of transubstantiation, a belief that he (rightly) regarded as physically impossible. The church was deeply embarrassed by these attacks, but did they constitute heresy? In purely theological terms that was hard to say. Wyclif was not denying any of the church's classical doctrines, but he caused such a stir that the authorities had to silence him, and accusing him of heresy was by far the best way to do that.[28]

No one before his time, and few people since, attracted as much official condemnation as Wyclif. Even today, a long list of accusations against him is preserved in the minutes of the great Council of Constance in 1415, as evidence of just how seriously the church took his threat. Wyclif was forced to leave his teaching post in Oxford but died in his bed, because he had support in high places and the king was not prepared to act as his executioner. In fact, Wyclif represented a new generation of intellectuals who rejected what had become the accepted way of thinking and wanted to replace it with new and (to their minds) better concepts. If the church had endorsed ideas that they thought had to be rejected, then the church was wrong to have done so and ought to change. But could the church ever be wrong? To suggest that was to call its authority into question, and it was this, more than anything else, that caused such alarm.

As far as the Scriptures were concerned, there was no law against translation into the language of the people, which Wyclif promoted, but the church feared that if ignorant laypeople got hold of the Bible they would misinterpret it and use it to support heresy.[29] Wyclif's supporters, known as Lollards, became

27. See H. Fichtenau, *Heresies and Scholars in the High Middle Ages, 1000–1200* (University Park, PA: Penn State University Press, 1998); W. L. Wakefield and A. P. Evans, *Heresies of the High Middle Ages* (New York: Columbia University Press, 1969); G. Leff, *Heresy in the Later Middle Ages: The Relation of Heterodoxy to Dissent* (Manchester: Manchester University Press, 1967). Can it be accidental that the major studies of this subject have been published by university presses?

28. On Wyclif, see S. E. Lahey, *John Wyclif* (Oxford: Oxford University Press, 2009); G. R. Evans, *John Wyclif: Myth and Reality* (Oxford: Lion Hudson, 2005).

29. Wyclif is often regarded as a Bible translator, but he was not. There were, however, two English translations produced by some of his followers that circulated in manuscript.

quite prominent after his death, and some of them were later implicated in a revolt against the English Crown. In response, the church made it illegal to translate the Bible into English and forced preachers to acquire a license before mounting the pulpit. In that way they hoped to contain Lollardy and ensure that nothing they found unpalatable would reach the general public. The University of Oxford was subjected to regular and intense scrutiny, because it was there that the trouble had started. In the minds of many, ideas were dangerous, and new ones were bound to be wrong. The church was now the establishment that did not want to be disturbed by any kind of change, but it was fighting a losing battle. Wyclif and the Lollards were suppressed, but the forces they represented could not be so easily contained; when they finally erupted, the church itself would be the great loser in a battle that it could not hope to win.

Increasingly, heresy came to be determined in relation not to objective doctrines such as the Trinity (although, of course, denying such things remained deeply heretical) but to opinions and behavior that challenged the church's authority. Attacking corruption in high places, refusing to pay tithes, questioning the power and role of a priestly hierarchy that had no biblical warrant in the critics' view—all of these things could be regarded as "heretical" if the church so chose. The threat of condemnation for heresy thereby became a means of controlling dissent of any kind. As the fifteenth century progressed, the ills of the clerical establishment proved harder and harder to conceal, and the voices of protest grew louder. Could they be silenced by an increasingly corrupt papacy, or would the kings of Europe finally grow bold enough to resist such ecclesiastical tyranny and reassert their right to decide which of their subjects should be put to death and why?

In the end, the question of what to do about heresy was to prove decisive for the fate of the medieval Western church. On the one hand, it was a fundamental principle that the church should remain as pure and spotless in the sight of God as possible. False teaching had to be identified, condemned, and rooted out if this goal were to be achieved. But it is one thing for a private organization to discipline its members and quite another for a public institution to do so, especially when that institution has a commanding position in the state. The church did not possess the power to execute anyone, but did it have the right to demand that secular rulers should act on its behalf? What could it do if they refused to comply with its wishes?

In the sixteenth century these questions and others like them rose to the surface and had to be addressed. In some places, such as Spain and parts of Italy, the church gained the upper hand and was able to exercise its discipline in and through the organs of the state. The result was the infamous

Inquisition, a procedure by which specially appointed investigators sought to root out heretics. Appointed by the church, these investigators were nevertheless agents of the state, and their decisions had the force of law. In other places, though, the state authorities proved to be less compliant. Most of the time they were prepared to uphold the basic principles of the established church, but they were less eager to put dissenters to death. Some were even prepared to consider whether a man such as Martin Luther had something worthwhile to say and was being unjustly targeted by a church that did not want to hear it. When that happened, the church could no longer rely on secular rulers to do its bidding, and its relationship to the state entered a new and critical phase.

The Sacramental System

At the heart of the medieval church lay the sacramental system, which it developed and which for many people was both their main point of contact with the church and its chief raison d'être. Seven rites were administered to members of the church at different times in their lives, some only once and others frequently—even, in some cases, daily. The system was not developed until the Middle Ages, and then only in the Western church; the East retained a more primitive pattern that even today can only superficially be harmonized with its Western equivalent.

Whether there were "sacraments" in the New Testament church is an interesting question. The word means "oath" and was first used by Tertullian around AD 200, when he described baptism as the "oath of allegiance" that a believer takes to Christ. Tertullian was using a military metaphor that he felt he could apply to the church because its members were soldiers of Christ who were prepared to die for him just as a regular soldier was prepared to die for the emperor. He regarded the water of baptism as the divinely appointed means by which a spiritual truth was conveyed to the one who received it.[30] This is what made it a sacrament in his eyes, and its effectiveness was assured both by the promise of God in his Word and by the presence of his Spirit in the sacred elements. In the Middle Ages, it was universally believed that a person must be baptized in order to be cleansed from original sin and admitted to membership of the church, which was the promise of eternal life. In consequence, those who died unbaptized went either to hell or to a nebulous place known as the *limbus patrum*, or limbo,

---

30. Tertullian, *De baptismo* 3.

where it was thought that the souls of the righteous who had died before the coming of Christ were kept in a kind of suspended animation. This was a matter of speculation, but whatever the actual state of those who died without baptism, the church taught that it was best not to take any chances. Since the consecrated water had its own saving properties, it was not necessary for the person being baptized to make a profession of faith. Baptism was like vaccination; it worked whether the recipient was aware of what was happening or not. In a world where infant mortality rates were extremely high, the fate of unbaptized infants was a major preoccupation. Ideally, baptism would be performed by a priest as soon as possible after birth, but such was the anxiety that could be aroused, that the church authorized laypeople, especially midwives, to perform the rite privately if they thought that the infant was in danger of dying.

Another important fact was that the name given to a child in baptism had a legal force that trumped everything else.[31] It was a sign of belonging to the company of the saved, both living and dead, and many babies were given the name of the saint whose memory was commemorated on the day of baptism. Martin Luther, for example, was so called because he was baptized on November 11, 1483, which was St. Martin's day.

The other rites and ceremonies that came to be regarded as sacraments were a mixed bag of practices, only some of which had a clear New Testament warrant. Most of them had grown up over the centuries, and at least one (matrimony) was not of Christian origin at all.[32]

The most obvious and important of these ceremonies was the Lord's Supper, which was clearly prefigured in the Last Supper of Jesus and his disciples and for which clear instructions are laid down in the New Testament. Very early on, its celebration was reserved to the bishop and delegated to his presbyters, a pattern that by medieval times had become the norm. Over time, theories were developed to explain what happened during the Supper and why it was so central to the church's life. The focus was on the elements of bread and wine, which stood for the body and blood of Christ. Quite what the connection was between the symbols and the realities they represented was unclear for a long time, but everybody believed that in partaking of the consecrated bread and wine they were entering into communion with Christ himself. Hence the Lord's Supper came to be known as Holy Communion,

31. Even today, in a country like England, a child's baptismal (or "Christian") name is more important than the one he or she may have been registered under at birth.

32. For the history of the individual sacraments, see J. Martos, *Doors to the Sacred: A Historical Introduction to the Sacraments in the Catholic Church* (Tarrytown, NY: Triumph Books, 1991).

a rite in which the members of the church drew closer to its head by taking his presence into themselves.[33]

That this communion was primarily spiritual in nature was never questioned. But the Son of God had become a man in Jesus Christ, and it came to be felt that just as his physical body played an essential role in the salvation of the human race, so his spiritual presence in Communion must be accompanied by an equally essential material aspect. In this way, the belief grew up that the bread and wine became the body and blood of Christ in something more than a purely symbolic sense. He was held to be objectively present in the elements, giving them a spiritual power of their own, quite apart from the service of the church. It was therefore possible to set the consecrated elements aside and venerate them as if they were Christ himself, and a host of devotional practices grew up around them as a result. It was even thought that they could be stolen and used for occult purposes in the so-called Black Mass.

Mention of this reminds us that most people called the Lord's Supper the "Mass," a corruption of the Latin word *missa*, which has no theological meaning of its own. It comes from the closing words of the liturgy, which were *Ite, ecclesia missa est* (Go, the church is dismissed), and was taken over to refer to the service by people who did not understand Latin. After the Protestant Reformation the word came to be used by Roman Catholics to emphasize their belief in the change wrought in the elements by their consecration, which (in their eyes) made the Mass entirely different from the Lord's Supper as practiced by Protestants.

As early as the Fourth Lateran Council in 1215, this change in the elements was called "transubstantiation," a term that reflects Aristotelian physics, which was widely accepted at that time. According to this theory, all reality could be analyzed into substances and their accidents, in other words, into what was fundamental and what was merely transient, or accidental. Bread, for example, was a substance that remained what it was, although it could accidentally appear in different colors, with different weights, and so on. This way of analyzing matter has been rejected in modern times, but the legacy of the medieval church lingers on, especially among Roman Catholics, where transubstantiation remains the church's official teaching. Theologians and liturgical reformers within the Catholic Church have struggled to redefine this, but with little success so far, and popular piety remains stubbornly conservative. It is still possible in Catholic circles for a priest to say Mass on his own or for particular "intentions" divorced from the main body of the church,

33. See G. Macy, *The Banquet's Wisdom* (Akron, OH: OSL Publications, 2005), for a short history of the different theologies of the Lord's Supper.

and the devotional practices associated with the reserved elements continue much as they always have done. Here more than anywhere else, we can see how the sacraments remain constitutive of the Roman Catholic Church in a way that cannot be said of their Protestant counterparts.

Of the other five recognized sacraments, confirmation is really an extension of baptism, and many people deny that it is a sacrament in its own right. It exists primarily in order to ensure that a child baptized in infancy makes a personal profession of faith. For Catholics this typically occurs when the child is about six years old, but Protestants who practice confirmation almost always defer it to the teenage years, when (it is assumed) children are more able to assent to their baptismal vows in a conscious and responsible manner.[34] In the Middle Ages hardly anyone was baptized as an adult, so the question of whether confirmation was always necessary did not arise. By the time it did, there was a general consensus that it was a distinct sacrament, and so even baptized adults now have to be confirmed, illogical though that is.

Next comes *paenitentia*, which may be translated as "penitence," "penance," or "repentance." Repentance, a heartfelt sorrow for sin and a turning away from it, is what it should be and is what the rite symbolically represents, but the normal word used to describe it is "penance," which is just an abbreviation of "penitence." Penance developed into a series of works imposed as penalties for sin. Christians would go to the priest before taking Communion, confess their sins, and be told what they must do in order to demonstrate that they were truly sorry for what they had done. Usually this would mean saying extra prayers or doing a good deed of some kind. Once the penance was accomplished, the penitents would return to the priest and be absolved, which would make it possible for them to receive Communion.

The practice of confession to others and demonstrable repentance could certainly claim New Testament support, but it was never organized in a systematic way in the New Testament.[35] Likewise, biblical authority could be claimed for refusing to allow impenitent sinners access to the Lord's Supper, but that was part of a wider public discipline and not confined to a semiprivate ritual controlled by a priest. Sacramental penance was a major cause of legalism in the medieval church, because each sin had to be weighed and measured so that the right degree of sorrow for it could be manifested. This produced elaborate calculations and led people to think of their sins as debts that had to be paid off. That in turn spawned a host of other practices,

34. Nowadays most American Catholics defer confirmation to the teenage years, but this is a recent development and is still far from universal.

35. See James 5:16–17.

including so-called works of supererogation, which people would perform in order to pay off sins of which they might be unaware, and the granting of "indulgences," or pardons for sins committed. Indulgences could even be sold to people with the money to pay for them, a scandal that was the immediate cause of the Protestant Reformation.

Worst of all, though, penance led to the belief that most people died in spiritual debt, not having paid off their sins in full. That led the church to invent a place called "purgatory" where the souls of the faithful departed would go and continue to work toward their ultimate salvation. The biggest problem with this, which is not generally perceived today but formed one of Martin Luther's main objections to the whole idea, was that it gave the pope jurisdiction over those who had died and gone to a spiritual realm that fell short of heaven. How could an earthly authority, however exalted, claim such power? As Luther saw it, by selling indulgences the papacy was not just engaging in a corrupt practice but also legislating outside its sphere of competence. Just as a court in one country cannot reduce the sentence of a criminal in another jurisdiction, so the papacy could not mitigate the sufferings of those beyond the grave. In claiming to do this, the pope was exceeding his authority and stepping into the shoes of Christ, whose vicar (representative) on earth he claimed to be. It was for this reason that Luther's revolt was more than the usual protest against corruption. It struck at the root of the pope's authority and led to a full-blown questioning of the nature of the church that he claimed to govern in Christ's name.

Another so-called sacrament was extreme unction, more commonly known as the last rites. This is the anointing with oil that precedes death. Originally it was meant to be an anointing for healing, and as such it can find support in the New Testament, but mortality rates were so high for so long that the original purpose was soon lost sight of.[36] Instead, it became a kind of assurance to the dying person that he or she was departing in a "state of grace," which would at least smooth the person's passage into purgatory, if not bypass it altogether.

The last two sacraments were matrimony and holy orders, which came to be seen as mutually exclusive. Matrimony was not a specifically Christian rite, and for many centuries the church did not celebrate weddings. Christians were warned not to marry unbelievers, but that was all. Marriage was a secular rite entered into for secular purposes; those whose eyes were concentrated on going to heaven tended to avoid it altogether. In the twelfth century that tendency to celibacy was formally imposed on all priests (it had been imposed

36. See James 5:14–15.

on bishops in 692), something that has remained characteristic of Roman Catholic clergy to this day.[37] At the same time, matrimony for laypeople fell into the hands of the church, which had to act because the instruments of civil Roman society had broken down in Western Europe, leaving the church as the only institution capable of providing the necessary legal guarantees.

As it took over civil matrimony, however, the church sought to impose Christian standards—notably by insisting that both parties should consent to the marriage, that no one should marry within certain broadly defined degrees of consanguinity and affinity, and that no divorce should be permitted. In the course of Christianization, marriage came to be regarded as a sacrament because it was a holy ordinance, prescribed by God and used in the New Testament to symbolize the relationship between Christ and the church, which is his bride. In this respect, matrimony could be seen as the most ecclesial of the sacraments, even though it was the one with the most ambiguous relationship to Christianity.

Medieval Mission and Expansion

In many respects the Middle Ages appears as a time when the horizons of the ancient world had contracted. The breakdown of civil government and the decline of secular learning can make it seem that way, but that is only one side of the story. From another point of view, the Middle Ages saw a great and lasting expansion of European culture and of the Christian church, which was now largely identified with it. In the century following the death of the prophet Muhammad in 632, Arab armies, propelled by their devotion to the religion of Islam, subtracted Syria, Egypt, North Africa, and most of Spain from the world of Christendom, though in most of these places Christians remained the majority of the population for several centuries. In later centuries, Spain was reconquered for Christendom, and Asia Minor (now Turkey) was permanently lost to Islam; otherwise this frontier has remained remarkably stable for the past fourteen hundred years.

But if there were great losses to the church on its southern flank, there were also considerable gains toward the north, though most of these occurred somewhat later. Arianism penetrated beyond the frontier of the Roman Empire in the fourth century, when it went to the Goths beyond the Danube frontier. Those Goths subsequently invaded the empire and settled there, leaving their

37. See C. Cochini, *The Apostolic Origins of Priestly Celibacy* (San Francisco: Ignatius Press, 1990); R. Cholij, *Clerical Celibacy in East and West* (Leominster: Fowler Wright, 1988), for a modern justification of the practice from a Roman Catholic point of view.

former homelands to pagans. Ireland in the fifth century became the first non-Roman country (apart from Armenia, which had treaty relations with Rome) to be evangelized. The origins of the mission there have been obscured in legend, but when the mists cleared there could be no doubt that a distinct kind of church had emerged.

Roman Christianity was urban based, because the Roman Empire was essentially a confederation of cities. Ireland did not have cities, so the mission there had to take a different form. Since the first missionaries were monks, they established monasteries, which became the focal points of evangelization. Settlements later grew up around these monastic churches, many of which became bases for local bishops and hence cathedrals. This kind of informal arrangement remained in place until the twelfth century, when a diocesan structure along Roman lines was finally introduced.[38]

Long before, however, the monastic church concept had spread across Great Britain and much of northern Europe that the Romans had never reached. Even in parts of the old empire where urban life had broken down, monastic churches could be found, bringing with them a new form of church order. The traces they have left can still be seen today in place names containing the word *minster*, *münster*, or *moutier*. Unlike the ancient churches of the Roman world, they did not grow naturally out of local social life. In Italy, the prefect (mayor) of Milan could become its bishop, as the great Ambrose did, but such a transition was impossible further north. Instead, the bishops tended to be abbots of monasteries, or at least monks, and they lived in a way that was quite different from that of the people around them. As monks, they were celibate and therefore highly mobile, making it possible for them to spread the gospel far and wide. Between 500 and 1000 most of northern Europe was evangelized, largely thanks to their efforts.

Elsewhere, the breakdown of urban life helped to facilitate the development of territorially based churches where the authority of a bishop could extend to a diocese that covered vast and often thinly populated areas. Within such a diocese there would be a number of local congregations, which gathered in buildings that, more often than not, had been specially built for worship. The building came by popular consent to be known as the "church," and the transfer of the original meaning of the word became so common that today when most people think of the "church" in their community, it is the building used for public worship that they have in mind. The catchment area of this

---

38. For the details, see A. Gwynn, *The Irish Church in the Eleventh and Twelfth Centuries* (Dublin: Four Courts Press, 1992); M. T. Flanagan, *The Transformation of the Irish Church in the Twelfth Century* (Woodbridge: Boydell & Brewer, 2010).

building was its parish, a word derived from the Greek *paroikia*, which just means "habitation." From the tenth century onward, the countryside was divided into parishes of manageable size, whether or not they had a church building in them, and a priest was appointed to minister to them.

The theory was that a parish would be small enough for every resident to come under the pastoral supervision of the local clergy. Ideally, this would include education, health care, and the provision of marriages and funerals, but standards varied enormously, and it was not always possible to meet expectations. Parishes that did not have a church building were expected to build one, but the funds for this were not always easy to obtain. Ideally, the diocesan bishop would provide this, but the need was almost always greater than the resources he could muster. So in many cases local landowners were asked to put up church buildings, in return for which they became their patrons. The patron of a church was given the right to appoint the resident priest, who could be anyone who was validly ordained.[39] The bishop was still expected to install him, as he did in churches that he himself had built, but this was a formality in most cases, and the bishop would normally only refuse if there was a very good reason for doing so.[40]

Over time, many noblemen used this right, or "advowson," as it is called in English (from the Latin *advocatio*), to put their younger sons into churches, since they had to find something respectable for them to do. It was not the most edifying way to find ministers, and we should not be surprised that there were so many failures of this type of "vocation." The astonishing thing is that it worked as well as it did, not least because a nobleman's son was more likely to have had some kind of education and was therefore able to read the service—in Latin. Patrons, it should be said, had responsibilities as well as privileges. If the resident clergyman died or left, the patron had to replace him within six months or forfeit his right of presentation to the bishop. He was also responsible for repairing the chancel of the church building (where the priest stood), sharing this with the rector, who was responsible for the nave (where the congregation sat).

This pattern was codified at the Fourth Lateran Council in 1215, when Pope Innocent III instituted a system of "benefices," which are best described as clerical posts that had enough revenue behind them to support a resident priest. A benefice, or "living" (to use the English term), would normally be a parish that raised enough tithe income for a priest to be appointed, but a

---

39. See S. Wood, *The Proprietary Church in the Medieval West* (Oxford: Oxford University Press, 2006), for a detailed study of this phenomenon.

40. The installation of a priest in a church owned by the bishop is called a "collation." In a church owned by someone else, it is an "institution."

nonparochial position (in a cathedral, for example) could also come into this category. The man who held the benefice was called the "incumbent," though in popular speech he was often known as the *persona*—the "person" of the parish, from which the English word "parson" is derived.

The parochial system eventually covered the whole of Western Europe, but there were exceptions to the general rule. The most obvious of these were the cathedral churches, which were the seats of the bishops (*cathedra* is the Greek word from which "chair" is derived). The bishop did not run the cathedral himself, however. That was the responsibility of the *decanus*, or "dean." Around the dean were a number of other clergy who together constituted the cathedral chapter that elected him. Deans and bishops were therefore quite separate; in the folklore of the church there is a long history of conflict between them, which unfortunately has more than a little evidence to support it. The members of the chapter were called *canonici*, or "canons," because they were appointed according to a rule, or "canon," which they were then expected to observe in the running of the cathedral. Some canons were residentiary, but others were not—there was great flexibility here. Canons who were supported from revenue derived from estates owned by the cathedral were called *praebendarii* (prebendaries) because they lived off a *praebenda* (prebend), which was the name given to such sources of income.

Tied to the cathedral chapters were a number of offices known as "dignities," of which the most important were those of archdeacon, treasurer, precentor, and chancellor. In theory, the archdeacon was the diocesan manager. It was he who was supposed to visit parishes to make sure that everything was in order and who examined candidates for the priesthood. In large dioceses, this task was too great for one man, so extra archdeacons were appointed; the diocese of Lincoln, for example, had eight of them. The treasurer looked after the finances, the precentor controlled the music and therefore the daily worship in the cathedral, and the chancellor looked after its legal business. Usually these men were also canons, but that was not necessarily the case, and the two roles remained quite distinct, although in some cases a dignity would be tied to a canonry so that the man who held one necessarily held the other as well.

In England, uniquely, this system was modified by a spiritual reform movement that wanted to turn all cathedrals into monasteries. In one sense this was a throwback to the early period of the Irish missions, but it developed independently at a later time. In the end, about half the medieval cathedrals in England were converted into monastic establishments, with two in a kind of halfway state. These were in the dioceses of Coventry and Lichfield and of Bath and Wells. Coventry and Bath were monasteries that were attached to the secular cathedrals of Lichfield and Wells but were not merged into them.[41] In monastic cathedrals, the "dean" was replaced by a "prior," and there were no canons or prebendaries. The tasks of the chapter were carried out by monks attached to the cathedral, who did not receive a personal income from the church and were therefore thought to be less open to corruption than those who did.

Another exception to the parochial system consisted of so-called peculiar jurisdictions, which were churches, chapels, or other places of worship that were exempt from the local bishop's jurisdiction. The reasons for granting peculiar status were many and varied, but the overall effect was to create a number of churches that lay outside the normal diocesan administration. The head of a peculiar, like the head of a cathedral, was called a "dean" and was vaguely answerable to the archbishop of the province in which the peculiar was located, but in practice he operated more or less independently. University college chapels, for example, were peculiars, as were royal chapels. Over time, a number of other places, many of them parishes in their own right, acquired peculiar status, especially when they fell into the hands of a bishop who was not the local diocesan. In England, for example, the bishops of Durham were notorious collectors of parishes outside their diocese, which became their peculiars.[42] The archbishop of Canterbury had peculiars in London, of which the most famous was Lambeth Palace, where he normally resided. Another one consisted of thirteen parishes grouped around the Church of St. Mary-le-Bow ("of the Arches"), where his vicar-general, the chief legal officer in the province of Canterbury, eventually established himself. As a result, to this day the president of the ecclesiastical courts in England is called the dean of the Arches, and (after a gap of several centuries) his court once again sits in the crypt of the church for which it is named.[43]

Another feature of the landscape was the so-called extraparochial area, which usually consisted of uninhabited tracts of land that nobody wanted—swamps, forests, and so on. These areas lay outside all normal ecclesiastical jurisdiction and were therefore often used as places of refuge for those who fell foul of the church. The most famous of these extraparochial areas was Sherwood Forest, where Robin Hood and his merry men were said to gather—fugitives from justice and society in general. But even there, the church could be present, as the figure of Friar Tuck reminds us.

41. Coventry was separated from Lichfield in 1877, but Bath and Wells remain linked to this day.

42. F. Barlow, *Durham Jurisdictional Peculiars* (Oxford: Oxford University Press, 1950) studies them in detail. They survived the Protestant Reformation intact and were not dissolved until the mid-nineteenth century.

43. See F. D. Logan, *The Medieval Court of Arches* (Woodbridge: Boydell & Brewer, 2005).

Friar Tuck belonged in Sherwood Forest because the friars were also men on the margins of society. Monasteries had a recognized place in the system, but over time that meant that they became rich and lost their zeal for propagating the gospel. From the tenth century onward there were a number of reform movements that basically started new monastic orders. The traditional monasteries had all followed the rule of St. Benedict, who had been the abbot of Monte Cassino in southern Italy in the mid-sixth century. But the new foundations followed more "modern" (and invariably stricter) rules devised by the reformers, of whom the greatest was undoubtedly Bernard of Clairvaux. His Cistercian order spread rapidly in the twelfth century but was by no means alone. The great abbey of Cluny in Burgundy had its own network of Cluniac houses, and there were a number of others, including the Gilbertine order, founded by Gilbert of Sempringham and incorporating both male and female establishments, something otherwise unheard of at that time. Women had their own convents, some of which became quite famous, but because they seldom engaged in trade in the way that the men did and were unable to appropriate parishes because they could not supply them with priests, they were much poorer and less influential than their male equivalents were.[44]

Around 1200, however, some people began to realize that reforming the monasteries was practically impossible as they kept reintegrating into the existing system and the standard forms of corruption reappeared after a generation or so. To deal with this, radicals such as Francis of Assisi and Dominic struck out on their own. They determined to lead an independent life of poverty, chastity, and obedience, depending entirely on charitable donations for their survival. These were the friars. Gradually, in order to earn a living, they turned to teaching or to what we would now call "social work." Many of them became famous preachers and theologians. As universities were founded across Europe, they were often staffed by friars, who had the freedom to step outside the existing system and start something new. Of course, in a very conservative society such as Western Europe at that time, such innovation was highly suspect—which is why the clergyman in Sherwood Forest was a friar, and not a monk or an ordinary parish priest.[45]

As far as church worship was concerned, there was both great uniformity and great variety. The uniformity was seen most obviously in the language

44. See C. H. Lawrence, *Medieval Monasticism: Forms of Religious Life in Western Europe in the Middle Ages* (London: Longman, 1984).

45. See C. H. Lawrence, *The Friars* (London: Longman, 1994). For more detailed coverage of individual orders, see J. Moorman, *A History of the Franciscan Order* (Oxford: Oxford University Press, 1968); B. Jarrett, *The English Dominicans* (London: Burns, Oates & Washbourne, 1921).

used, which was almost invariably Latin. Classical Latin rapidly ceased to be spoken in anything like its pure form once the Roman Empire disintegrated, but for many centuries most people who lived in the former provinces still thought that it was the language they spoke, albeit in dialect form. It was only in 812 that a decree of Charlemagne recognized the *lingua rustica* of France, which he authorized for use in preaching—the first indication that what we now call French was emerging. In the countries of the north, Latin had never been spoken, but it was introduced by the missionaries, who used it in preference to the local vernacular. There were some translations, into Irish and English, for example, but these were never in official use. The Western church used Latin, whether people understood it or not, and this was regarded as a sign of its unity, as well as of its connection to New Testament times. After all, when Pontius Pilate ordered the inscription placed above the head of Jesus on the cross, he made sure it was in Hebrew, Greek, and Latin.[46] But Hebrew was the language of the Jews, who had rejected Christ, and Greek was used by schismatics in the East. So only Latin was left—the holy tongue that bound all the West to the cross of Christ.

Apart from that, however, there was considerable diversity. Many local dioceses and regions developed their own liturgies, which were broadly similar but far from identical. Few people traveled much, so it made relatively little difference, but when the unity of the church was challenged by the Reformation, this variety was one of the first things that had to be tackled. Diversity could no longer be allowed because it might be an open door to heresy, and each church that came out of the sixteenth-century divisions set about establishing its own norm—or what in England was called "uniformity" of worship—which ensured that its congregations all used the same forms and were taught the same doctrine.

How much of an impression did all this make on the average person? It is impossible to gauge this with any degree of certainty, because the evidence we have is circumstantial and liable to be misleading. It is often those who stand out as exceptions whose names and doings are recorded, but this only tells us what was not expected, not what most people actually did. We do know that very few people could understand the church services, which were conducted in Latin, because when the priest raised the consecrated bread and said, "*Hoc est corpus meum* [This is my body]," it was heard by many as "hocus pocus"—a phrase that is now used to describe pseudomagical nonsense. That suggests that many people must have seen the liturgical celebrations in that way—as a means of warding off evil spirits, perhaps, or of

46. John 19:20.

obtaining favorable treatment from God—without having any idea about what was really going on.

Another feature of the Middle Ages that seems strange to us today is that almost no one possessed a Bible, and few could have read one if they had. Books were prohibitively expensive, and reading and writing were of little practical use to most people. Even priests were often barely literate. Many of them were sons of the soil who lived close to their flocks and may have been excellent pastors for that reason, but their formal education was rudimentary, and often they had little more need of it than anyone else in their parish. As long as they could say the services, which many of them would have known by heart, and sign their name, little more was required of them most of the time.

The contents of the Bible were not unknown, however. Its stories were conveyed to a wider public through stained-glass windows and mystery plays that told the stories of creation and redemption. Wandering preachers would teach the sayings of Jesus and the apostles, and the great drama of salvation was codified in the church year. This began four weeks before Christmas, when the coming ("advent") of Christ was announced and the prophecies of the Old Testament were rehearsed. But Advent also pointed forward to the second coming of Christ—the past and the future were both caught up in the present. Christmas was the great feast of the incarnation, which was followed by the life of Jesus, which culminated in Good Friday and Easter. After that came the Ascension and Pentecost, which marked the end of the cycle and the beginning of the present, or "ordinary," time of the church.

In addition to this basic framework there were any number of saints' days and other commemorations that would remind people of the great events in the life of Jesus and of the church. Many of these festivals were closely tied into the rhythm of agricultural life and thus became a kind of baptized paganism. Christmas, for example, was placed where it was because it marked the dying and rebirth of the light at the winter solstice. Easter absorbed many of the traits of a fertility cult, as its eggs and bunnies still attest. All Saints' Day (November 1) commemorated those who had died in the faith, and it was appropriately placed at the end of the agricultural year, when the harvest was in and the leftover shreds were burned. In preparation for this, the demons had to be cast out, which was done on the night before—All Hallows' Eve, or Hallowe'en, as it has come to be known. The intermingling of Christian and pagan themes went so deep that it was often impossible to separate the two. Santa Claus, for example, was a Christianization of the pagan "Father Frost," but his name is that of St. Nicholas, a fourth-century bishop of Myra in what is now southern Turkey, who had nothing to do with Christmas and would doubtless be deeply shocked to discover how he is remembered today.[47]

What popular devotion lacked was a deep understanding of the teaching of the New Testament epistles, which were more cerebral in content and almost impossible to dramatize or portray in visual art. The apostle Paul was well known to monks and intellectuals, but his sometimes complex arguments were mostly lost on ordinary people. It is no accident that the Protestant Reformation of the sixteenth century was rooted in a rediscovery of Pauline theology, which many people had never encountered before. Martin Luther did not invent justification by faith, but when he began to preach it, many of his hearers heard and understood it for the first time, perhaps because it was something that a stained-glass window or a mystery play could not convey to a wider public.

What the imperial church created was cultural Christianity, or Christendom, a world in which everything was expressed in Christian terms or related to Christian themes. What individuals believed did not matter very much (unless they were theologians or teachers liable to influence others) because it was all caught up in the wider net of the church. Even today, despite generations of secularization, remnants of this traditional culture persist. Non-Christian parents may still bring their children for baptism, and most people expect the church to have some involvement in weddings and funerals, even if they would be hard put to say what else it is for. In one curious respect, the legacy of the centuries of Christendom remains very much with us. In the ancient Roman world, Christians were sometimes accused of atheism because they did not believe in the pagan gods. Today, however, an atheist is not someone who rejects Jupiter or Venus but someone who denies the existence of the God of the Bible.

The Eastern Churches

Most of our discussion so far has concentrated on the Western church, which developed in the orbit of Rome and on the ruins of the Western empire. But there was always another church, or group of churches, that never came under the sway of the Roman pope and that offer us a different perspective on the development of the institutional church within what was originally the same imperial framework. Broadly speaking, there was no real difference

47. His feast day is December 6, and in some countries like the Netherlands, this is still celebrated as the day for giving presents. In Greece, the Father Frost figure has been identified with St. Basil, whose feast day is conveniently fixed on January 1.

between West and East as long as the Roman Empire remained intact. As late as the seventh century, it was still possible for someone such as Maximus the Confessor (580–668) to travel freely between the two halves of the Christian world, and even for a Greek (Theodore of Tarsus) to become archbishop of Canterbury.[48] The popes were subjects of the Eastern emperor until 751, when the last Byzantine possessions in north and central Italy were lost to the Lombards, and even after that, the memory of the connection remained alive. Geographically, politically, and historically, Rome was closer to the East than anywhere else in Western Europe, and the effects of that continued to be seen for centuries.

The seeds of eventual discord were first sown in 800, when Charlemagne resurrected the Roman Empire in the West, a development that Byzantium never accepted as legitimate. In the following century his theologians engaged in polemic against the East, largely in order to justify this rejection of Byzantine authority.[49] Matters became more serious when the evangelization of the Slavs got under way. The great missionaries to the Slavic peoples were Constantine (or Cyril, to use his monastic name) and his brother Methodius. They were Greeks from Thessalonica who spoke the local Slavic dialect and who were brought to the Balkans by sixth- and seventh-century invaders.[50]

Cyril and Methodius went to Moravia (now part of the Czech Republic), where they converted the king and a number of his subjects. Moravia, however, was on the border of the Western empire, whose rulers felt that the mission from the East was a threat. To ward this off, Cyril went to Rome to ask for the pope's help, but he died there and was unable to secure what he needed. Threatened by both the Western empire and the pagan Magyars (Hungarians) who were arriving from the East, Moravia buckled and eventually collapsed. Methodius left and relocated to northern Macedonia, not far from his original home. There he evangelized the Bulgarians, who had already made approaches to Rome. The Bulgarians knew that they would be forced to convert to Christianity but were hoping to submit to the Western church and so escape the clutches of nearby Constantinople. That, of course, was perceived as a threat in the East, and the Western mission to Bulgaria was thwarted much as the Eastern one to Moravia had been.[51]

48. He served in that capacity from 668 to 690 and was the chief architect of the institutional Church of England in its earliest phase.

49. See R. Haugh, *Photius and the Carolingians* (Belmont, MA: Nordland, 1975).

50. On the conversion of the Slavs to Christianity, see A. P. Vlasto, *The Entry of the Slavs into Christendom* (Cambridge: Cambridge University Press, 1970); D. Obolensky, *Byzantium and the Slavs* (Crestwood, NY: St. Vladimir's Seminary Press, 1994); J. Meyendorff, *Byzantium and the Rise of Russia* (Crestwood, NY: St. Vladimir's Seminary Press, 1989).

51. R. Browning, *Byzantium and Bulgaria* (London: Maurice Temple Smith, 1975).

A line was being drawn across Europe that would eventually extend all the way to the Arctic Ocean, leaving Bulgaria, Serbia, Romania, and (most important of all) Russia on the Eastern side, but Croatia, Hungary, Poland, the Baltic States, and Finland in the West. It is a fundamental division that remains intact today, even if its importance for both religion and culture is not always properly recognized. There was also a buffer zone between the two halves of Christendom where neither tradition dominated and which was therefore open to other influences. In the south, both Albania (including Kosovo) and Bosnia fell into this zone, which helps to explain why so many of the people there converted to Islam when the region fell under Turkish control. Further north, what is now the Romanian province of Transylvania became home after the Reformation to Protestants and Unitarians, who also flourished for a while in Poland, an officially Catholic state that ruled large tracts of Orthodox Ukraine and Belarus and was therefore obliged to tolerate different religious bodies.[52]

One big difference between the Western and the Eastern churches that became clear at this point was that the East did not insist on uniformity of language. Whereas Rome imposed Latin on northern Europe, Constantinople did not do the same with Greek. Instead, the Eastern missionaries translated the Bible, the liturgy, and a number of theological texts into Slavonic, a language based on a Bulgarian dialect but easily understood throughout the Slavic world. They also established autonomous (or "autocephalous") local churches that were not immediately dependent on Constantinople. In the Balkans this process was compromised by political considerations, so that when the Byzantines were strong enough to incorporate Bulgaria into their dominions, the Bulgarian church was also assimilated, but this was never the case in Russia. There, a pattern developed by which the head of the Russian church, the metropolitan bishop of Kiev, would be alternately a Greek and a Russian, a practice that maintained the link with Constantinople without leading to the domination of one church by the other. It was not until 1444, when the Byzantine Empire was in its death throes, that the last Greek metropolitan was deposed and a Russian elected to take his place.[53]

The survival of a strong civil society in the Byzantine Empire also meant that the institutional church never came to occupy the commanding position that it held in the West. Many laymen were accomplished theologians, and the emperors were deeply involved in church affairs. Monasteries were a

---

52. Poland also became home to many Jews, who remained a significant element of the population until they were annihilated in the Second World War.

53. See D. Obolensky, *The Byzantine Commonwealth* (London: Weidenfeld & Nicolson, 1971).

prominent feature of Eastern church life, but the monks tended to be much
more individualistic than their Western counterparts, and many were revered
for their sanctity and skill as spiritual directors. There was never any equivalent
to the orders of Western monasticism, and Eastern monks did not involve
themselves in worldly affairs to anything like the extent that their Western
counterparts did. Western monks produced famous cheeses and wines, for
example, but not Eastern ones. The Eastern monks were also relatively unin-
volved in education, which remained secular as long as the Byzantine Empire
lasted. Sometime in the tenth century, monastic communities began to colo-
nize Mount Athos, in northern Greece, where they developed a network of
independent foundations that still exist today. Athos was not unique in the
Byzantine world, but it survives as the only living relic of a culture that has
virtually disappeared everywhere else. It is a closed society where women are
not allowed and most of the creature comforts of modernity are unknown.
The monks who live there dedicate themselves to prayer and spiritual direction, serving as a resource for the entire Orthodox world. There is nothing in
the West even remotely comparable to it, and it stands as a reminder of the
central position that monasticism has occupied, and continues to occupy, in
the Eastern Christian world.

The Eastern church did not develop a parochial system in the way that the
West did, but every village had its church and its priest. These priests were
not only allowed to marry but were often almost compelled to do so. To this
day an Orthodox priest is expected to project a masculine image, complete
with beard and a large number of children, in a way that the West has never
attempted to impose on its clergy. The primacy of celibacy was observed by
enforcing it for bishops, who in practice were almost always monks. This
led to the emergence of a distinct class of "priest-monks" ("hieromonks"),
who were virtually the only people who could aspire to a bishopric. Western
monks could also be priests, of course, but this special connection with the
episcopate was (and is) unknown.

As for church buildings, the East never experienced the great architectural
revival that produced the Gothic cathedrals of the West, but in other ways it
gave greater importance to places of worship than the Roman church ever did.
As early as the sixth century, the emperor Justinian I (r. 527–65) erected the
magnificent Church of the Holy Wisdom (Hagia Sophia) in Constantinople,
which at that time was the largest building of its kind in the world.[54] The
interior of the church was decorated with magnificent mosaics and frescoes

54. Even today it is surpassed only by the Basilica of St. Peter in Rome, which was built a
thousand years later.

depicting the life of heaven, with Christ seated in glory (in the dome) and the saints gathered around him. This trend was resisted by the iconoclasts of the eighth century, who wanted to keep (or return to) the more austere church decoration of an earlier time, but they failed and the use of visual imagery was enshrined in public worship to a degree that was never true in the West. To this day the overwhelming presence of icons and other pictures inside an Orthodox church sets it apart from its Roman Catholic counterparts, even if Catholics do not object to the images on principle, and, of course, this feature distinguishes the Orthodox even more from Protestants. But Western Christians must appreciate that this is not just a matter of style and tradition, since iconography plays a role in Eastern Orthodox theology and worship that is unknown in the West.[55]

The great renewal of the Western church under the papacy, which began about 1050 and maintained a steady momentum for over 150 years, had no counterpart in the East. The patriarch of Constantinople was never in a position to dominate the emperor, and the canon law of the Eastern church, though it existed and was expounded by competent jurists, never threatened to rival civil legislation.[56] One result of this was that the Eastern church could not abolish divorce and had to accept a compromise by which a man (no one thought of a woman in this situation) could marry three times—but not a fourth. This was not a theological principle but a political decision, justified by what the Easterners call "economy," which means the prudent application of principles according to circumstances. Divorce was not wanted, but it could not be entirely avoided, so "economy" was used as a means of coming to terms with it. This way of resolving the ever-present tension between principle and practice allowed the Eastern church to live with anomalies that in the West were liable to provoke division or to force the church hierarchy to legislate more precisely than it might have wished.

One area where the Eastern church practiced economy was in its dealings with Islam. From the time the Muslim Arabs invaded Syria in 636 to the fall of Constantinople in 1453, it could not escape the Islamic presence and had to learn how to live with it. In theory, Muslims were infidels and the Eastern church should have been doing everything it could to defeat them. In practice, it never did so. After the Arabs failed to take Constantinople in the early eighth century, the Byzantines settled down to a largely peaceful coexistence with them. The majority of the inhabitants of Syria and Egypt were still Christian,

55. See C. A. Tsakiridou, *Icons in Time, Persons in Eternity: Orthodox Theology and the Aesthetics of the Christian Image* (Farnham: Ashgate, 2013).

56. W. Hartmann and K. Pennington, *The History of Byzantine and Eastern Canon Law to 1500* (Washington, DC: Catholic University of America Press, 2012).

and the emperor felt a responsibility for their welfare, even if they were mostly monophysite in their theology. For nearly four hundred years theologians on both sides debated with one another, but at the grassroots level there was a lot of cooperation and tolerance.

It was not an ideal situation, but the Eastern church did what it could to protect its people who were under Muslim rule and was generally successful in this. It was not until the Western church arrived on the scene with the Crusades that this equilibrium was seriously disturbed. The West accused the East of laxity in its dealings with Islam, and the Muslims responded by stepping up their efforts to convert Christians, so as not to give the crusaders the excuse that they were an army of liberation. This was an example of Eastern "economy" that was designed to make the best of difficult circumstances, and it gives us a good picture of how the two halves of the Christian world differed in their approach to a common problem.

To sum up a highly complex situation, the Eastern church was "imperial" in the sense that it was the state church of an empire while the Western church, in contrast, was an empire in its own right, competing with a number of different secular rulers rather than complementing them, and claiming the right to discipline them if and when they stepped out of line. In the late Middle Ages the imperial vision of both churches was to undergo a transformation, but for completely different reasons. The imperial church of the East fell with the empire to which it belonged, though it resurfaced later by managing to transfer its ideology to the newly emerging grand duchy of Moscow, which came to be regarded as the third Rome. The imperial church of the West, on the other hand, collapsed when the secular states that it had tried to dominate became too strong and turned the tables on the papacy, even to the point of supporting its enemies in order to gain their own freedom.

The Doctrine of the Church

When assessing the way in which the medieval church looked at itself, we must bear in mind two factors. The first is that institutionalization produced its own dynamic for definition. The Roman Empire had long survived without any equivalent to the church, so when the church emerged on the scene a place had to be found for it. What role should the church play in society? What privileges should it have, what powers should it be given, and what boundaries should there be between it and other organs of the state? Everything from the celebration of religious holidays to tax exemptions for the clergy had to be covered—and justified. If the church was necessary for the public good, then it would be relatively easy to make a case for giving it privileges and exemptions. But if it was just another religious cult of no particular value to anyone except its own members, it would be much harder to justify giving it any special consideration.

In this situation, the church itself had its own part to play in convincing people that its presence was both necessary and beneficial. Before long the Western church found itself the only social institution with any stability or continuity, which gave it a foundational role in society. Legal business was transacted by clerics, and at a higher level, popes and bishops legitimized secular rulers. Community life was increasingly shaped by the rites and rules of the church. Pagan customs were frequently taken over and "baptized" and their previous associations soon forgotten. Just outside Paris, for example, an enormous cathedral was built in honor of St. Denis, and the kings of France were buried there. The church was erected over the shrine of the pagan god Dionysus, who was simply recycled as "Denis," but later generations did not know or believe that. In their minds, Denis had been a third-century bishop of Paris who was beheaded for his faith. Miraculously, he picked up his severed head and walked ten miles with it, before dropping to the ground on the site of the church built in his name.

This extraordinary legend circulates to this day as the "official" story, and readers may judge for themselves how likely it is to be true. But whatever we make of it, the past was rewritten to conform to a Christian view of the world, and in that picture the church obviously had a vital part to play. It was the church that canonized the legend, rewrote history, and put itself and its mission at the center of human endeavor. People whose loyalties had previously been directed to Rome or to some barbarian tribe now found themselves classified as Christians, a new people bound together in the church, which knew neither race nor language and was expanding until, in principle, it embraced the entire world.

The great architect of this vision was Augustine of Hippo (354–430). For him, Christ was the head and the church was his body, "not just the local church, but both the local church and the church throughout the whole world; not the present church but the church that exists from the time of Abel and extends to all those who will be born in the future and who will believe in Christ."[57] Past, present, and future blend into one in the church, which embraces them all. But at the same time an important distinction had to be observed. As Augustine put it:

57. Augustine of Hippo, *Enarrationes in Psalmos* 90.2.1. The same theme recurs in his *Sermones* 4.11.

Let me recall the two hauls of fish that the apostles gathered in at Christ's command—one before his suffering and the other after the resurrection.[58] In these two catches the entire church is represented, both as it is now and as it will be after the resurrection of the dead. Now it has multitudes without number, both good and bad, but after the resurrection it will have only the good, and a fixed number of those.[59]

Here we see in parabolic form a distinction between what theologians call the church militant here on earth and the church triumphant in heaven. On earth the church has an open-door policy. Everyone can come into it, and the good mix with the bad. But in heaven, only the good will be present. The good will always be members of the mixed visible church during their earthly pilgrimage; God alone knows his own and in the end will separate them out for salvation.

The implications of this for a doctrine of the church were enormous. Before Augustine's time, most people thought of the church as the company of the saved; those who belonged to it were going to heaven, and those who were not members were condemned to hell. The problem with this picture was that it was plain to everyone that too many members of the church were not leading genuinely Christian lives. Did that mean that the church was not the body of the saved that it claimed to be? The Donatists answered that question in the affirmative and seceded to form their own church of the truly saved. Augustine countered them, not by calling black white and pretending that the obviously unworthy were not that bad after all, but by stating that there are two different faces to the church, one temporal and the other eternal. They were not mutually exclusive but overlapping, so that all those chosen for salvation would belong to the church as of right, but the visible institution on earth would also contain a good many false members. True believers did not have to worry about them because, in the end, they would not make the cut.

It is safe to say that Augustine's understanding of the church made the growth and development of the medieval institution possible. Had the church maintained a kind of Donatist view of purity, it would have devoured itself as members separated from one another whenever they detected any hint of sinfulness. But there was also an element of truth in Donatism that had to be acknowledged and provided for. There was a pure church hidden in the visible institution but revealed in its full glory in heaven. Could a believer have the assurance that he was one of the elect? To this Augustine had to answer in

58. The references are to Luke 5:4–8 and John 21:6–8, respectively.
59. Augustine of Hippo, *Sermones* 248.1.

the negative, because no one can know the mind of God. But at least we can know that the elect are all members of the visible church, so that belonging to it is a necessary step on the way to glory. The best that believers could do was to stick with the church, despite its problems, knowing that outside it whatever hope of salvation they had would be lost.

Augustine made predestination central to the identity of the church. Christ knew who were his, and God sent him into the world at the right time. It is not for us to try to be wiser than he; rather, we are to submit to his sovereign will and rejoice that we have heard the gospel while others have been passed over. The blessing that has come to us has nothing to do with our merits, real or imagined, but is entirely an act of God's grace, predetermined from before the foundation of the world.[60] Knowing this relieves us of the anxiety of trying to please Christ in order to gain favor with him. He is the bridegroom; we are the bride he has chosen. Our duty is to submit and obey him as a wife is called to submit to her husband and obey him.[61] There is no need to try to be more attractive to him; he has already chosen us and will give us the beauty that he wants us to have.[62]

Augustine's understanding of the church promoted another aspect of which he may have been unaware at the time. This was the sense that the church was primarily one throughout the whole world. That had never been denied, of course, but in earlier times the emphasis had been on the local congregation gathered around its bishop, who then communicated with other churches in his province and (occasionally) further afield. The legalization of Christianity gave the church an opportunity to hold councils on a wider basis, but it was Augustine, more than anyone else, who provided a theological underpinning for this newfound sense of unity. A church that was primarily spiritual, united to Christ as his body and present in eternity, could hardly be anything but one, and its local manifestations in time and space had to be evaluated in terms of that. As Augustine understood it, the universal church transcended the limitations of the created order and was spiritually perfect. What we see around us are visible expressions of that church, all of which are to some extent defaced and corrupted by the world we live in. Believers therefore must learn to distinguish what is eternally valid from what is only a local phenomenon and prefer the former to the latter in cases of conflict or discrepancy.

This emphasis on the oneness of the church tied in with the confession of faith adopted by the First Council of Constantinople in 381 and known to us

60. Augustine of Hippo, *De praedestinatione sanctorum* 18.1.
61. Augustine of Hippo, *Enarrationes in Psalmos* 147.18.
62. Augustine of Hippo, *Sermones* 262.5.

as the Nicene Creed.[63] It defined the church as "one, holy, catholic, and apostolic," four adjectives that have come to be known in subsequent theology as its "marks" or "notes." The precise definition of these marks has varied over time and occasionally proved to be contentious, particularly in the wake of the Protestant Reformation, but to the generation that first confessed them their meaning seemed clear enough.

The unity of the church, as we have already seen in Augustine, went beyond the bounds of time and space. Commenting on Ephesians 4:6, where Paul says that there is "one Lord, one faith and one baptism," John Chrysostom (d. 407) said: "What is this one body? It is the faithful throughout the world, both those who are, those who have been, and those who will be. Even those who lived before the coming of Christ and who pleased God belong to it, because they also knew Christ."[64] The unity of the church was spiritual, given by the Holy Spirit at Pentecost and maintained by those who remained faithful to his teaching. It was manifested in baptism and in the Lord's Supper, but these outward rites were meant to reflect an inner bond of spiritual love that bound Christians together.[65] What is remarkable is that it was never expressed in terms of institutional conformity, as it would be in later centuries. Individuals were expected to be in communion with their bishops, and the bishops were meant to share the faith with one another, but this was a spiritual thing measured by conformity to the teaching of Holy Scripture, and not a legal connection imposed by a church hierarch, however exalted he might be.

The holiness of the church was likewise a spiritual quality. In line with the two aspects of the church that we have already noted, Augustine stated quite clearly that the holy church was the Jerusalem that is above, our heavenly mother, the city of God.[66] His contemporary Rufinus of Aquileia (345?–411) said much the same, adding only that the holiness of the church was characterized by the purity of its doctrine, which was clearly stated in the Apostles' Creed.[67]

As for the church's catholicity, the best and most complete definition of this was given by Cyril of Jerusalem as part of the catechetical instruction that he prepared for new believers:

63. The creed was confused with that of Nicaea I (325) but is now universally regarded as independent of it. See J. N. D. Kelly, *Early Christian Creeds*, 3rd ed. (London: Longman, 1972), 205–367, for a full explanation.

64. John Chrysostom, *Homiliae in Ephesios* 10.

65. Augustine of Hippo, *Sermones* 229A.1–2.

66. Augustine of Hippo, *Sermones* 214.11. The allusion is to Galatians 4:26.

67. Rufinus of Aquileia, *De symbolo apostolorum* 39. Rufinus was using an earlier version of the creed that we now recognize under that name.

> The church is called "catholic" because it extends over the whole world . . .
> and because it teaches universally and completely all and every doctrine that
> human beings need to know about things visible and invisible, heavenly and
> earthly. It is also called "catholic" because it subjects the entire human race to
> the demands of godliness.[68]

Once again we are struck by the emphasis placed on doctrine and morals,
rather than on institutional structures. All Christians were expected to model
the catholicity of the church by their words and behavior, which would necessarily include active membership in its visible structure but could not be
defined by it.

Finally, the apostolicity of the church was determined above all by the purity of the faith that it preached. Athanasius (296–373) was very clear about
this. In writing to an Egyptian bishop called Serapion, he stated quite clearly:

> The very tradition, teaching and faith of the catholic church from the beginning
> was preached by the apostles and preserved by the fathers. On this the church
> was founded. If anyone departs from this, he neither is, nor any longer ought
> to be called, a Christian.[69]

The imperial church that emerged in later centuries developed more fixed
and institutional interpretations of these marks, but it always insisted that
they were the signs of the true church. For the better part of a thousand years,
that claim went unchallenged and was little discussed. Only when a growing
number of people began to suspect that the marks of the church were no
longer visible in the institution to which they belonged was their true meaning questioned, and when that happened, the imperial church was plunged
into a crisis from which it never fully emerged.

68. Cyril of Jerusalem, *Catecheses* 18.22.
69. Athanasius, *Ad Serapionem* 1.28.

5

The Crisis of the Imperial Church

The Crisis of Authority

When Pope Innocent III (r. 1198–1216) summoned what was to become the Fourth Lateran Council in 1215, he and his church were at the height of their power and influence. The council turned out to be the last of the great reforming synods that had met over the previous century in the Lateran, the papal palace in Rome, in order to establish ground rules for administering the vast international network that the Roman church had become. The First Lateran Council had assembled in 1123, after a gap of some 250 years, and legislated against what it saw as the chief abuses of its time. These were the sale of church offices (known as "simony"),[1] the cohabitation of priests with women, and the interference of laypeople in the business of the church. The agenda was clear: the church had to put its house in order and create as much distance as it could between its internal affairs and the people to whom it ministered. The Second Lateran Council in 1139 reinforced the previous one by going into greater detail regarding particular abuses, but it also took note of heretics who denied or perverted the sacraments and called on the secular rulers of Europe to stamp them

---

1. The name was taken from Simon Magus, the Samaritan who had tried to buy the gift of the Holy Spirit from the apostles. See Acts 8:18–24.

out.[2] The Third Lateran Council was held in 1179 and was mainly concerned with correcting abuses in the election of bishops and other clergy,
in addition to the problems that had surfaced earlier but had still not been
resolved satisfactorily.

It was the Fourth Lateran Council, however, that was to make the most
far-reaching changes and have the longest-lasting impact on the church.
As we would expect from Innocent III, it launched a broadside attack on
heresies, which were now seen to be a major danger to the church. The
neo-Manichaean Albigensians (or Cathars) in the south of France were
denounced, and a Crusade was subsequently organized to suppress them,
which it did with the help of the French king. The mystic prophet Joachim
da Fiore (d. 1202), whose writings were to exercise great influence on later
generations who were inspired by his predictions of the coming reign of the
antichrist, were also condemned.[3] Peter Lombard's *Sentences* were cited for
the first time as the chief authority for the church's doctrine, and after that
his work became the standard textbook for theological students across the
Western church. Other matters covered included the regulation of confession
to a priest, which was strengthened by the imposition of what is known as
"the seal of the confessional," that is to say, the obligation imposed on the
priest not to reveal anything confessed to him, even if it was a crime against
the law.[4] The council also legislated against clandestine marriages by insisting
that public notice should be given on at least three occasions beforehand.
This created what is known today as the reading of the "banns," a practice
still found in some Anglican and Presbyterian churches.[5] It was also the
time when the benefice system for clergy appointments was established,
and the pentarchy of patriarchates originally established in 381 was finally
recognized by Rome.

At a time when secular government in Europe was divided and weak, the
church provided a unifying force that gave real meaning to the idea of a common Christian civilization. After 1204 Rome even managed to extend its reach
to Constantinople when that city fell to the crusaders, and there were hopes
that its position in Palestine, which had been weakened by an Islamic revival
there, was still recoverable. On July 16, 1212, a major battle at Las Navas de
Tolosa in Spain had broken the back of the Islamic states in the peninsula,
and it looked as though the whole country might soon be brought back into

2. Canon 23.
3. See M. Reeves, *Joachim of Fiore and the Prophetic Future* (London: SPCK, 1976).
4. The validity of this "seal" is still being contested today.
5. It is a legal requirement in the Church of England and in the Church of Scotland, for
example.

Christendom.[6] The Western church was on the move, and for a time it seemed that its progress was unstoppable.

A century later, however, the papacy had left Rome for an indefinite stay in Avignon, where it was under the watchful eye of the French king. Constantinople had been lost to the Byzantines in 1261, and the crusading ideal was dead. In Western Europe the church was still by far the most important social institution, and most people continued to identify with it more than with anything else, but it was no longer dominant in the way that it had been a hundred years before. No one at the time could have known it, but the church was about to enter three centuries of internal decline and conflict that would not be halted until 1648, when the Peace of Westphalia ended the Thirty Years' War and established a religious equilibrium in Western Europe that has remained essentially unchanged ever since. The price of peace, however, was the effective separation of church affairs from secular politics. Even in the still-extant Holy Roman Empire, the papacy would no longer play any significant role in European affairs.

How did this happen? It is in the nature of institutions to rise and decline, and the papacy had certainly gone through hard times before. The onslaught of Islam in the seventh century and the Viking invasions in the tenth did great damage to the church, and there were times when it must have seemed that Christianity would be overwhelmed in Europe just as it had been in its ancient Middle Eastern heartland. But the church had recovered and gone on to flourish in a way that it had never done before (and was never to do again). Why was it that this pattern did not repeat itself in the thirteenth and fourteenth centuries?

One of the unforeseen results of the Crusades was the increased contact they brought with the Arab and Muslim world. This was particularly noticeable in Spain, which had a flourishing Muslim culture, despite its distance from the main centers of Islam, and which was gradually reconquered by the Christian princes of the north in the course of the thirteenth century. Another place where there was considerable interaction between Christians and Muslims was Sicily, where the rebellious emperor Frederick II (1194–1250) spent most of his time. Frederick encouraged interfaith dialogue, and if that upset the pope, then so much the better from Frederick's perspective. People like him, and the crusaders in general, could hardly fail to notice that the Muslim lands and the Byzantine Empire had a much higher level of culture than Western Europe at that time. They soon discovered the riches of Arab learning, although much

6. As it turned out, that had to wait until 1492, but the Muslims were never again in a position to threaten the Christian kingdoms to the north.

of that had originally been borrowed from the ancient Greeks and Hindus. Muslim scholars had long been debating questions about the relationship between faith and reason, which had been forced on them by the interaction of the Qur'an with ancient Greek science, represented above all by the pagan philosopher Aristotle.[7]

Aristotle was a name that was barely known in Europe, and even the Byzantines paid little attention to him or the school of thought that went under his name. It was different with the Arabs. They took to his writings and saw in them a source of intellectual enlightenment quite independent of any kind of divine revelation. Subjects such as mathematics, astronomy, and medicine, to name only a few, were dealt with by this corpus of Greek writings, and what we call the "scientific method" of discovery by experiment was promoted by them. Of course, we now know that the ancient Greeks were more often wrong than right, and that has given many modern people a negative attitude toward them. But this discovery did not come until the sixteenth and seventeenth centuries. To those who first encountered it some three hundred years earlier, ancient Greek learning, as transmitted by the Arabs, opened up a whole new world of knowledge that had remained hidden from their eyes before that time.

This discovery inevitably hit the church, which regarded itself as the sole guardian of all knowledge. Moreover, that knowledge had come to it not by scientific investigation but by divine revelation. The early Christians had fought against the pagan philosophies of their day and had done so successfully, but for the most part it was polytheism that they attacked rather than what we would now call the natural sciences. That side of ancient learning either passed them by or was accepted (as it was in Byzantium) as the "exterior wisdom," that is to say, the wisdom of this world, which was of minor importance compared to the "interior wisdom." That was the spiritual understanding that a person needed if he or she wanted to get to heaven, which is what all right-thinking people were primarily interested in.

There was an overlap between the material and the spiritual worlds, and it was one that caused more difficulties for Christians than for Muslims. The Muslim view of God was purely spiritual, so they could keep heaven and earth in separate compartments more easily than Christians could. Christians confessed that God had become a man in Jesus Christ and that the church was in some sense an extension of that incarnation—the body of Christ on earth. For that reason, the material world could not be separated from the

7. See I. Najjar, *Faith and Reason in Islam: Averroes' Exposition of Religious Arguments* (Oxford: Oneworld, 2001).

divine or interpreted in a way that would exclude the possibility of any clash between them. A good example of what this meant can be seen from the way in which the creation of the world was understood. For Muslims the doctrine of creation was axiomatic but vague; God had made the world, certainly, but precisely how and when remained a mystery. Christians, however, read in the Bible that God made the world in six days, which they assumed were twenty-four-hour periods in historical time. Scholars and theologians added several layers of nonliteral meaning to the text, but as time went on their taste for allegory diminished, and from the thirteenth century onward it came to be thought that the book of revelation (the Bible) must coincide with what God reveals to us in the book of nature (the world that is subject to rational investigation).

The stage was thus set for the historic clash between "religion" and "science" with which we are familiar today and which the church always seems to be losing. Already in the thirteenth century, schools were appearing in places such as Paris and Oxford that were challenging, if not the church as such, then at least the monasteries as the chief providers of education. For many centuries a young man who wanted to be a priest (or whose parents wanted him to become one) could go to a monastery, get a basic education, and then be ordained and placed in a parish, which in many cases would be in the gift of the abbot. Monastic education had a very practical side; a priest trained there would probably know how to farm the land, milk cows, and so on. Such skills brought him close to the people he was called to serve and came in handy if he had to provide for himself.

The schools, on the other hand, turned out a very different kind of ordination candidate. A man who graduated from one of them would be able to debate philosophy and theology, but in the nature of things that was more likely to lead to disputes and have very limited appeal at the parish level. Indeed, a persistent theme of the later Middle Ages was the need for these schools, or universities as they came to be called, to find employment for their graduates. Their chancellors begged reluctant bishops to find benefices for them, but perhaps inevitably, many graduates preferred to work in administration—ecclesiastical, secular, or both. In this way, the kings of Western Europe were able to find a pool of highly trained men who would work for them and could use their skills to counteract the influence of the church.

Needless to say, the church was aware of these dangers and did what it could to maintain its control over education. From the beginning, Aristotle was perceived as the chief enemy, and in 1277 there was a decree that his works should no longer be taught at the University of Paris. By then, however, it was too late. A wiser course had already been charted by men such as Thomas Aquinas (1225–74). He recognized that Aristotelian science and biblical theology were complementary, not contradictory, disciplines. What Aristotle had to say could be accepted as true as far as it went, but theologians insisted that it did not go far enough. To complete the picture of universal knowledge, divine revelation of truths that lay beyond the power of reason to discover was necessary, and that revelation could be interpreted only by the church, to which it had been entrusted. Superficially, this distinction between truths accessible to human reason and truths that lay beyond might appear to resemble the one between the exterior and interior wisdom so familiar to the Byzantines, but the conceptual framework was different. The Byzantine scheme of things allowed for allegorical and mystical interpretations of the Bible, but these were increasingly frowned upon in the West, especially in university faculties of theology.

To the new breed of Western philosopher-theologians, the difference between the Bible and Aristotle was one not of genre or even of purpose but of source. They were talking not about the same things in different ways (as the Byzantines assumed) but about different things in the same way. As the schoolmen saw it, the Bible supplied knowledge that the Aristotelian method was incapable of obtaining, but that knowledge was not of a fundamentally different character. In itself it was just as rational as anything that the natural sciences could come up with, but the limitations of the human mind were such that it could not be discovered in that way. The Bible picked up where Aristotle left off—in other words, what was knowable by nature was supplemented by what could only be known by grace. It was taken for granted that the two worlds of learning connected with each other, so that Aristotelian science, properly understood, did not contradict biblical revelation, and vice versa. If there was a discrepancy, it could always be blamed on Aristotle, who was a pagan and therefore could not have been expected to have it right all the time. Problems arose only when the Aristotelian method turned up something that was (or seemed to be) incompatible with the biblical revelation.

To the generation of Aquinas, this picture of the two sources of knowledge appeared to safeguard the position of the church, but it was not long before it was being called into question. Miracles were a particular problem. It might be possible to defend something like the resurrection of Jesus as a one-off occurrence that would be expected of a man who was also the divine Son of God, but what about the so-called miracle of the altar, in which priests transformed ordinary bread and wine into the Savior's body and blood thousands of times every day? Was this really plausible? Even if such a miracle were possible, how could the church be the dispenser of divine grace when so many of its ministers were ignorant and corrupt, unable even to read the

Scriptures that they were supposed to be guarding and interpreting? Could it really be the case that a man who had been taught to pray in a monastery knew more about theology than one who had learned how to study and debate it in a university?

By 1300 these questions were starting to be asked, and every time the church tried to suppress them the problem merely got worse. But the intellectual weakness of the church's position was not fully exposed for a long time because the debates were relatively abstract and hard for ordinary people to understand. Much more telling in their eyes was the financial issue that arose from the exemption that the church claimed from secular taxation. In the church's eyes, money that had been given to it was money given to God and therefore not taxable by the state. But in the state's eyes, the church was a social parasite, demanding protection from its enemies (pagans, heretics, and Muslims) but unwilling to pay for it. The failure of the Crusades brought this problem home to many. Huge sums of money had been raised and spent by (or under the auspices of) the church in a cause that had failed. Meanwhile, the kings had to promote the rule of law and order at home, a task that could often be frustrated by a church that demanded special privileges—for instance, the right to try its own officials even if they were accused of a secular crime such as theft or murder. The idea that there was one law for laypeople and another for clergy took root, and this apparent injustice had at least some basis in fact, since anyone who could sign his name could claim "benefit of clergy" and escape some of the harsher punishments of the law as a result.

Resentment of the privileges of the church helped a man like King Philip IV of France (r. 1285–1314) to engage in a long-running duel with the papacy from which he eventually emerged victorious. When he demanded the right to tax the goods of the church, all the pope could do was excommunicate him and issue a papal decretal (*Clericis laicos*) condemning the seizure of ecclesiastical property by a secular ruler. The pope had a certain moral authority, but the king had an army behind him, and as long as that army stayed loyal, he was bound to win. By the time Philip IV died, he had forced the popes to leave Rome and install themselves in Avignon, where they were to remain until 1377. This period, known to subsequent generations as the "Babylonian captivity" of the church, was detrimental to the papacy because it called the nature of its authority into question. If the pope was the bishop of Rome, the place where the apostle Peter had been martyred, why did he not have to live there? More to the point, how could he accept a situation in which he was effectively at the mercy of the king of France?

This question became more acute after 1328, when the failure of the male line in the French royal house led to a conflict between the French nobility (who wanted the next male relative of the deceased King Charles IV to succeed him) and King Edward III of England (r. 1327–77), who was the son of Charles IV's only daughter, Isabel, and claimed the right to inherit the French crown through her. The result was the Hundred Years' War between England and France, in which it might be said that the English won almost all the major battles but the French won the war—in the end. Of course, this ongoing conflict called the neutrality of the papacy into question, and it is no accident that Edwardine England was one of the first places in the West where resistance to the pope and his claims surfaced in a serious way.

The ground for this had already been prepared by William of Ockham (1287?–1347), an Englishman whose dedication to Aristotelian principles of reason and logic was second to none. Ockham had a checkered career, to put it mildly, and died in Germany as a fugitive from papal justice—though the fact that the Germans gave him refuge shows that England was not the only country to have an interest in undermining the Avignon popes. Another important influence in the same direction was that of Marsilius of Padua (1280?–1343), a contemporary of Ockham who wrote a devastating critique of the papacy known as *The Defender of the Peace*.[8] Marsilius demonstrated that the papacy had vastly overstepped the bounds of its authority in its attempts to dominate Europe, and in truth, he had little use for the institution. His book became a clarion call for root-and-branch reform, and in later times, it was assumed that everyone who questioned papal authority had imbibed the teaching of Marsilius, whether that was true or not.

But it was to be not Marsilius but John Wyclif, a man influenced by Ockham though not directly taught by him, who would lead the charge against the papacy, in circumstances that seemed peculiarly favorable to him at the time. As a student at Oxford, Wyclif absorbed Ockhamist ideas, along with a heavy dose of Aristotle and the scholastic theology of men such as Thomas Aquinas. But perhaps the deepest impact on his life came not from them but from something else altogether. Beginning in late 1346 and extending over a three- to four-year period, Western Europe was ravaged by the bubonic plague, popularly known as the Black Death. Carried by fleas that infested rats, the plague was highly contagious, and within a very short time somewhere between a third and a half of the European population died. The clergy were hit especially hard, because they ministered to the sick and dying and thus caught the plague from them.

8. Two recent English translations of this work are available. One was translated by A. Gewirth and known by its Latin title as *Defensor pacis* (Toronto: University of Toronto Press, 1980); the other was translated by A. Brett and is known by its English title, *The Defender of the Peace* (Cambridge: Cambridge University Press, 2005).

No one understood how or why the plague caused such devastation, but explanations were not slow in coming. In a world where it was assumed that the church prayed to God for the protection of his people from such calamities, it was not difficult to point to the abnormal conditions in which the church then found itself as the true cause of the people's misery. The plague could easily be presented as God's judgment on a corrupt church. Wyclif was not primarily concerned about the papacy's move to Avignon, nor did he worry unduly about financial irregularities and so on. What bothered him most was doctrinal error, a sin that to his mind lay at the heart of everything else that was wrong. He thought that false beliefs would inevitably produce false teaching and lead to wrong behavior, which would then invite the just retribution of God.

Wyclif did not attack the institution of the papacy as such, but he did home in on two fundamental beliefs that the popes were keen to promote. The first was the idea that the Bible and church tradition were authorities of equal importance, so that what could not be found in written form in the Scriptures might nevertheless be part of divine revelation by having been handed down through the tradition of the church.[9] Since both authorities were ultimately controlled by the pope, it made little difference which was used; either way, the church got what it wanted. The second belief was transubstantiation, which Wyclif believed was scientific nonsense but which the papacy was promoting as one of the chief aspects of the ministerial priesthood.[10] For Christians to draw closer to Christ, they had to partake of the sacrament, but that sacrament could be consecrated only by a legitimately ordained priest. Hence the authority of the church over people's lives was closely connected with the power of the priest to bring God's grace to them—or, even more important, to withhold that grace if they misbehaved. To the church were given the keys of the kingdom of heaven, and it was the duty and the privilege of the priesthood, headed by the pope himself, to accept or reject those who sought to enter.

Wyclif insisted that ultimate authority in the church belonged not to the pope but to the Bible, which was God's self-revelation to the human race. The fact that the popes had been able to take over the church to the degree that they had was due to popular ignorance of the Scriptures—as we might put it today, the average Christian did not know what his or her "rights" were. The extreme scarcity and unreliability of translations of the Bible ensured that only those with a good knowledge of Latin had any hope of understanding its teaching.

9. This point was made by the papal legate Othobon in 1268, in a speech he made to the clergy of the English province of Canterbury. Othobon was promulgating a new set of canons for the English church, and he thanked God that it was possible to supplement the teaching of Scripture in this way. He later became Pope Hadrian V (1276).

10. This was yet another legacy of the Fourth Lateran Council in 1215.

This, of course, gave the clergy a privileged position. To understand how this felt, we might compare the role that lawyers often play today. In theory, anyone accused of a crime can defend himself or herself in court, but the law is so complicated and arcane that only foolhardy individuals would attempt to do so. Instead, people seek out lawyers, whose job is essentially to find a way for clients to be acquitted, whether they are guilty or not. Medieval priests were not unlike this. Some of them were lawyers as well, administering the canon law with the same assurance with which they taught the Scriptures and expecting others to accept their conclusions without complaint. The result was that people with influence could often get what they wanted—an annulment of their marriage, for example—whereas humbler folk were at the mercy of the system.

Because Wyclif promoted Scripture and opposed the doctrine of transubstantiation, later generations of Protestants saw him as the "morning star of the Reformation" and claimed him as their spiritual forebear, though this view has been contested in more recent times. Of course, everyone must agree that Wyclif could not have seen the Reformation coming; it did not break out until more than one hundred years after his death. By then, the issues that provoked the division of the church were different, and Martin Luther never appealed directly to Wyclif as his inspiration. Nor did Wyclif's surviving followers, known as Lollards, make much impression in the sixteenth century. Those who still existed melted into the Protestant movement without leaving any trace, and even the Wycliffite translations of the Bible, though they must have been known, played no part in the reformed church. In any case, they were based on the Latin version of the Scriptures, not on the original Hebrew and Greek texts, and thus would have been of little interest in the sixteenth century, when people were eager to go back behind the Latin to the original languages of the text.

But if it is problematic to view Wyclif as the forerunner of the Reformation, there were certain aspects of his teaching that raised issues that would come to feature very prominently in it. His assertion of biblical authority over against church-approved tradition and his rejection of a scientifically untenable doctrine of transubstantiation were symptomatic of the kinds of things that would later raise the question of the church's authority in a way that he would have recognized, even if it went beyond what he himself was trying to do.

Institutional Disintegration

One effect of the plague was to diminish the supply of monks. In earlier times, monasteries, and the clerical vocation in general, had been a useful safety valve to contain the danger of overpopulation. Peasants needed large families to run their farms and to compensate for the very high death rate, but they did not want their land to be subdivided to the point where it was no longer profitable to work. So unwanted sons (and unmarried daughters) could be handed over to the church, where they would lead comfortable and respectable lives, perhaps even rising to a position where they could help their impoverished families. The plague put a sharp and sudden end to all that. The problem of a surplus population gave way to a shortage, and few young men could be spared for the monastic life. Monks and the clergy had also suffered disproportionately, as we have already noted. As a result, monasteries that had once been full declined to the point where they had only a handful of members, and vast tracts of arable monastic land lay fallow because there was nobody to till them. Labor, which had once been cheap and plentiful, now became scarce and more expensive, allowing skilled craftsmen, for example, to establish small businesses that could lift them out of rural poverty. Slowly but surely, a middle class began to emerge that could afford to educate its children but did not particularly want them to enter the celibate world of the institutional church.

These developments did not presage a decline of faith—far from it. From the late fourteenth century onward we come across new experiments in Christian community living, no longer rooted in traditional monasticism but reflecting a desire to live in the normal human way, with marriage and family forming a key part of the consecrated life. The most important of these was based in the Netherlands and was associated with the name of Geert Groote (1340–84). Groote was instrumental in founding a community known as the Brethren of the Common Life; its practices were called the "modern devotion" because of their novelty at the time.[11] Groote met with a good deal of opposition, but in the course of the fifteenth century, the modern devotion spread across the Low Countries, attracting, among others, the great Thomas à Kempis (1380?–1471), whose classic work *The Imitation of Christ* is still widely read today. It used to be thought that the Brethren were forerunners of the Protestant Reformation, but this is now considered anachronistic, and in fact they were hostile to Protestants when they first encountered them. On the other hand, there is no doubt that their way of life was more attractive to people such as Martin Luther than traditional monasticism was, and it seems that once the Reformation was under way, people who might earlier have joined the Brethren became Protestants instead.

11. See R. R. Post, *The Modern Devotion: Confrontation with Reformation and Humanism* (Leiden: Brill, 1968).

There was also a greater emphasis on individual spirituality, which could be practiced by both celibates and married people. Female devotion, never absent, became more common in the literature of the time, and educated women such as Lady Margaret Beaufort (1443–1509) in England became prominent benefactors of the revival of learning that began in earnest in the fifteenth century.[12] The church was diversifying, and in many ways ordinary Christians were becoming less dependent on the traditional structures. Of course, we must be careful not to exaggerate this phenomenon. For the vast majority of people, things would hardly have changed at all, and the age-old routines of parish life must have continued as they always had. But whatever its limits, change was at least becoming possible and accepted in a way that it had not been a century or two earlier.

The decline of the monasteries led to a corresponding decline in the kind of education that they had to offer, though here again, we must not exaggerate. There would still be people going into monasteries for their theological education in the early sixteenth century—Martin Luther was one of them. But after the plague there can be no doubt that the impact of the universities increased, and the value of the education they provided was more widely appreciated. Friars, who as a group had been on the fringes of church life in the thirteenth century, became more central as time went on, and the freedom they had to move around was of great help in their establishing themselves as teachers and freelance preachers. There was certainly a tendency for them to institutionalize their orders in the way that the monks had done before them, but there were also strong forces of renewal within their ranks that kept at least some of them fresh and faithful to the original vision of men such as Francis of Assisi. In the early sixteenth century, the Franciscans experienced a revival among the so-called observants, that is to say, men who returned to the strict rules of the order as originally laid down by Francis. These observants were particularly influential in Ireland and have been credited by some with having staved off Protestantism by their own program of reform.

In many places where preaching had been little known, the friars were able to bring the Word of God to the people, sometimes with dramatic effect. In Florence, for example, the Dominican friar Girolamo Savonarola (1452–98) had such a powerful impact that for a short time he became the effective ruler of the city and introduced a moral reformation there that continues to astound modern observers. Savonarola was regarded as a dangerous radical and was soon put to death for his temerity, but that he was able to get as far as he did,

12. She was the mother of King Henry VII (r. 1485–1509) and founded two Cambridge colleges (Christ's and St. John's), as well as endowing a professorship of divinity that is named after her.

when both church and state were ranged against him, shows the strength of the movement he represented and the appeal it held for many ordinary people.

But whatever influence these and other "outsider" movements had on the church between 1350 and 1500, nothing can compare with the dramatic implosion of the papacy itself, the linchpin of the entire medieval system. At the very time when Wyclif's enemies were making his "heresies" known to the wider church, the popes were on their way back from Avignon to Rome, partly thanks to English victories against France that had weakened the French monarchy and made it less able to prevent the papacy from returning to the place where it belonged. In theory, the return of the papacy to Rome should have been welcomed by everyone, but although the wider Christian world was happy to see it restored to its rightful home, those most directly involved— the cardinals and the French nobility—were not. After nearly seventy years in Avignon, all the cardinals were French and had no desire to settle in a city that to them was not only alien but also half-ruined by neglect.

When the pope died in 1378, the cardinals agreed to elect one of their number as his successor, provided that he return immediately to Avignon. Unfortunately for them, the new pope reneged on his promise, taking the name Urban VI, a clear indication of his determination to stay in the eternal city (*urbs*). Flabbergasted by this betrayal, the cardinals withdrew to Pisa, where they deposed Urban VI and elected a more compliant pope instead. He promptly did their bidding and returned to France, which was only too glad to support him. There were now two popes, each claiming the legitimate authority of election by the College of Cardinals. For a church that had come to rely so heavily on the pope as the focus of unity, this was a disaster because it split Western Christendom in two. England was at war with France, so, of course, it sided with the Roman pope over against the Avignonese one. Scotland, on the other hand, was allied with France against England, so it plumped for Avignon. And so it went across Europe. Virtually no one took sides for theological reasons; the whole affair was political from beginning to end, bringing doubt and discredit on the entire institution of the papacy.

The Great Schism, as this episode was called, continued until 1417, when it was patched up at the Council of Constance, which had been summoned by the emperor for precisely that purpose. Even then, it was some time before the last remnants of the schism finally died out and it could truly be said that there was once again a single pope recognized by all. Unfortunately, this otherwise happy outcome was marred by a scandal that was to reverberate through church history and is still alive to some extent today.

Criticism of the church along the lines of John Wyclif was not confined to England. In Bohemia, Jan Hus thought much the same thing, and the

Hussites were inspired by their English colleagues. Since they all used Latin, it was easy for their ideas to spread, and as a result, today some of Wyclif's works survive in manuscript only in Central Europe, where the Hussites had copied them. Hus was a Czech speaker in a country that had come increasingly under German domination, so nationalism played a role in his opposition to a church that seemed to favor the more powerful. Other Czechs were concerned that the papacy was allowing Communion in one kind only (the bread but not the wine), a practice that they regarded as unbiblical. No one really knows how this custom originated, but one theory is that it was a hygienic measure taken to avoid the spread of plague and other diseases that could easily be caught by sharing a common cup. Whatever the truth of the matter, there can be no doubt that Communion in both kinds (*sub utraque specie*) was the New Testament norm and had been the universal practice of the church until fairly recently.

Instead of recognizing this and restoring the cup to the laity, the church authorities chose to regard Utraquism, as this movement was called, as a challenge to be fought off, and they came up with a number of ingenious arguments in defense of the innovation. One of them was that since a body contains blood, persons who eat the body of Christ also consume his blood, so there is no need to give it to them separately. Hus was not originally an Utraquist, but he fell into that camp quite naturally, and it was as a defender of that position that he was summoned to the Council of Constance to await the judgment of the church. The emperor promised him safe-conduct, so Hus went, believing that he had a chance of vindicating himself before the universal episcopate.

Tragically, not only was Hus condemned, but his safe-conduct was ignored and he was burned at the stake as a heretic. This caused a furor in Bohemia, where large numbers of people effectively broke communion with Rome. It was a slap in the face to the emperor, whose prestige suffered a serious blow as the papacy reasserted its right to determine who had the right to speak for the church as a whole. Perhaps most worryingly, it was a clear example of how a traditional practice—in this case, a recent tradition to boot—could prevail over the clear biblical witness, merely because the pope and a church council said so. Did they have the authority to do that?

It is important to stress that the decision to condemn Hus was taken by both the pope and the council; it was not imposed by the former on the latter (or vice versa). This must be said, because one of the provisions agreed on at Constance was that in the future the church would be run, not as a dictatorship based in Rome, but along quasi-parliamentary lines. The intention was that ecumenical councils would meet every five years to decide matters of supreme importance for the government of the church, and the pope would be their executive officer, charged with carrying out their decisions but not permitted to impose his own will on them. The pope did not want to be hobbled in this way, of course, but his position was still weak, and no one was prepared to start a fresh division over something that was designed to bring people together. In any case, as the executive officer charged with implementing the decisions arrived at in common, he had a long-term position that was strong and could perhaps be used to restore what he thought his proper authority should be—as in fact turned out to be the case.

In the meantime, the church experimented with what is known as "conciliarism." Had modern means of communication been available in the fifteenth century, this proposal might have worked. As it was, bishops and officials had to travel all across Europe at regular intervals to attend councils that had a way of continuing longer than anyone wanted. Conciliarism was an idea that was implemented before its time and without the resources needed to make it work on a long-term basis. Another problem was that no one wanted the councils to meet in Rome, not least because it was a hard place to reach. But of course that meant that the pope would have to travel to northern Europe if he was to preside over them, and it was unlikely that he would be able or willing to do that on a regular basis. After the Council of Constance closed in 1418, Pope Martin V (r. 1417–31) dragged his feet, and nothing was done during his lifetime. When he died, pent-up frustration forced his successor Eugenius IV (r. 1431–47) to summon a council to meet at Basel, which continued in one form or another until 1449.

Eugenius IV had no intention of going to Basel himself, and eventually he transferred the location to Ferrara. From there it went to Florence and finally ended up in Rome, which was just what the conciliarists did not want. By the time it ended, even many of the original supporters of conciliarism were disillusioned by the result, and a countermovement stressing papal authority was well under way. Finally, at the Fifth Lateran Council (1512–17), conciliarism was formally condemned and the papal monarchy fully restored—or so it seemed.

The Papal Revival

The revival of the papacy in the century after 1417 is one of the most surprising and least understood phenomena in the history of the church. Although there was a widespread desire to see the end to the schism that had lasted for a generation, few people at the time imagined that it would be possible to return to the situation that had prevailed in the heady days of papal supremacy in Western Europe. But the popes were determined to restore the power of their see, and Eugenius IV was clever enough to know how to do so. It must also be said that events played into his hands, and in a way that few could have foreseen.

After the recovery of Constantinople by the Byzantines in 1261, there was an attempt to restore the Eastern Empire to its former glory. This never really succeeded, and the next two centuries are a story of slow but inexorable decline until finally the city itself fell to the Ottoman Turks. The Turks had invaded Asia Minor in 1071, and although kept at bay, they had never been dislodged. After 1300, they regrouped under a gifted leader, Osman (Ottoman), who laid the foundations for the empire that would bear his name and last until 1922. In 1354 the Turks established a bridgehead in Europe and quickly overran most of the Balkan Peninsula. Constantinople itself held out, as did a number of places in Greece, some of them ruled by the Byzantines and others by the Venetians or the Genoese, who naturally promoted Western Christianity as much as they could.

Western influence was very strong in Byzantine intellectual circles at this time, and a number of leading figures either supported Western ideas or were converted to the Roman church. Whether this meant that they left the communion of the Byzantine church was not clear—most of them apparently did not. The Byzantines had always accepted Roman primacy on the basis of the Petrine claims, but they did not acknowledge papal jurisdiction as the inevitable consequence of that. Nor did they accept a number of Western theological positions, including the doctrine of transubstantiation, the existence of purgatory (which they doubted), and the double procession of the Holy Spirit from the Father and the Son, the so-called *filioque* clause that the West had introduced into the Niceno-Constantinopolitan Creed around 1014. The Eastern churches had never pronounced on these questions, so it was theoretically possible for members to hold the Western view on them if they wished. What they did not accept was that the papacy had any right to force these doctrines on the Eastern churches, which had never assented to them and which contained many members (probably the majority, in fact) who explicitly rejected them.

In 1274 the Second Council of Lyons attempted to reunite the Eastern and Western churches but failed, not least because it was a political project of the emperor Michael VIII (r. 1258–82), who wanted to protect his empire against possible Western attack and would sign almost anything to achieve that. Michael was regarded as a traitor by many in the Eastern church, and his supporters were persecuted after his death. The next century saw a revival of Byzantine monasticism, which was deeply anti-Western in practice, even though a number of its leading figures were well disposed to certain aspects of Western theology. Positions would harden later on, but in the fourteenth century it was still possible for conservative Eastern writers to be sympathetic to Western ideas and integrate them into their own theology without encountering serious opposition.[13]

Things might have gone on like this indefinitely, but in the fifteenth century the Turks were strong enough to launch the final assault on Constantinople, which now stood like a Greek Christian island in a Turkish Muslim sea. The Eastern emperor John VIII (r. 1425–48) knew that his city's days were numbered and was desperate for Western aid, which was the only thing that could save him. He knew that the price he would have to pay would be formal reunion of the churches and that there was no hope of that unless it could be arranged on a global scale, with everybody concerned involved in the process and consenting to the final decision. The Byzantines did not particularly trust the conciliarists and preferred to deal directly with the pope, who they thought had greater authority and would be more likely to obtain the result they desired. Eugenius IV, for his part, saw this as just the opportunity for which he was waiting. It was in order to make life easier for the Byzantines, who did not want to stray beyond Italy, that he moved the council that was already in session from Basel to Ferrara. John VIII and a delegation of clerics that included the patriarch of Constantinople made their way there, but an outbreak of the plague forced them to transfer the council to Florence. It is therefore as the Council of Florence that the fateful synod of reunion is generally known today.[14]

After months of negotiation, the Byzantine delegation agreed to accept the Western demands in return for autonomy in its internal affairs and (most important) an army to relieve Constantinople. The papacy, which had never renounced its crusading ambitions, now found a real reason to renew the call for a holy war against Islam, because not only were the Turks threatening Constantinople, they were making their way into Hungary and Central Europe as well. The rulers of the West were therefore persuaded that it was in their own interests to gather an army to attack the Turks, but in 1444 that army was destroyed at Varna and the crusading ideal was dead. Nine years later, on May 29, 1453, Constantinople fell to the Turks, and any pretense of union between East and West was abandoned.

13. On this period, see D. Nicol, *Church and Society in the Last Centuries of Byzantium* (Cambridge: Cambridge University Press, 1979).

14. See J. Gill, *The Council of Florence* (Cambridge: Cambridge University Press, 1959), for the history of the council, written from a Western point of view.

What happened in reality was that "union" with the West had been bought at the price of dividing the Eastern churches in two, a scenario eerily reminiscent of what had happened a thousand years before after the Council of Chalcedon. Political arguments played an important role in this, of course, but on balance it must be said that they weighed more heavily with the unionists than with their opponents. Those who rejected the compromise of Florence knew that the alternative was Turkish rule, which they did not particularly relish, but they were prepared to accept it as the lesser of two evils. They knew that the Turks would tax them but otherwise leave them alone. The papacy, on the other hand, would leave them politically independent (and unprotected) but would do all it could to subvert their churches and traditions by forcing them to conform to Western norms as much as possible. Where the Eastern Christians could reject union openly, as in Russia, they did so immediately; elsewhere they had to wait until the fall of the Byzantine Empire, but that was not long in coming. After 1453, church union was no longer a practical possibility, and East and West went their separate ways.

Many of the Byzantines who had supported the union left for Italy, but the Uniate tradition, as it is now called, did not die with them. The principles agreed on at Florence in 1439 were later used to promote union with a number of Russian Orthodox churches in what is now Ukraine and also with the Romanian Orthodox in Transylvania. Both these areas had come under Western rule (Polish or Hungarian), and desire for union with Rome was sometimes genuine, but the long-term effect of what happened was negative and remains so. Ukraine, for example, is still divided between "Greek Catholics," as the Uniates are called, and the Orthodox. Similar situations exist elsewhere, though usually on a much smaller scale. The Council of Florence also approved "unions" with the Armenians (1439), the monophysites (1442), and the Nestorians (1444), all of which had the same effect as the reunion with Byzantium—these churches were divided and only a minority entered the Roman communion, leaving a bad taste in the mouths of the others and making it more, not less, difficult to achieve any lasting reconciliation.

One of the more surprising results of all this was that Turkish rule gave the Eastern churches much more power than they had ever had before and transformed them out of all recognition. Previously the patriarch of Constantinople had been little more than an imperial state official, who could be removed more or less at the emperor's pleasure. The Turkish sultan stepped into the emperor's shoes, but being a Muslim, he did not find it so easy to interfere in church affairs. The Turks did contrive to ensure that the patriarchs were men to their liking, and they often engineered depositions and fresh elections that destabilized the church, but in return they granted the patriarch something that no Byzantine emperor could ever have done. The patriarch became the head of the Orthodox Christian *millet* (nation) and was entrusted with the internal government of that community. Overnight, the patriarch became even more powerful than the pope, at least among his coreligionists. As time went on, the previously autonomous Bulgarian and Serbian patriarchates were suppressed; the ancient sees of Antioch, Jerusalem, and Alexandria were likewise subordinated to Constantinople when they fell under Turkish rule.

By the beginning of the nineteenth century, the patriarch of Constantinople was not just the head of the church but the head of the "nation" as well, that "nation" being understood as Orthodox and basically Greek. Nationalist movements led to revolts, first in Greece and Romania, then in Serbia and Bulgaria, and one of the basic criteria for the reestablishment of nationhood in those places was the restoration of an autonomous Orthodox church. To this day, the fusion between Orthodoxy and nationality in Eastern Europe is so strong that people who otherwise speak the same language and have a great deal in common (like Serbs and Croats) find themselves attacking each other because one is Orthodox and the other Roman Catholic—and never the twain shall meet. The failure of church union in the fifteenth century thus continues to play itself out in the politics of the Balkans and Russia today, with unfortunate consequences for all involved. Secularization and the spread of atheism have done little to check this, with the result that many Eastern churches find themselves in the unenviable position of having thousands of devoted adherents who are declared unbelievers. For them, and for many observers of the local scene, it is the cultural heritage that the church represents that is determinative, not any kind of belief.

None of this could have been imagined by Eugenius IV as he worked toward the reconciliation of East and West. For him the goal was the reunion of the church as it was meant to be: the spiritual nexus of a Christendom that was presided over in secular affairs by the emperors of East and West. He did not think it unnatural for the Eastern delegation at Florence to be headed by the emperor, but whether he would have said the same if his Western counterpart had turned up is more than doubtful. It was the pope's belief, as it was that of his contemporaries, that when Constantine I transferred the capital to Byzantium, he had granted the bishop of Rome jurisdiction over the West. This Donation of Constantine, as it was known, was a document extant in the papal archives that had been used by generations of popes as proof of their right to claim the authority they did. But in the run-up to the reunion negotiations with the East, documents and claims of this kind had to be revisited because the Eastern church knew nothing about them.

Lorenzo Valla (1407?–1457), an Italian humanist in the vanguard of what we now call the Renaissance, examined the Donation carefully and proved that it was a forgery, made most probably in the ninth century by monks who wanted to protect the papacy against the depredations of the Carolingians. The amazing thing is that when this was discovered, it had very little (if any) immediate impact on the church. The papacy was so secure and the emperors of both East and West so relatively weak that it no longer mattered. The Eastern Empire soon disappeared, but the Western one was about to acquire a new lease on life. The Babylonian captivity of the papacy had been possible because the king of France was strong enough to make his will prevail over the pope and because there was no rival power in Europe equal to France at that time.

The Hundred Years' War weakened France, at least temporarily. The Holy Roman Empire was not initially in a good position to benefit from this, but things began to look up as the Habsburg dynasty consolidated its power over it. The Habsburgs had long been powerful rulers in what is now Austria, but in the fifteenth century they began to branch out. In 1477 they acquired the Low Countries (now Holland and Belgium), and in the next generation married into the royal house of Spain. This was to be a key move. Spain had always been on the periphery of Christendom, but its centuries-long struggle to reclaim the Iberian Peninsula from the Arabs gave it a crusading mentality that was largely absent elsewhere. For Spaniards, spreading the gospel and the church by conquest was practical politics, not just a vague aspiration, as it was in most other places. After Granada, the last Muslim kingdom in Spain, fell to the Christians in January 1492, the Spaniards were in an expansive mood. One of the things the queen of Spain did to reflect this was to fund Christopher Columbus, who thought he could sail west and reach India.

The sequel is well known. Columbus never got to India, but he discovered a new world and claimed it for Spain. The Portuguese, who were great explorers and mariners, and whose sponsorship Columbus had originally sought, were upset by this, so the pope intervened by dividing the world in two. The result was that by the Treaty of Tordesillas Portugal got eastern South America (now Brazil), Africa, and Asia, while Spain got the rest of the Americas and the Pacific Ocean as far west as the Philippines.[15] Both countries were committed to evangelization; the extension of their secular empires had as its goal the mission of the church to preach the gospel to every creature.

15. There were actually two treaties, because the first one did not give Portugal enough of South America. As a result, the line of division was moved westward, making Brazil a Portuguese, rather than a Spanish, colony.

By marrying into the Spanish royal family at just the right moment, the Habsburgs were able to draw on the immense wealth that now started flooding into that country from its new possessions and to consolidate their rule in Central Europe. The man on whom this inheritance devolved was the emperor Charles V (r. 1519–58), who was also King Charles I of Spain (r. 1516–56). At last there was a Holy Roman emperor who did not have to depend on his German subjects for his income and who could make a plausible claim to be the universal ruler of Christendom. In theory, the church should have been delighted with this turn of events, but was Charles really its protector? Would he bow to the will of the pope, or would he make the pope his vassal as earlier emperors like Frederick II had tried to do? The answer, it turned out, would be given not by Charles or the pope but by a relatively humble German monk and university professor whose interests were rather different from theirs. For it was just at the moment that Charles took charge of his inheritance that Martin Luther burst onto the scene, with revolutionary new ideas that would change the church forever.

Closely tied to the politics of the time was a financial crisis that threatened to overwhelm the papacy, which had never fully recovered from the vast expense of the Crusades. In the fifteenth century the Italian cities were booming as the Renaissance reached its height. Venice and Genoa grew rich on trade, while Florence and Milan were important banking centers. Rome was expected to compete with them, but it had no source of income other than the church. To increase its revenues, the popes resorted to various forms of taxation. For example, when a new bishop was appointed, he was obliged to pay to the papacy a sum equivalent to one year of his future income. In some cases, the popes placed their own retainers in vacant sees that they never visited but whose revenues went straight to Rome. The English parliament legislated against this twice (in 1351 and again in 1393), and the French king was so incensed that in 1433 he forbade any form of papal taxation in his dominions.[16]

The warning signs were there, but the popes found it almost impossible to rein in their expenses, and the search for further sources of funding continued unabated. The situation became particularly bad under Pope Leo X (r. 1513–21). In the words of the historian J. N. D. Kelly:

Easygoing and pleasure-loving, the patron of artists and re-founder (Nov. 1513) of Rome university, Leo was recklessly extravagant, so desperate for money that he pawned his palace furniture and plate. In addition to his pleasures, he had to pay for his wars, the projected crusade, and not least the construction

16. The prohibition was not lifted until 1516.

of St. Peter's; to raise money he borrowed extensively and sold offices, even cardinals' hats.[17]

One ingenious way for the church to raise more money was by the sale of indulgences, a practice that had been created several centuries earlier. An indulgence was a declaration that the purchaser would spend less time in purgatory than he or she would otherwise have expected. No one knew what gave the pope the right to regulate what happened after death, but the fear of purgatory was enough to persuade many people that buying time off was a good idea. When the papal coffers were at risk of being depleted, a new campaign for the sale of these indulgences would be launched in the hope of replenishing them. It was one of these campaigns that ignited Martin Luther's protest, and in the fallout the Reformation was born.

The Protestant Reformation

No event has ever shaken the church as profoundly as the sixteenth-century Protestant Reformation. There had been schisms before, such as that of the Donatists, but they had been peripheral. There had been splits caused by extraneous factors, such as the isolation of the Celtic churches after the fall of the Roman Empire, but they had been healed fairly easily once contact was restored. There had even been breakaway movements caused by theological disagreements, such as that of the monophysites of Egypt and Syria and the Nestorians, but they did not touch on the fundamental character of the church itself. However much they disagreed with one another, all sides in these disputes claimed an episcopal succession that they could trace back to the apostles, and they organized their ministry and worship in much the same way. The Donatists and the Celtic church have now disappeared, but the non-Chalcedonian churches still survive and are regarded with sympathy by the Eastern Orthodox, who recognize the fundamental similarities between them—similarities that they do not share with either the Roman Catholics or the Protestants of the Western tradition. It was the Reformation that challenged this common pattern and forced the Christian world, or at least its Western half, to think through its principles of ecclesiology for the first time.

In the early sixteenth century there were still a few dissenting groups from earlier times, but they were localized and not very influential. Some Lollards survived in England but were so obscure that almost nothing is known about

17. J. N. D. Kelly, *The Oxford Dictionary of Popes* (Oxford: Oxford University Press, 1986), 258.

them, and there were Waldensians in the Alps, survivors of a medieval dissident movement originally led by Peter Waldo (1140?–1218?).[18] The Hussite movement in Bohemia was far more influential than either of these, but it too was a regional phenomenon that did not spread beyond its Czech-speaking homeland. The pope did not lose much sleep over them, nor did he worry unduly about the Eastern churches, most of which were under Islamic rule or else so remote (in Russia and Ethiopia, for example) that they hardly mattered from a Western perspective.

Protestantism was something else altogether. The surviving Lollards, Hussites, and Waldensians quickly aligned with it—not the other way round—and it was to leave an indelible mark on the Christian world. In the course of a single generation, from about 1520 to about 1560, Western Christendom was torn in two and a new kind of Christianity came into being. At the heart of this revolution was the doctrine of the church. As we have already seen, the church as a theological principle had not been entirely neglected in earlier times, but its identity had never been at the heart of any passionate debate. Everybody agreed with the creedal formula, which said that it was "one, holy, catholic, and apostolic," and most people instinctively understood what that meant, or thought they did. The unity of the church was confessed in its common creed, and a Christian could go anywhere in the world and receive Communion at the hands of the local priest. Popes and bishops might excommunicate one another, but at the grassroots level there was a common sense of belonging that was only occasionally disrupted by schism and/or heresy. Even in the East, it was common for parish priests to give Communion to Western Christians long after the schism, and in some places the practice did not end until the eighteenth century.

The holiness of the church was hard to define, but no one doubted that it applied to the saints and martyrs in heaven, whose example was constantly being held up for the church "militant here on earth" to emulate. Clergy, monks, and nuns were treated with special respect and regarded as holier than the average layperson—at least in theory. There were lapses and scandals that dented the reputation of some of them, but on the whole, the sacrifice of celibacy and the distinctive lifestyle imposed on the professionally religious had their effect. The church, as an institution, had a central place in society, and its goods, buildings, and officers were immune from the normal power and pressures of the law. The details of this might be debated—as they certainly were in the matter of taxation—but the principle that the institutional

18. They still survive, and the main Italian Protestant church today is known as the *Chiesa Valdese*.

church was not to be vandalized, even when a city was captured, was accepted. Fugitives from the law could seek sanctuary in churches, and although that was sometimes violated in practice, it was nevertheless upheld in principle. To shed blood inside a church was a major offense, as the knights who murdered Thomas Becket in his cathedral at Canterbury discovered to their cost. Becket's tomb became a shrine and was used as a reminder to kings and others that the holiness of the church and its officials was not to be trifled with.

The catholicity of the church meant that it was fundamentally the same everywhere. All baptized persons were Christians, whatever language they spoke and wherever they came from. Nationality in the modern sense had no meaning, and it was perfectly possible for someone like Erasmus of Rotterdam (1466–1536) to travel across Europe and feel at home wherever he went. The Latin language, though it was no longer anyone's mother tongue, served as a common denominator among the educated and guaranteed that anything of interest would be read and circulated everywhere. Even in the East, the use of Latin was spreading, and in some places (for instance, Ukraine) it even became the medium of theological education. The advent of printing in the late fifteenth century merely speeded up the process of European integration and made it more efficient; Luther's Ninety-Five Theses crossed the continent in a matter of weeks, faster indeed than they probably would today, since translation into two dozen different languages would now be necessary.

The church's apostolicity was guaranteed by two things: confession and succession. Educated people knew that the Apostles' Creed was not the work of Peter and his colleagues, despite a medieval legend that claimed it was, but they had no doubt that its contents went back to them. The New Testament was the apostles' legacy to the church, and everyone knew that it was a fundamental source of Christian doctrine. The church's authority to interpret Scripture was guaranteed by an unbroken episcopal succession from Peter, the first bishop of Rome, to his current successor in the Lateran Palace. There was no doctrine of papal infallibility at that time, but although most people knew that some popes had been less than distinguished in their office and that there had been times when rival popes competed for recognition, they believed that God had preserved his church in spite of all its troubles, and that the gates of hell had not prevailed against it.

In the early sixteenth century, these fundamental beliefs were the shared convictions of virtually everyone, including Martin Luther. When he posted his Ninety-Five Theses on the church door in Wittenberg on October 31, 1517, he had no idea that he was about to witness the breakup of the institution that he and everyone else had known all their lives. As the theses reveal, Luther believed that the sale of indulgences was wrong, and he disputed the right of the pope to claim jurisdiction over the dead in purgatory, but this did not amount to an attack on the church, its sacraments, or its authority. Luther had spotted an abuse that he wanted to see corrected, and initially he believed that once he had made his case, the rest of the church would come to see that he was right.

Things did not turn out that way. What Luther may not have fully realized at first was that after the suppression of the Hussites and the defeat of conciliarism, the locus of authority in the church had shifted decisively in the direction of the papacy. Luther could advance all the arguments he wanted against the sale of indulgences, and on his premises he was no doubt correct. But if the pope said that selling them was permissible, his approval trumped any logic that Luther might muster on the other side, because the pope had the power to decree what was right and what was wrong. He did not need scriptural authority to back him up, because as the successor of Peter he was a living apostle and therefore an independent source of doctrine for the church. To call his rulings into question was to attack the church itself. As this realization dawned on Luther, his attitude toward the papacy and the church changed. He came to believe that the only way the church could be brought back to its basic principles was by overthrowing papal power. That in turn led to searching questions about everything the pope stood for. Were the doctrines he taught really revealed by God, or were they merely human inventions that the papacy had adopted because they suited its purpose?

Once questioning began, it could not be stopped. Before long other voices were being raised, many of them far more radical than Luther's. The claims of the papacy were not an isolated aberration; they rested on a whole series of assumptions that had developed over time and had seldom been questioned, though it was clear to any reader of the New Testament that they had little basis in the teaching of Jesus and his disciples. Legitimate practices, such as Holy Communion, had been exaggerated and misinterpreted, leading to superstitious abuses. Others, like the anointing of the sick, had been twisted out of context and misapplied. Above all, the way of salvation had been turned into a ladder of achievement, whereby believers were expected to earn their heavenly reward by their own efforts in cooperation with the grace of God, rather than by depending exclusively on the grace of God. According to the Lutherans, Christians go to heaven by placing their faith in the saving work of Jesus Christ, not by trying to do similar things themselves. No longer was it merely the sale of indulgences that was wrong; the entire system was a lie. There were no indulgences, not because the pope had no authority to grant them, but because there was no purgatory for the souls of the departed to be delivered from.

Suddenly it became clear to Luther and his followers that the sacramental system on which the church relied was based on a number of false assumptions, even if many of the rites were valid in themselves. Above all, there was no supernatural priesthood, cut off from (and lifted above) the main body of the church by sacramental ordination and compulsory celibacy, and empowered to perform miracles like that of transubstantiation. The Bible painted a very different picture of what the church should be, but ordinary laypeople did not realize this because they had no access to the Scriptures. It was therefore imperative that the Bible be translated into the spoken tongue, distributed to all who could read, and taught from the pulpit on Sunday morning. The celebration of Holy Communion was not to be abolished but to be put in its place as an extension of the preaching of the Word of God and as something to which only those who heard that Word and received it had access.

The medieval Mass had been surrounded by what Lutherans considered superstitious practices, such as the reservation of the consecrated elements, which were thought to be the body and blood of Christ. These practices had to go, because they were inconsistent with the Lutheran understanding of the true nature of the sacrament. The authority of the Bible was called upon as the standard by which the traditions of the past, however ancient and venerable, must be judged. The Bible canceled anything popes or councils might say that contradicted it. As the locus of authority was increasingly concentrated in the Bible alone, the church and its practices came to be seen in a different light. Could nonbiblical traditions be justified, or was it necessary to abandon them, whether they were harmful or not? Who was to decide what could be kept and what had to be discarded? Could the ancient ecclesiastical institution be reformed, or was it necessary to scrap it altogether and make a new start?

These were the questions that surfaced once Luther's ideas took hold, and that determined the nature and development of the Reformation. Scholars debate whether there was a single movement for change or a number of separate developments that led to different reformations in different places. If we look at the details of what happened, we can see that there were indeed many kinds of reformation. Had everything followed the same course under a single leader, there would be only one Protestant church today, but the impulse for reform was felt in many ways, not all of which were easily compatible, and the result was the emergence of several different churches, which sometimes competed with one another just as much as with Rome. The Catholic Church also changed in reaction to Protestantism. Traditionally this has been dubbed the "Counter-Reformation," but while it was no doubt partly that, it is nowadays generally understood that it was a reform of its own kind. An elderly Catholic in the 1570s would not have recognized the church of his youth in what he saw going on around him, even though he would have been worshiping among people who claimed that they were in direct continuity with that church.

In 1517, all that still lay in an uncertain future. Luther's theses were soon being debated all over Western Europe, and in Zurich Huldrych Zwingli was emboldened to make a protest of his own against the church and its sacramental theology. Zwingli acted independently of Luther, but in the general commotion of the time the two men were thrown together in what was to prove an uneasy association. Before long, other voices were being heard, some of them in support of Luther, some in support of Zwingli, and some in support of neither. Erasmus of Rotterdam was typical of many intellectuals. A severe critic of the papal church, he initially welcomed Luther's protest and hoped that it would lead to genuine reform. But when he realized that Luther was not just a moral reformer but was propounding a theology of grace different from the one that Erasmus adhered to, he changed his tune and launched an attack on him instead. Luther replied in kind and in the process distinguished his reformation from the well-meaning but theologically lightweight humanism that had become popular in academic circles.[19]

Luther was summoned by the emperor to explain his position before the German parliament, or diet, as it was called, and against the better judgment of some of his supporters, he agreed to go. The subsequent encounter has become legendary, and the facts have been obscured as a result, but whatever actually transpired, Luther came away more determined than ever to stand his ground. The emperor had promised him safe-conduct, but after the diet he outlawed him, making his immediate future highly precarious. Mindful of what had happened to Jan Hus a century earlier, his friends took no chances. They abducted him and concealed him in the Wartburg castle for the next three years. There, Luther spent his time translating the Bible into German and writing tracts in defense of his position. When he was finally released, he had become a national hero; it seemed for a moment that the whole of Germany might follow him.

In desperation, Leo X turned to the kings of Europe for support, but they refused to do anything to help him. The only exception was Henry VIII of England, who wrote a treatise on the seven sacraments in which he attacked Luther, for which the pope thanked him by granting him the title "Defender

---

19. The two tracts are published together in E. F. Winter, ed., *Erasmus and Luther: Discourse on Free Will* (London: Continuum, 2007). See also M. Luther, *The Bondage of the Will*, trans. J. I. Packer and O. R. Johnston (London: James Clarke, 1957).

of the Faith," which his descendants still bear today.[20] Leo excommunicated Luther in 1521, but by then it was too late to turn back the tide of protest.

The next few years were ones of confusion. The emperor Charles V was a loyal Catholic and wanted to preserve the unity of the church, but even he recognized that the papacy needed a thoroughgoing overhaul. His solution was to summon a council of the church to deal with the crisis, but unlike the Eastern emperor a century before, he could not do that on his own. He needed the pope to act, but Clement VII (r. 1523–34), a cousin of Leo X, did nothing. In 1527 Charles's troops invaded Rome and made the pope his prisoner. Clement bowed to the inevitable and agreed to accept the emperor's terms for his release, but he never managed to summon the desired council.[21] In the meantime, Henry VIII petitioned for his marriage to Catherine of Aragon, who happened to be the emperor's aunt, to be annulled on the ground that she had previously been married to Henry's elder brother.[22] Catherine appealed to her nephew, who made it clear to the pope that the pope could not grant her husband's wish without causing grave offense to the whole Habsburg family. Seeing that he would not get his way, Henry gradually moved toward a break with Rome, which was consummated in 1534.

Meanwhile, Luther and his followers, at the emperor's request, had presented a confession of their faith to the German diet that met at Augsburg in 1530. It was in this confession that they "protested" (i.e., "proclaimed") their faith, after which those who signed it were known as Protestants. It was a recognition that the imperial church had broken in two and would not be put back together again in the foreseeable future. The only question now was how far Protestantism would extend and on what conditions it could achieve a long-term modus vivendi with the Catholic Church.

---

20. The irony, of course, is that the faith they now defend is not that of the pope but of Luther.
21. It would eventually convene at Trent in 1545 and sit, off and on, for eighteen years.
22. Arthur, the brother in question, had died, and his father, Henry VII, had procured a papal dispensation for the marriage to his second son to take place.

6

What Is the Church?

The Disunity of the Post-Reformation Church

The most obvious problem that the sixteenth-century Reformers faced was the fact that by rejecting the authority of the papacy they were breaking the unity of the medieval church. In purely institutional terms this might not have mattered too much, because there had never been a time when all Christians had acknowledged the supremacy of Rome, but Protestantism went much further than that. It was not just the traditional hierarchy that the Reformers repudiated but the whole basis on which it had been established. The creedal confession that the church was "one, holy, catholic, and apostolic" was maintained, and often vigorously asserted, by Protestant theologians, but the content that these words came to have was different. Furthermore, not all those who broke away from Rome did so in the same way or for the same reasons, so the nature of this difference varied from one Protestant group to another. At the same time, all sides in this dispute continued to insist that there was (and could be) only one church. How could that doctrine be reconciled with the reality of division?

Conservative Reform

There were essentially three different responses to this question. The first was conservative and reactionary in intention but often radical in practice, as it tried to shore up the traditional structures of the medieval church and justify them in the face of criticism. Though not always united in strategy or intention, those who chose this path stayed in the Catholic Church and tried to influence its policy from within. Some of these people, such as Reginald Pole (1500–1558) or Giovanni Morone (1509–80), were relatively sympathetic to Luther and might be regarded as "liberal." Both of these men became cardinals and played a prominent part in early attempts to achieve common ground with Protestants, but as time went on and positions hardened, they were squeezed out. Pole ended up as the archbishop of Canterbury who reconciled England briefly to the papacy during Queen Mary's reign, and Morone became one of the most influential men behind the scenes in Rome. Yet it was symptomatic of the atmosphere there that in 1557 both men were accused of being secret Lutherans. Pole was in England and out of harm's way, but Morone was imprisoned, and it is thought that this incident cost him the papacy nine years later.[1]

In the end, the liberal wing of the Catholic Church was eclipsed by a resurgent ultraconservatism, spearheaded by Ignatius Loyola (1491–1556). Loyola was a Spanish soldier who had a conversion experience when he was convalescing from a battle wound, and he decided that what the pope needed was an army of men who were totally loyal to him. He founded the Society of Jesus, a new kind of missionary order that dedicated itself to furthering the cause of the Catholic Church and of papal supremacy within it. The Jesuits, as the members of this order were called, became tutors and confessors to much of the European nobility and used their influence to instill a sterner form of the traditional faith into the hearts and minds of those in their care. Before long, the Jesuits were feared all over the Protestant world, because they were recognized as the most effective proponents of the old religion. The Jesuits were the shock troops of the Catholic Counter-Reformation, but theirs was a broad vision. Not only were they determined to rescue as many souls from Protestantism as they could, but they were also dedicated to overseas missions. Spanish and Portuguese explorations and conquests had added vast new territories to their respective crowns, and the church lost no time in embarking on mission work in them. Whether it was in Mexico or India, Jesuit missionaries were in the forefront of expansion, with the result that far more people joined the Roman Catholic Church in the sixteenth century than left it to become Protestants.

1. Morone is little known in the English-speaking world, but there is a good recent study of Pole. See T. F. Mayer, *Reginald Pole: Prince and Prophet* (Cambridge: Cambridge University Press, 2000).

For those who remained within the Catholic fold after the Reformation, being in communion with the pope was *the* touchstone of orthodoxy. It might be possible to hold to all the doctrines of the Roman church and even to celebrate its liturgy, as Henry VIII still did after his break with it, but that was not enough. Henry was considered a Protestant, not because he believed any specifically Protestant doctrine but because he was out of communion with Rome. That, and that alone, was the touchstone by which everything else was now to be measured.

Pragmatic Reform

The second response was to favor a pragmatic kind of reform, dealing with particular abuses and restructuring the church to the degree that was considered necessary. This was essentially what happened in Germany, Scandinavia, and England, where the structure of the medieval church was often left intact and the changes were mainly theological. Where secular rulers had a free hand with the church, as in England, for example, they would typically take control of senior appointments and make sure that any laws enacted by the church were subject to their approval but otherwise leave the existing pattern more or less untouched. In the English case, this meant that many of the abuses that the Reformers complained about were not dealt with at all. Absentee priests were still absentees, and only fitful provision was made for educating the clergy. Even public worship was little affected at first; it was a full fifteen years after the break with Rome before services were conducted in English rather than Latin. In Germany there was more change in this respect, but even there traditional rights and privileges were usually upheld, including those of bishops. When a bishop became Protestant, for example, his diocese would often be secularized and his office taken over by the local ruler rather than abolished outright. At a lower level, church courts, the tithe system, and other such matters would remain virtually untouched, so that the institutional church continued to function more or less as it had before.

Martin Luther's most important backers were German princes who were alarmed at the possibility of a Habsburg takeover of the Holy Roman Empire. For them, having a church that was out of communion with Rome was an advantage, because it weakened the central state and gave them the autonomy they craved. Some of them were genuine followers of Luther's theology, but that was seldom their main concern. They wanted to be free of the pope, less closely tied to the emperor, and firmly in control of religious affairs in the territories over which they ruled. To that end, they supported (and even enforced) religious uniformity *within* their dominions, but, of course, they could do nothing about what happened in jurisdictions that they did not control.

The result was that the unity of the church was circumscribed by the reach of the state, which ended up producing almost as many separate churches as there were secular rulers. Even those that claimed to be Lutheran did not necessarily follow the same church order, since each ruler was free to impose whatever system he wished. As long as Luther himself was alive, he could exercise some influence over the way things developed, but after his death there was no one of comparable stature, and Protestantism quickly came to acquire something of the ecclesial variety that we are familiar with today.[2]

The pragmatic, or "magisterial," Reformers, so called because they worked alongside the *magisterium* (secular government) and in harmony with it, could never escape the government's clutches. For one thing, they relied on the state for protection. Luther would almost certainly have been burned at the stake like Jan Hus if the princes had not come to his rescue, and without their support Protestantism could never have established itself. In 1555 Charles V finally agreed to let each German ruler choose the religion his territory would follow, adopting the principle known as *cuius regio eius religio*, which was a formal acknowledgment that the state had the right to determine the form of the church within its borders.

The Peace of Augsburg, as the agreement of 1555 came to be called, tried to solve the problem of the Reformation by recognizing it where it was already established and containing it within those limits. Given that the Reformation was still expanding and diversifying, this agreement could not satisfy people for long, and even when it was first promulgated there were significant problems. One of them concerned the empire's ecclesiastical territories, which in theory belonged to bishops who were in communion with Rome. But in the chaos of the years before 1555, several of them had been occupied by secular Protestant rulers who did not want to give them up. The unofficial solution was for the emperor to acknowledge these Protestant rulers as "administrators" rather than bishops, an odd and unsatisfactory compromise that sowed the seeds of future trouble. A similar difficulty occurred with monasteries and other religious houses that had been seized by Protestants—should they be returned to their original owners or not?

There was also the issue of minorities, Catholics in Lutheran territories and vice versa. As we might expect, given their respective presuppositions,

---

2. For recent studies of this situation, see J. Whaley, *Germany and the Holy Roman Empire 1493–1806*, 2 vols. (Oxford: Oxford University Press, 2012), and P. H. Wilson, *Europe's Tragedy: A New History of the Thirty Years War* (London: Allen Lane, 2009).

the Catholics wanted to expel dissenters without compensation, whereas the Lutherans wanted them to be tolerated or allowed to emigrate legally. The emperor, who was himself Catholic, was in a difficult position because, although he was supposed to be an impartial adjudicator of the disputes that arose, he was determined to suppress all forms of Protestantism in his own hereditary lands, including those where Protestants were a majority of the population. Overall, the majority of the empire's subjects remained Catholic, but most of its subordinate princes became Protestants. There was a growing possibility that they would come to dominate the German parliament (diet) and even elect a Protestant as emperor, which they very nearly did in 1618.

Yet another question that the peace did not resolve was the nature of what was recognized as "Protestantism." Officially, this term embraced those who subscribed to the Augsburg Confession (*Confessio Augustana*) of 1530, but there were many Protestants who had moved on from that and become more radicalized. Secular rulers who moved in that direction were tolerated in practice but not in principle, and their long-term status was uncertain. The Catholics did not want them, of course, but neither did the "authentic" (or Gnesio-) Lutherans, who thought that these radicals had gone too far. There were also places that became Protestant after 1555, especially in the Netherlands, which were still formally provinces of the empire. No provision was made for them, and they had to fight for their rights, as the Dutch did for more than two generations. In Germany, therefore, the peace of 1555 sowed the seeds for further conflict, which duly erupted when the circumstances were right.

What the religious peace succeeded in doing was defining Protestantism according to a confession of faith in which its adherents expounded the doctrines that set them apart from others. Confessionalism of this kind had not existed before, but it came to be characteristic of the Protestant churches. As a general rule, these confessions began with a short rehearsal of the basic beliefs of the Christian church as a whole, with particular reference to any points on which they might differ from the general consensus. Belief in God, the Trinity, the divinity of Christ, and the inspiration of Scripture was held in common by virtually all Christians, so the confessions seldom went into them in detail. Much more important were the doctrines concerning salvation, the church, the ministry, the sacraments, and relations with the state. The way of salvation set Protestants apart from Catholics, but on the other subjects, the different Protestant groups were just as likely to disagree with one another as with Rome or the Eastern churches.[3]

3. It should be said that few (if any) Protestants took the views of the Eastern churches into consideration when framing their particular doctrines. On the other hand, some of them wanted

The English Reformation was even more dependent on the state than its German counterpart, but because England was much more centralized than the Holy Roman Empire, the outcome was markedly different. King Henry VIII (r. 1509–47) had initially supported the pope against Luther, but eventually he broke with the papacy over the annulment of his marriage to Catherine of Aragon. The pope refused to grant this, officially for theological reasons but in reality because he was the prisoner of Catherine's nephew, the emperor Charles V. Political considerations forced Henry VIII to make allies among the Protestant princes of Germany, but he had no desire to reform the Church of England in anything like a Protestant direction. Instead, he made himself its supreme head and gave the archbishop of Canterbury those papal powers that he, as a layman, could not arrogate to himself. But everybody knew who was in control, and the Church of England changed only to the extent that Henry permitted. By the end of his reign, there were a vernacular Bible and a few prayers in English, along with some theological primers intended for the instruction of the laity, but that was about all. Initially these textbooks tilted toward Protestantism, since they were written by theologians who had been influenced by the Lutherans, but when Henry realized that, he called a halt and even rewrote some of the material himself, in order to keep the church as conservative and "Catholic" as possible.[4]

Henry was succeeded by his nine-year-old son Edward VI (r. 1547–53). Because he was a minor, a regency council ran the government on his behalf. That allowed Thomas Cranmer, the archbishop of Canterbury, to initiate a real reform of the church, which he managed to introduce largely because there was no one of sufficient authority to stand in his way. But when Edward was succeeded by his Catholic sister, Mary I (r. 1553–58), England went back to the Roman fold, with the agreement of Parliament.[5] Cranmer and a number of his colleagues were arrested and eventually put to death, giving "Bloody Mary" her now famous reputation, but when she was succeeded in turn by her sister, Elizabeth I (r. 1558–1603), the Protestantism of Edward VI was restored. Throughout this process it was the will of the ruler that prevailed, a

to link up with the East against their common enemy the pope. For a survey of these attempts, see S. Runciman, *The Great Church in Captivity* (Cambridge: Cambridge University Press, 1968).

4. See R. McEntegart, *Henry VIII, the League of Schmalkalden, and the English Reformation* (Woodbridge: Boydell & Brewer, 2002); A. Ryrie, *The Gospel and Henry VIII: Evangelicals in the Early English Reformation* (Cambridge: Cambridge University Press, 2003). Also useful, though unfortunately marred by vitriol against fellow scholars in the field, is G. W. Bernard, *The King's Reformation: Henry VIII and the Remaking of the English Church* (New Haven: Yale University Press, 2007).

5. For a recent and judicious assessment of Mary, see J. Edwards, *Mary I* (New Haven: Yale University Press, 2011).

will underwritten by several "acts of uniformity" that were passed by Parliament at the monarch's request.[6] As in the German principalities, everyone in England was obliged to worship in the same way, and church attendance was made compulsory to make sure that they did. Those whose sympathies still lay with the papacy had to conceal the fact, particularly after Elizabeth was excommunicated by the pope in 1570.[7]

In Ireland, which was theoretically under English rule, the change of religion was never secure; by the end of Elizabeth's reign, only a small minority of the Irish population had become Protestants. Various expedients were tried, including the establishment of a Protestant theological college in Dublin and the settlement of large numbers of English and Scottish Protestants in different parts of the country, but mainly in the northeast, where they became (and have remained) a majority of the population. The subsequent history of the country, where Protestantism has traditionally been associated with British rule and Catholicism with opposition to it, traces its roots back to this time.[8]

This pattern was repeated with only minor variations everywhere in Western Europe. Countries that remained Catholic proscribed any form of Protestant worship, and Protestant countries did the same in reverse. For most people there was little choice, and church membership came to be regarded as more dependent on nationality and political allegiance than on particular doctrines, however much theologians and the official voices of the churches stressed the latter over the former. In a world where every Portuguese was Catholic and every Swede Protestant *by definition*, how could it have been otherwise?

Radical Reform

The third response to the divisions of the Reformation was more radical. It came from people who believed that the traditional structures were either too corrupt to be reformed or unbiblical and therefore to be abolished on principle. Their aim was to reconstruct the church along New Testament lines, which they thought was possible on the basis of a careful study of the evidence. Most of the systems of church structure and government that were

6. The texts of these and of other material relating to the English reformation can be found in G. L. Bray, *Documents of the English Reformation*, 2nd ed. (Cambridge: James Clarke, 2004). For a good but little-known study of the theoretical underpinnings of the English church at this time, see H. F. Woodhouse, *The Doctrine of the Church in Anglican Theology, 1547–1603* (London: SPCK, 1954).

7. See A. Walsham, *Church Papists* (Woodbridge: Boydell, 1993).

8. See M. Tanner, *Ireland's Holy Wars: The Struggle for a Nation's Soul, 1500–2000* (New Haven: Yale University Press, 2001); A. Ford, *The Protestant Reformation in Ireland, 1590–1641* (Dublin: Four Courts Press, 1997).

devised on this basis could claim some kind of biblical support, but none was overwhelmingly persuasive. As a result, churches that chose this third option were prone to subdividing, because no group could persuade the others that its interpretation of the New Testament was demonstrably superior to any other.

The most successful attempt to rebuild the church starting from first principles was made by those churches that we now call Reformed or Presbyterian. They followed the teaching of John Calvin (1509–64), who was basically conservative in the way he tried to adapt the existing church pattern to what he saw as the requirements of Scripture. The essence of his ecclesiology was a belief in collective leadership, grounded in the principle that there was no difference in the New Testament between bishops and presbyters and that the earliest congregations were led by more than one individual. Calvin did not rule out some form of presidency, however, and in that way a Reformed church could incorporate bishops in the medieval meaning of the term, though with a reduced status and function. He also believed that the church had to be independent of the state in the sense that it should be free to govern itself, but he did not object to having an established state church, as long as it was free to act as the conscience of society and not be subordinate to secular rulers and their wishes.

Calvin's ecclesiology was especially influential in the small city-states and territories within the Holy Roman Empire that had what we would now call a "republican" form of government. Geneva, where he himself was based, had been ruled before the Reformation by its bishop, but he was thrown out in 1532, and the city council was left to determine what its confessional allegiance would be. It chose a form of Protestantism, but when Calvin turned up a few years later and tried to enforce a church discipline that was stricter than what the councillors were prepared to tolerate, they threw him out and invited him back only when they saw that the church was drifting into anarchy. Calvin returned in 1541, but despite his formidable reputation as a church leader and reformer, he had to battle the city council for the rest of his life. He is frequently blamed for the judicial execution of Michael Servetus (1511?–1553), an antitrinitarian heretic, but in fact it was the council that sentenced Servetus to death and Calvin who tried to mitigate the sentence, without success.[9]

Calvin's troubles in Geneva reflect the problems that were bound to occur when a reformer tried to put theological principles ahead of practical politics. The idea that a person should enjoy freedom of conscience in a state that was officially committed to a particular form of Christianity was beyond the comprehension of most people at that time. If what they believed was

9. See B. Gordon, *Calvin* (New Haven: Yale University Press, 2009), 217–32.

the truth, then deviations from it had no place in society and would almost certainly be harmful if allowed to exist without punishment. Even so, there is some evidence that the Reformed churches were less intolerant than the others. Their belief that the unity of the church was spiritual, not visible, and that true believers would recognize one another, whether they shared the same outward expressions of their faith or not, enabled them to accommodate people who differed from them, as long as the differences were of an acceptable kind. Because the Reformed believed that worship should be in the spoken language and that the church should be organized by each nation according to its own customs, they were usually prepared to accept foreigners more or less on their own terms.

Thus we find that as early as the reign of Edward VI, Protestant England granted refuge to Continental Protestants without obliging them to submit to the worship and discipline of the Church of England. Men like Martin Bucer (1491–1551) and Peter Martyr Vermigli (1499–1562) were even given university posts and allowed to teach theology without having to become members of the national church. Similarly, cities such as Frankfurt and Geneva opened their doors to English subjects fleeing the persecution of Mary I without inquiring into their particular beliefs and practices. It was enough for them that their guests shared a common vision of the gospel and the church. Of course, this generosity had its limits. A Frenchman could turn up in London and join the French church there, which organized itself along Genevan lines, and he would be perfectly accepted by everyone. But an Englishman who advocated the same kind of church government for his own people would be in trouble with the authorities, because it went against the law of the land.

Tolerance of those who held different views but belonged to the same nation was much slower in coming. Even among the Reformed, it was the product of necessity rather than genuine conviction, at least at the beginning. In the Netherlands, for example, the revolt against Spain that lasted from 1566 to 1648 was guided and directed by Calvinists, who were a minority of the total population and therefore had to tolerate others in order to gain support for the war. By the time the struggle was over, these others had gained certain rights of their own and were accepted as residents of the country, but they were not allowed to vote or take part in the government. In that respect, the Netherlands followed the principle laid down by Calvin in Geneva, where the civil government was independent of the church, but only church members could serve in it.[10]

---

10. On the Dutch situation, see J. Israel, *The Dutch Republic: Its Rise, Greatness, and Fall, 1477–1806* (Oxford: Oxford University Press, 1995).

Calvin's style of Reformed church made considerable headway in France, but it was never strong enough to take over. Instead, the country was plunged into a generation of religious wars, which sharpened the differences between Catholic and Protestant and made any compromise impossible. In 1589 a dynastic accident brought the Protestant Henri IV to the throne, but the citizens of Paris would not allow him to enter the city unless he converted to Catholicism. After four years of hesitation he finally did so, but soon afterward he granted Protestants a limited degree of official toleration, the first time that any European state had done so. The Catholics had to live with that, unhappy though they were, and for a while the Protestants managed to create what was almost a state within the state. Unfortunately, toleration was an idea ahead of its time and in the French context proved to be unworkable. Privileges were gradually whittled down until finally, in 1685, Protestants were forced to convert to Catholicism or be expelled. Many chose exile and went to the Protestant countries of the north, where they joined the local established churches, even though they kept their French identity for many generations.

Meanwhile, disputes within the Dutch Reformed Church forced the secular authorities there to summon a synod, whose purpose was to define what Reformed Christianity actually was. It met at Dordrecht (Dort) in the winter of 1618–19 and was the only occasion before modern times when Protestants from all over Europe met to establish a basis of unity among themselves. The French Protestants were not allowed by their government to attend, but the British delegation made a deep and generally favorable impression—the first, and so far only, time that British theologians have enjoyed such influence on the world stage.[11] Dort was a Dutch synod, and its decisions were not formally adopted elsewhere, but they set the tone for what constituted a Reformed theological position, and in that respect they still play an important role today. They were particularly influential in Britain, though neither England nor Scotland ever officially recognized them.

The reasons for that were complex. When Queen Elizabeth I reestablished a Protestant church in 1559, she also provided the Scottish reformer John Knox (1514?–1572) with an army he could use to take over his native land. Knox was too radical for Elizabeth, but he was reliably Protestant and in 1560 succeeded in persuading the Scottish parliament to vote for the Reformation. Contrary to what many people think, Knox did not abolish the Catholic system of church government, but he modified it to allow for more

11. See A. Milton, *The British Delegation and the Synod of Dort* (Woodbridge: Boydell & Brewer, 2005).

collegial participation.[12] After his death, a presbyterian movement gained great influence, but a residual episcopate managed to survive. When James VI (r. 1567–1625) became king of England in 1603 (as James I), most people thought that he would introduce a similar system of church government in England. Elizabeth I had maintained the episcopal establishment although she had little time for bishops, but James, whose position in England was weak, saw their value as a prop to his regime. Instead of introducing a Scottish form of church government into England, he decided to attempt the opposite: to make the Scottish church conform to the English one.

James understood the Scots and knew his limitations, so he seldom pressed his agenda beyond what the Scots would take, and on the rare occasions when he did, he quickly backtracked in the face of opposition. His son, Charles I (r. 1625–49), was less skillful at this and far less diplomatic. Charles was an aesthete drawn to the outward show of religion, but although he was sincere in his faith, he was not a theologian in the way that his father had been. The result was that he appeared to promote a Catholic form of worship without showing any corresponding zeal for Reformed theology. When Parliament objected, he closed it down. When Scotland rose in revolt against his policies, he attacked the country and tried to force his views down people's throats. Worst of all, he teased the Irish Catholics with promises of toleration that he was powerless to grant, a foolhardy policy that merely convinced the English that he was about to unleash an Irish army on them in order to enforce his ideas about worship and church government.

In the end, the Scots abolished episcopacy altogether, and the exasperated English joined them in revolt. There followed a civil war, one of the main purposes of which was to decide how the church was to be governed and what relationship it was to have to the state. When the war broke out, the English parliament summoned an assembly to meet at Westminster for the express purpose of establishing a Reformed church for the three kingdoms of England, Scotland, and Ireland.[13] The Scots had the upper hand because their representatives, though few in number, were united in advocacy of presbyterianism and had an army to support them. Before long, the English were obliged to subscribe to the Scottish vision of what constituted a Reformed church, and the Westminster Assembly eventually produced a church settlement that conformed to that. Remarkably, however,

12. See A. Ryrie, *The Origins of the Scottish Reformation* (Manchester: Manchester University Press, 2006); G. Donaldson, *The Scottish Reformation* (Cambridge: Cambridge University Press, 1960).

13. See C. Van Dixhoorn, ed., *The Minutes and Papers of the Westminster Assembly, 1643–1652*, 5 vols. (Oxford: Oxford University Press, 2012).

its confession of faith avoided dealing with matters of church government, so that it was possible for a broad range of Reformed believers to accept it. It quickly became the benchmark of English Reformed Protestantism, and its influence spread far and wide. Even Congregationalists and Baptists could accept most of it, and their own confessions were only relatively minor modifications of it.[14]

Unfortunately, a number of the English present were less enthusiastic, and the parliamentary army, once it took shape, was led by men who were definitely opposed to presbyterians on the matter of church government. What they favored was congregationalism, or "independency," as it was usually known at that time. This gave each local church the right to settle its own form of ministry and worship, as long as it adhered to the broad outlines of Reformed theology. A few of the English members of the assembly would have been content to keep the bishops, but episcopacy had been so discredited by the policies of Charles I that there was no hope of that. By 1649 the king had been put to death, the episcopate had been abolished, and a presbyterian form of church polity had been established—on paper. But the army would not enforce it, and congregationalism became the default option in practice, if not in theory. This led to a struggle between the English and the Scots, which the former won hands down. By the time the civil war was over, the church had been set free from its traditional masters, and there was almost complete freedom of speech—except for Catholics, episcopalians, and Scottish Presbyterians, who refused to accept the abolition of the monarchy.

Despite these limitations, the victors were remarkably tolerant for their time. Baptists, Quakers, and a host of other groups that have since disappeared were permitted to express their ideas more or less freely, and people got used to being allowed to have their own opinions in theological matters. Of course, it was impossible to operate a national church on such a chaotic basis, and the attempt to do so soon fell apart. In 1660 a Scots Presbyterian general invited King Charles II (r. 1660–85) to regain his throne, and the old order was reestablished. Those who dissented from episcopalianism were driven out of the church and persecuted—in Scotland as well as in England. This went on for more than twenty years, until finally the nightmare that everyone had feared occurred. The throne was inherited by Charles II's brother James II (VII of Scotland) (r. 1685–88), who had become a Catholic in 1673. There was no law to prevent him from succeeding, although the English parliament had tried hard to pass one while there was still time to do so.

14. This is particularly true of the (Baptist) Second London Confession of 1689 and the Philadelphia Confession of 1742.

James II claimed to be in favor of religious toleration, but that was widely perceived as a means of restoring Catholicism—the most intolerant form of Western Christianity—by the backdoor. He was eventually driven out, and his son-in-law, the Dutch William of Orange, became king as William III (r. 1689–1702). William introduced the Dutch form of toleration into his new kingdoms. Dissenting Protestants were allowed to worship freely, Catholics were excluded from any participation in politics, and the established churches (episcopalian in England and presbyterian in Scotland) were strongly encouraged to be as broad-minded in theological matters as they could be.[15] There was opposition to this policy, of course, but it was unsuccessful. Reformed ecclesiology had proved able to accommodate different kinds of church polity within a single state without sacrificing the principle of a national church. Exclusion from the Church of England or from the Church of Scotland would henceforth be the choice of individuals wishing to leave rather than of dissidents being thrown out, though more stringent rules continued to apply to clergy, preachers, and members of the universities, as one would expect.

As time went on, the success of limited toleration encouraged the state to grant more, and the dual system of having a national church that embraced everyone alongside dissenting congregations that worshiped as they pleased enabled a Christian government to permit freedom of conscience without the risk of being undermined by it. Eventually it would even be possible to disestablish the church, as happened in the United States after the American Revolution, without seriously upsetting this balance. Because of it, American Christians today can feel generically Christian and yet remain loyal to a particular denominational tradition, without sensing any contradiction in this essentially dual allegiance—to the universal church, on the one hand, and to the local congregation, on the other.

The Reformed tradition is a conservative or moderate example of the radical approach to ecclesiology in the Protestant world. There is, however, a more extreme variant, which in its original form insisted on what it saw as strict biblicism and rejected any connection between the church and the secular state. Advocates of this position were often pacifists and insisted that oath taking before a secular judge was ungodly, but even if they did not go that far, they still believed that infant baptism had no biblical justification and that those who practiced it were denying the very nature of the church. To the extremists (or as they would see it, consistent radicals), the church was

15. In Ireland the established church was episcopalian, but presbyterians were given some recognition and a state subsidy for their clergy. Catholics, however, were severely discriminated against, at least on paper, and they were the vast majority of the population.

a gathered company of professing believers, and baptism should therefore be administered only to those who had already made a profession of faith. Because the first generation rejected the baptism they had received as infants and "rebaptized" themselves as adults, they came to be called Anabaptists, though of course they rejected that designation.[16]

In the Anabaptist understanding of the church, it would no longer be possible for a local congregation to be coterminous with a village community. Only those who came out from the world could belong to the church, and that would inevitably exclude a significant number of people who might otherwise think of themselves as members. Could this be done in a place where everyone knew everyone else and most people were related? What kind of church community would result, and how would it be sustained from one generation to the next? As the different options available played themselves out, the answers became clear—and often they were not at all what the original Reformers had in mind, as the Anabaptists were the first to demonstrate.

To the Anabaptists and those who thought like them, the spiritual fellowship of believers was paramount; how they then worked together in community was secondary. The theory sounded good, but it was not long before problems arose. Their leaders tended to have their own ideas about what should and should not be tolerated within a Christian fellowship, and it was not long before they were laying down rules for determining who was (and who was not) a true Christian. Inevitably, the emphasis fell on those who had to be excluded from the community, and here some very strict criteria could be applied. It was not unknown for people to be disciplined for very minor infractions of rules. They were not stoned or put to death, but they were "shunned," as the expression went—excommunicated from the fellowship. In a closed society, that could be a very effective and often quite cruel form of punishment, especially when it divided one member of a family from the rest. Sad as it is, those who joined together to escape the tyranny of a state church all too often found themselves creating an even more oppressive system than the one they had left behind.

In the end, the radical Reformation found itself regrouping its members in sectarian communities that lived apart from the rest of the world. In theory they might believe that individuals had to decide for themselves whether to be Christians; faith could not be inherited from one generation to the next. Infant baptism was therefore excluded, and those who wished to join the church were rigorously examined. But as time went on and a second generation emerged, these communities that had separated themselves from the

16. The Greek prefix *ana-* means "re-."

rest of society found that they had to accommodate their children somehow. Children might not be baptized until they made a profession of faith, and perhaps not all of them would do so, but there is no doubt that before long the Anabaptists had become a distinct group, almost a different nationality, of their own. Even today, there are old Mennonite, Hutterite, and Amish families that can trace their spiritual ancestry back to the sixteenth century in a way that very few others can. Those most opposed to the idea of a national church have become a kind of nation themselves.

What united the two types of radicals was a common desire to abolish the distinction between clergy and laity and to impose a common (and strict) discipline on every member of the church. In order to achieve this, the conservative Reformed churches expanded the presbyterate to include people who in other churches would be regarded as laymen because they lacked specific theological training and were usually not paid by the church. However, these elders shared in the ministry of church discipline, and their large number was meant to ensure that no church member would be neglected. The Anabaptists achieved the same result by restricting church membership to begin with and by expecting all professed believers to discipline themselves, though a form of eldership was also required in order to make sure that this was actually happening.

It must be remembered that the three main tendencies that asserted themselves in the fallout after the Reformation were not hermetically sealed compartments, and various combinations were possible. Obviously, the reactionaries in the first group who remained Catholics were the ones least open to any form of cross-fertilization, but over time they were subtly influenced by Lutheran and especially by Calvinist ideas, though of course they never acknowledged them as such. For example, they began to produce vernacular translations of the Bible, to organize seminaries for the training of priests (which was originally a Protestant idea), and to prepare catechisms for the young (another Protestant innovation). Those in the second group might adopt a Reformed (Calvinist) theology while retaining a medieval Catholic structure, the Church of England and the Anglican tradition that stems from it being the most obvious example of that. Finally, the radicals might reject Calvinism and in some cases adopt views oddly similar to Roman Catholicism, particularly in their understanding of grace and the sacraments. This happened in some of the more extreme sectarian communities on the fringes of English Puritanism, which taught the possibility of spiritual perfection through the sacraments and other forms of religious devotion. The rich variety of Protestant traditions today is due in large part to this tendency toward eclecticism, which creates tensions between those who insist on a consistent

Reformed position, including both doctrine and church order, and those who are prepared to compromise, though usually only on questions of order and not of faith.

The belief that the unity of the church was primarily spiritual did not disappear in Protestant circles, and it was to enjoy a new lease of life in the late seventeenth century with the emergence of a movement known as Pietism in Germany and associated with Methodism and the Evangelical revival in the English-speaking world. Pietism was essentially a reaction to the divisions among Protestants that had hardened in the course of the religious controversies of the later Reformation era. German Lutherans and the Reformed churches were anathematizing each other almost as much as they were the Catholics, and neither had any time for the radicals. In England, adherents of the state church were at war with dissenters for reasons that had far more to do with politics and society than with Christian belief. Could any way be found to overcome these difficulties and restore the spiritual unity that the churches ought to be manifesting but were not?

The answer the Pietists gave to this was that spiritual experience and devotional practice could overcome theological differences. The unity of the church could be demonstrated by practical Christian living in a way that was obscured (or even denied) by theological argument. Thus, for example, Lutherans might not admit the Reformed to Holy Communion because they differed about the precise nature of the sacrament, but they both read the same Bible, prayed the same prayers, and often sang the same hymns. They were one in the Spirit, even if they were confessionally divided, and those who had no particular theological ax to grind were aware of this. Not surprisingly, perhaps, Pietism was very influential among laypeople, and it is fair to say that among Pietists the ancient distinction between clergy and laity, which the radical Reformers had so longed to abolish, came closer to being eradicated than almost anywhere else in the church.[17]

The influence of Pietism took some time to be felt, but in the early nineteenth century it helped to make a union of Lutheran and Reformed churches in Prussia possible—though not without some opposition on the Lutheran side—and in its Evangelical form it was to have a major impact in the English-speaking world. It is no exaggeration to say that the unity of Protestants is most clearly visible today among Evangelicals, who are the modern inheritors of the Pietist tradition. They pay relatively little attention to "denominational distinctives," move from one tradition to another with great ease, and often prefer (or create) a generic, nondenominational type of church, whatever denomination it may

17. Only the Quakers are equally indifferent to this distinction.

(or may not) belong to. The unity they have is one of the Spirit, and formal divisions that might stand in the way are simply brushed aside.

The Holiness of the Church

No one could doubt that the Protestant Reformation shattered the institutional unity of the Western church. Most people, then as now, regretted this, but many Protestants claimed that it had to be done because the church was corrupt. The clergy were often living in ways that belied their vows and profession. The laypeople were generally ignorant and left to their own devices. Only a thoroughgoing reform could put these matters right, and it was the resistance of the hierarchy and its supporters that caused the division. Had everyone seen the need for change and supported it, there could have been a Reformation that transformed the entire church and preserved its outward unity on the spiritual principles that in theory defined its existence. Not surprisingly, therefore, the question of what makes a church holy and acceptable to God soon came to the forefront of the Reformation debates. It is in the different answers that were given to that challenge that we can see most clearly what set the different parties involved apart from one another.

Those who continued to support the claims of the papacy knew as well as anyone else that there were serious problems at the heart of the church's administration. Too many bishops were neglecting their duties, the clergy were not properly trained and disciplined, and laypeople were left at the mercy of Protestant predators who could point out how serious these failings were and promise them something better. The widespread willingness of ordinary people to listen to the Reformers was a clarion call to the church that it needed to put its house in order, and much of what happened in the so-called Counter-Reformation promoted by the papacy is best understood in that light. The main forum for defining the nature of Catholic reform was the Council of Trent, which was summoned by the pope in 1545.[18] The emperor Charles V had been pressing for such a council ever since the Reformation broke out, but the papacy had dragged its feet. It was held at Trent as a compromise between the pope's wish that it should meet in Rome and the emperor's insistence that it should take place on his territory. Trent was in northern Italy and thus reasonably accessible from Rome, but it was also in the Holy Roman Empire, and so under the emperor's direct rule. The Protestants were invited to send

18. See J. C. Olin, *Catholic Reform: From Cardinal Ximenes to the Council of Trent, 1495–1563* (New York: Fordham University Press, 1990); J. W. O'Malley, *Trent: What Happened at the Council* (Cambridge, MA: Harvard University Press, 2013).

representatives to the opening sessions, but they refused, and under pressure from the Jesuits the invitation was not renewed. Trent became, and would remain, a council at which the Roman Catholic Church would retrench and reform its practices by restating their underlying principles and seeking new ways to implement them more effectively.

What emerged in the end was a church that was much more uniform, both in appearance and in practice, than it had ever been before. Bishops and clergy were subjected to a rigorous discipline. Disputed doctrinal questions, like the extent of the biblical canon and the nature of justification by faith, were examined at length and explained in a way that was deliberately intended to counter Protestant claims. For example, the books of the Greek Old Testament that are not found in the Hebrew Bible (the so-called Apocrypha) were given canonical status in their Latin version, and it was formally declared that justification by faith meant nothing unless it was accompanied by "works"—a direct contradiction of what Luther taught. Moreover, it was in and through those "works" that the holiness of individuals could be measured, an assertion that would transform Catholic devotional life and make the differences between it and Protestantism obvious to all.

The Protestants had objected to a host of practices that they believed contradicted the gospel or were useless. These included things like fasting, enforced clerical celibacy, devotions surrounding the Mass (like the adoration of the consecrated elements), and so on. Trent responded by reinforcing them, cutting out obvious abuses like the sale of indulgences (but not the indulgences themselves), and establishing a regular pattern of confession and penance before Holy Communion that was designed to ensure that ordinary church members were doing what was expected of them. The Mass remained at the heart of devotional life and, if anything, became even more central than before. The many eucharistic rites that had existed in the pre-Reformation church were abolished, and a single pattern was authorized for the whole church. It was to be celebrated in Latin, so that a Catholic could attend it anywhere in the world and participate. The famous Tridentine Mass, as this was known, remained in official use for four hundred years, and today's conservative Catholics look back to it, not to anything that preceded it, as the benchmark of what the church should be doing in public worship.

The pre-Reformation patterns of monastic life were retained and strengthened, but laypeople were encouraged to take on as many monastic devotional practices as they could. As a result, exceptionally devout laypersons might go to Mass every day, wear a hair shirt under their clothes as a sign that they rejected the vanities of this world, make pilgrimages to sacred shrines, and spend time praying by rote in front of the reserved sacrament or a statue of the Virgin Mary or one of the saints whom they were expected to adopt as patrons or models for their own behavior. Protestant criticism, which in the early days of the Reformation had focused on the superficiality of so much popular devotion, now emphasized its futility. To their minds, Catholics were trying to earn their way into heaven and being encouraged to do so by the church, which acted as the dispenser of God's grace. From the Protestant point of view, these people were deluding themselves, because salvation was a free gift of God granted by his Holy Spirit and not something that could be obtained by human effort. They came to see the Roman Catholic Church as a massive institutional tyrant that was determined to keep its spiritual slaves in subjection by denying them access to the truth contained in the Scriptures and imposing on them a spiritual discipline that had more in common with the Pharisees' interpretation of the law of Moses than with the gospel of Christ. In other words, the more Rome reinforced its principles, the more Protestants were alienated from it and used the signs of Catholic reform as evidence that the pope was indeed the antichrist.

In contrast to the Roman Catholic Church, the internal unity of the Protestant state churches was upheld by the secular law, which also dictated how people were to behave in all walks of life—certainly in public, but to some degree in private as well. There were laws governing what they could wear, how they could spend what little leisure time they had, and what they could read. The Ten Commandments were the basis of public morality; magistrates were expected to uphold biblical principles as far as they could. Courts were supposed to ensure that the entire Christian society conformed as much as possible to norms laid down in the Word of God, and not least in the Old Testament. There had long been a tendency to adapt Mosaic laws to suit Christian needs, as the medieval tithing system demonstrated, but Protestants extended this to cover such things as the degrees of kindred and affinity that would prevent a marriage from taking place. The canon law had opted more or less arbitrarily for seven degrees of relationship, which were later cut back to four, but Protestants found their ideal pattern in Leviticus 18 and wrote it into their marriage laws.[19]

Where this left the holiness of the church as a distinct institution within that society is hard to say. On the one hand, the medieval distinction between the "church" and the "world" was abolished. There was no more monasticism, and the clergy were no longer expected to be celibate. Church worship was conducted in the local language, and congregations were expected

19. See Leviticus 18:6–18 and compare it to the list of prohibited degrees appended to the Anglican Book of Common Prayer.

to participate in the service to varying degrees. In most of the Reformed churches, laymen were appointed as elders and shared in church government with those who were formally trained and ordained to full-time ministry, though the pastor or "teaching elder" retained his special position and was not as different from the pre-Reformation priest as some of the more radical Protestants would have wished.

In many respects, it would be fair to say that Protestant state churches and the societies they served merged into one another. This was seen most clearly in Lutheran countries, where the church often became a department of state with its ministers paid out of public funds. No clear line was drawn between the sacred and the secular, so that the king was regarded as the chief bishop and church ministers acted as schoolmasters in their local communities. Reformed churches followed this pattern to some extent, but they maintained a greater independence from the state. For example, they continued to hold synods and pass laws of their own, which they then hoped the state would ratify. In some cases, the Reformed had little choice in the matter, because they were a minority and had to accept what they were given. This was particularly true in France, where the Protestants wanted to act within the bounds of the law, but the law was that of a Catholic state that found it difficult to recognize their rights. In the end, a compromise was worked out, but it was less than what the French Protestants wanted and was gradually whittled away to the point where they were suppressed and expelled from the country.

But if relations with the secular authorities varied enormously from place to place, the internal discipline found in the Protestant state churches was fairly similar in all of them. The key to achieving a holy church was education. The Bible was translated into the vernacular and preached from the pulpit at least twice every Sunday and often during the week as well. Worship services focused on the ministry of the Word, to which the sacrament was seen as a supplement. In theory, Holy Communion was meant to be administered fairly often, but in practice it was not. In some places it was limited to four times in the year, but this was not because it was not taken seriously. On the contrary, infrequent celebration allowed parishes to hold "Communion seasons," in which the sacrament would be preceded by a week or more of preparation, which consisted of daily services of prayer, repentance, and calls for conversion and amendment of life. Laypeople might not communicate very often, but when they did it was a solemn occasion that made a much greater impression on them than a weekly routine ever could.

To get a sense of what this was like, it is unnecessary to look further than the classic formularies of the Church of England. The Book of Common

Prayer, first published in 1549 and subsequently revised several times before reaching its classic form in 1662, shows very clearly what was involved. The service of Holy Communion contains a number of exhortations that were meant to guide pastors and congregations in preparing for the sacrament, and they give a clear indication of what was expected. Even more revealing are the two Books of Homilies, the first issued in 1547 and the second in 1563, which contain very detailed instructions about how a Christian should live. In fact, if the two books are compared, it becomes apparent that while half the sermons in the first book deal with matters of doctrine and half with practice, in the second book the balance shifts decisively in favor of the latter. This is evidence that concern for the visible holiness of the church and its members increased as time went on and that serious efforts were being made to inculcate a godly lifestyle among the population.[20]

What took place in church was backed up by a network of schools that were established to train the young. Schoolmasters were regarded as part of the ecclesiastical establishment and were subjected to the same doctrinal tests as the clergy, which tells us how important the school was as a means of training the next generation. Not every parish had a school, and only a minority of the youth was able to get an education, but this was still a great advance on what had obtained before the Reformation and was an incentive to the church to extend its provision as much as possible. The influence of this approach was long lasting. Even in the eighteenth century, as the population exploded and the Industrial Revolution overwhelmed the ancient parish structure in the rapidly expanding cities, the church responded by increasing the output of affordable Christian literature and creating Sunday schools for those children who had to work during the week. The need for education was never lost sight of, and the spiritual dimension remained fundamental to it for generations.[21]

The biggest challenge that the Protestant state churches faced was the scale of the provision that they had to make. Overnight they were expected to find learned pastors and teachers who shared and could communicate the vision of the Reformers. They also had to find the funding needed to sustain such an operation. At the time of the Reformation, many people, including the state, had taken advantage of the disarray of the church to seize its property and revenue. Getting this back proved to be almost impossible, and the Protestant state churches were in dire financial straits, despite their privileged

20. See P. Collinson, *The Religion of Protestants: The Church in English Society, 1559–1625* (Oxford: Oxford University Press, 1982).
21. This was true even in the United States, where school prayer remained part of the daily routine until it was challenged and ruled unconstitutional in the mid-twentieth century.

position.[22] Demand rapidly outstripped supply, and it soon became apparent that radical measures would have to be adopted if the goals of the Reformation were ever to be achieved. Unfortunately, progress in that direction was hindered by some of the very people who were expected to promote it. The leaders of the church were often well connected in society, coming from or related to the nobility and wealthy families who benefited from the church's financial hardships. In England, the bishops continued to live in their palaces and manage vast households, as they always had, and as sources of revenue dried up, they tended to lay their hands on as much of what was left as they could. Even Queen Elizabeth I got in on the act, suppressing bishoprics for years on end and diverting their income to her own treasury.[23]

It is therefore not surprising that there was growing concern about this within the church itself. Many pastors and laymen began to press for tighter controls over appointments and greater discipline over those already in office. They also believed that the English church needed to complete the process of Reformation begun a generation earlier but held back for political reasons. Even those who appreciated that it was better to move slowly as long as there was still a significant body of traditionalist opinion in the country came to feel that once the pope had excommunicated the queen (1570) and closed the door to any reconciliation with Rome, it was time to pursue reform of the church to its logical conclusion, as had been done in Geneva and in Scotland. Unfortunately, they met with resistance from the queen, who feared that any change to the religious settlement that she had imposed in 1559 would destabilize the country and encourage intervention by foreign powers (especially Spain) that were pledged to restore Catholicism as much as they could.

Those who advocated further change did not want to leave the state church and were not opposed to the queen's settlement as such but thought that it still contained too many elements left over from medieval times. Their desire was to root out those imperfections (as they saw them) and "purify" the church—hence the derogatory name "Puritan," which was soon attached to them. Puritanism was never really about doctrine; by and large, the Puritans were satisfied with that. Rather, it was about church discipline, which was left in the hands of the state, not those of the church.[24]

22. C. Hill, *Economic Problems of the Church: From Archbishop Whitgift to the Long Parliament* (Oxford: Oxford University Press, 1956).

23. Bristol, a poor diocese, was vacant for ten years (1593–1603), Ely for almost nineteen (1581–1600), and Oxford for twenty-one (1568–89) and then for a further twelve (1592–1604). Others experienced delays in new appointments ranging from two to four years.

24. See P. Collinson, *The Elizabethan Puritan Movement* (Oxford: Oxford University Press, 1967). For the original texts, see W. H. Frere and C. E. Douglas, eds., *Puritan Manifestoes: A Study of the Origin of the Puritan Revolt* (London: SPCK, 1907).

Inevitably, as the Puritans realized, this led to laxity in enforcement, since the lay authorities had no desire to rock the ecclesiastical boat over issues that (to them) were obscure and relatively unimportant. What members thought about predestination or the nature of the consecrated bread in Holy Communion was their business, and as long as they kept their views to themselves, the secular authorities did not worry. To the Puritans, this attitude was anathema. They wanted a church that did not merely conform outwardly for political reasons but that had a common mind because its members were genuinely convinced of the truth of the beliefs it confessed. For this reason, and because they perceived that there was a yawning gap between what they wanted and what they had to live with, the question of the holiness of the church became a matter of vital concern, and it is for that, as much as for anything else, that the Puritans are still remembered today.

It was not that the Elizabethan church lacked any mechanism for enforcing church discipline but that the existing structures were often employed in the wrong way. For example, instead of dealing with such matters as ignorance and drunkenness—both major evils in sixteenth-century England—the authorities preferred to attack clergy who refused to wear the vestments prescribed by canon law or who deviated from the official liturgy in what to them was a similarly trivial way. Outward conformity of this kind was accepted by some on the ground that it was a matter of indifference what one wore or what precise words one used in the services. But when matters like these became the be-all and end-all of church discipline, even the more moderate Puritans found it hard to swallow. Christianity demanded a change of life and of lifestyle, and if that did not occur, then the holiness of God was being profaned and the church was corrupt.

Typical of this attitude, and characteristic of British rather than of Continental Protestantism, was the growing obsession with the observance of the Sabbath. The Reformers had provided that after church on Sundays, lectures would be given to the congregations in what amounted to a form of adult Sunday school. But traditionally, after-church had been a time of socializing, when traveling salesmen would bring their wares and the community would set about drinking. It was even an established custom that the money paid for beer would be used to repair the church buildings; these occasions were therefore known as "church ales." When they were sufficiently tanked up, some of the men would start playing the games that lay at the origin of what we now know as football, cricket, and baseball.

To the Puritans, this was a profanation of the Sabbath and had to be stopped if at all possible. The government firmly resisted, even to the point that in 1618 King James I issued his infamous *Book of Sports*, which he ordered every clergyman to read from his pulpit. The *Book of Sports* made it unlawful to prevent the playing of games on Sunday. It caused such outrage that a number of Puritans prepared to leave the country—first for Holland but ultimately for America, where they felt they could establish a Puritan commonwealth free of Sunday sports and other impious activities. So great was the indignation that even a quarter of a century later, when Parliament revolted against the king and the ministers of the church were investigated for their soundness, one of the questions asked was whether they had read the *Book of Sports* to their congregations. If they confessed that they had, they were expelled from their pulpits as ungodly and unworthy of their high calling.

But the Puritans did not believe merely in enforcing public "holiness," with all its opportunities for private hypocrisy. Refraining from trade and sport on Sunday was intended not for simple rest but for training in godliness. People were expected to go to church and be instructed, often at some length, about their faith. They were then expected to go home and study the Bible for themselves, meditating on what they had heard in church. The church, in other words, became the great school for spiritual growth that the original Reformers had wanted it to be, with sermons and lectures forming the central part of its activities. The ultimate aim of this was to transform people's lives so that the public expression of godliness would flow naturally from the inward conviction of the leading members of society. The Puritans knew that not everybody would be happy to conform to their requirements, but they relied on those who were to keep the others in line. The "godly," as the compliant were known, were expected to take the lead, and very often they did so. It is well known that those who cultivate good habits of self-discipline are more likely to succeed than those who do not, and Puritanism benefited from that. What we now call the "middle class" owes its origins, at least in part, to their behavior, and the political upheavals that disturbed seventeenth-century England were to a large extent the result of their struggle for power over society as a whole.

The Puritans have often been caricatured and derided by their opponents, and their reputation has suffered as a result. In a fallen world, those who aim for perfection are bound to be accused of failing to achieve their goal, and accusations of hypocrisy are only to be expected. But fair-minded observers have increasingly recognized that for all their faults, the Puritans came closer to creating a church that exhibited the marks of true holiness than any of their contemporaries, and that it is the legacy of their work that underpins the most advanced democratic societies today.[25]

25. P. Benedict, *Christ's Churches Purely Reformed: A Social History of Calvinism* (New Haven: Yale University Press, 2002); J. Witte Jr., *The Reformation of Rights: Law, Religion, and Human Rights in Early Modern Calvinism* (Cambridge: Cambridge University Press, 2007).

In some respects the Puritans lived on the boundary between the Protestant state church and radicals like the Anabaptists and similar groups with which they are sometimes confused in the popular mind. This was partly because they wanted to apply the principles of Reformed Calvinism to the English state church, and partly because frustration at the opposition they encountered led some of them to separate from it. These separatists, as they are called, had to leave England, and many settled in the Netherlands, where they came across the Mennonites, a moderate Anabaptist group that had obtained a limited degree of toleration there. It was from this conjunction that the English Baptists emerged. They were radicals in terms of church polity, but not in other ways—they were not pacifists, for example, nor did they form distinct communities cut off from the wider society. Their mindset remained essentially Puritan, in that they preferred to work for change within the existing structures as much as they could, and they cooperated with other Protestant dissenters in England as far as their consciences would allow them to. One of their leading spokesmen was John Bunyan (1628–88), who insisted that even baptism should not be allowed to divide true believers from one another, and to this day, the chapel that he founded in Bedford has two membership rolls: one for those who baptize infants and the other for those who do not.[26]

The more extreme radicals, of course, believed that the only way to ensure holiness in the church was to cut it off from contact with the world as much as possible. It was to this end that they formed separate communities, and although many of their descendants have reintegrated into wider society over time, something of the original impulse still remains. Pacifism, in particular, is often promoted by them, as well as semi-utopian visions of social change. Generally speaking, it would be fair to say that other Christians often admire and respect them for their convictions but do not follow them because they recognize that, however desirable these goals may be, they are unattainable in a fallen world. In many ways, the radical Reformation stands as a reminder of what ought to be and therefore acts as the conscience of Protestantism, but by its very nature it is the faith of a minority and is likely to remain so until the return of Christ in glory at the end of time.

The Eastern churches were not affected by the Reformation and so escaped the debates about holiness that were so important in the West. Because of this, it is easy for Western observers to get the impression that Eastern Christians are not much concerned with the subject, but that would be a misunderstanding.

26. John Bunyan, *Differences in Judgment about Water-Baptism No Bar to Communion* (London: John Wilkins, 1673).

Many of the terms of the Western debates are incomprehensible to them because they are not used to making fine distinctions between grace and nature, Scripture and tradition, and so on. But there is no doubt that holiness in the Eastern churches is closely tied to monastic spirituality, which sets the tone there far more than in the West. It is by no means uncommon for Eastern Christians to retreat to a monastery for spiritual reflection, and laypeople often do this as a matter of course. This helps to explain the sympathy that many Orthodox people have for Evangelical Protestantism, which in some ways is an adaptation of monasticism to everyday life. Few Evangelicals today are aware of it, but their regular times of prayer, disciplined Bible reading, and practice of the presence of God at all times are monastic in origin and give them a practical spirituality that other Western Christians often lack. The Evangelical insistence that actions speak louder than words and that what people do says more about their relationship with God than what they say also appeals to the Orthodox, who instinctively believe that words cannot express the essence of their faith. Theological arguments do not appeal to them any more than they appeal to most Evangelicals, an attitude that gives them more in common with each other than might otherwise be expected.

A Universal Church?

The Reformation encountered its greatest challenge when it came to the third mark of the church, its "catholicity." What exactly did this mean? Rome insisted that it meant that the church was one and the same everywhere, recognizing the pope as its head. That vision had never been reality, of course, but before the Reformation it was relatively easy for Western Europeans to disregard the Eastern churches, most of which were under Muslim rule in any case. The advent of Protestantism made it harder for Rome to maintain its claim to universality, but the papacy had a worldwide vision and pioneered missionary work in the Americas, Africa, and Asia. The Spanish and the Portuguese believed that spreading the faith was an integral part of their colonizing mission, and in the seventeenth century the French followed them in this. Millions of people in what we now call the "third world" were baptized, but although the statistics were impressive, the reality was something different. In the Americas, Catholic missionaries founded outposts in places that later became big cities like Los Angeles, San Francisco, and Montreal, which for centuries served as bases for both commercial and spiritual expansion into the interior. Elsewhere in Latin America they built on existing social structures, which they used to the same effect.

It was the policy of the Spanish and the Portuguese crowns to control senior ecclesiastical appointments in the colonies, and the papacy acquiesced in this through a system known as the *padronado* (Spanish) or *padroado* (Portuguese). This ensured that only men born in Spain or Portugal could become colonial bishops, a policy that came to be resented by the colonial-born European colonists. After Latin America became independent, the system naturally had to change, but it was taken over by the local European elite, who did not extend their privileges to the mixed-race or native peoples they ruled over. As a result, popular Latin American Catholicism became a mixture of orthodox Christianity and pagan superstition, much of it recycled from pre-Columbian Indian cultures or from the ancestral religions of imported African slaves. The church was ill-prepared for the activities of Protestant (and especially Pentecostal) missionaries in the twentieth century, some of whom were remarkably successful in attracting these so-called Catholics to their own denominations. Rome still claims the majority of the population as members of its church, but what this means in practice is a matter of dispute, and the quoted statistics are highly unreliable guides to belief or regular church attendance.

In Asia, the Portuguese were less successful. Doors that were initially open closed after a time, and policies designed to make Christianity more intelligible and acceptable to local cultures were often combated by Rome, which feared that the approach would lead to syncretism. Matteo Ricci (1552–1616) was an extraordinarily successful Catholic missionary to China and made a great impression there, but his initiatives were not followed up, and in the end the indigenized form of Christianity that his followers wanted to introduce was condemned by the papacy, a blow from which the Catholic mission to China never recovered.[27] Elsewhere, reminders of this period crop up in church buildings scattered across Africa and Asia and occasionally in words that native languages borrowed from the missionaries.[28] Roman Catholicism remained at least as much Roman as Catholic, with the Latin language and baroque Italian culture dominating it into the twentieth century.

But despite the weakness of their claims, Roman Catholics have been able to monopolize the use of the word "catholic," a usage that is now seldom disputed by others and has received general acceptance in most places. The effects of this can be seen if we compare "catholic" to "orthodox," the word that is generally used to designate the Eastern churches. It is still possible for others to claim "orthodox" for themselves, as the Orthodox Presbyterians

27. See G. Minamiki, *The Chinese Rites Controversy: From Its Beginning to Modern Times* (Chicago: Loyola University Press, 1985).
28. In Indonesian, for example, "church" is *gereja*, from Portuguese *igreja*, and "Sunday" is *Minggu*, from Portuguese *Domingo*.

do, but it is hard to imagine them adopting the designation Catholic, even if its official confessional statements say that it is.

As this example confirms, most Protestants and Eastern Orthodox now avoid using the word "catholic" because of its associations with Rome, and some even prefer to translate the word in the creeds as "universal" instead, though what that is supposed to mean in practice is often difficult to say. Almost all Protestant and Eastern Orthodox churches are limited by political and cultural considerations to a single state or language group, and even when they are in fellowship with others, this seldom means much in practice. Without a common language it is difficult for people to worship together on anything more than a symbolic level, and almost never would one institutional church defer to another in matters of its internal government. Even the Orthodox have been divided over whether to adopt the Gregorian calendar in place of the earlier Julian one, which some of them regard as better because it was being used in the time of Jesus.[29] To the claims of culture and language must be added divisions over race, which have affected places such as the United States and South Africa to a degree that is hard for outsiders to understand or accept. There can be no doubt that Protestantism in those countries (and occasionally elsewhere) has been deeply marked by policies of racial segregation that continue to be felt in the church, where "black" and "white" congregations meet separately and often organize themselves in different denominations.

It is true that most mainline Protestant churches belong to international federations that are supposed to uphold some standard of unity among people who claim the same denominational label, but that is hardly the same as being "catholic" or "universal." The Lutheran World Federation, the Anglican Communion, and the Baptist World Alliance are all examples of these, but as their recent history demonstrates, they are susceptible to internal disputes, and none is well placed to engage in interdenominational dialogue or cooperation. The only Protestant body that comes close to that is the World Council of Churches, which represents a wide range of Protestant (and Eastern Orthodox) bodies, though many of the more conservative ones do not belong to it, and its influence, which was never very great, has declined considerably in recent years. Whether we like it or not, nationalism and denominationalism have

29. This controversy strikes most Western Christians as arcane, but it took most Protestants a long time to accept the Gregorian calendar, too. The problem was that it was introduced by Pope Gregory XIII in 1582, *after* the Reformation, and was therefore rejected by non-Catholics as a matter of principle. Most European Protestants finally accepted it in 1700, but the British held out until 1752. In Eastern Europe, Russia adopted it for secular purposes in 1918, and the other Orthodox countries followed suit in the 1920s, but although some of their churches accepted it, others (including the Russian one) did not and still follow the old calendar today.

conspired to weaken the catholicity of the non-Roman churches, a fact that apologists for Rome never cease to emphasize.

When the Reformers thought of the catholicity of the church, it was mainly to the ancient creeds that they appealed. They insisted that they were perfectly orthodox, subscribing to the Apostles' Creed, the Nicene (Niceno-Constantinopolitan) Creed, and the so-called Athanasian Creed, though most of them were unaware that the first and the last of these were not known in the Eastern churches. They did know about the *filioque* dispute but accepted the standard Western position on this. As time went on and the different Protestant bodies developed their own confessions of faith and theological traditions, cooperation among them declined and any serious notion of catholicity disappeared. Most of the national churches closed the door to regular intercommunion with others. There was still a willingness to accept refugees, such as the Huguenots, who were expelled from France after 1685 and were able to integrate into the Lutheran church in Germany and the Church of England without difficulty. But this was a special case. Lutherans did not normally open their pulpits to Anglicans, for example, and even if they had been willing to do so, few Anglicans had the linguistic skills needed to take advantage of such an offer. The Church of England, for its part, grew increasingly wary of foreign Protestants. It was hesitant to accept King George I (r. 1714–27), a Lutheran from Hanover who inherited the British throne because of his Protestantism, and to this day it has remained out of communion with the Church of Scotland because of the latter's presbyterian form of church government, even though its supreme governor, the monarch, is also a member of the Church of England.

Such denominational rigorism has often been even more acute in breakaway and radical groups. Baptists, for example, have always been extremely reluctant to accept people who were baptized as infants but not as believers, despite the pleas of men like John Bunyan. Presbyterians and Congregationalists (Independents) might agree about everything except how a church should be run, but that difference has often been enough to ensure that they could not work together, though in this case it seems that traditional differences have occasionally been overcome in modern times.[30]

Nowadays, secularization, missionary expansion overseas (where these ancient divisions often seem irrelevant), and ecumenical initiatives have blunted the force of denominationalism. Pan-Protestant cooperation is more common

---

30. In Canada, Congregationalists and Presbyterians joined (with Methodists) in 1925, to form the United Church. In England, they created the United Reformed Church in 1972, and in Australia the Uniting Church in 1976. But in both Canada and Australia, significant numbers of Presbyterians refused to unite in this way and have created continuing churches of their own denomination instead.

than since the sixteenth century, but we are still some way from the point where we can take it for granted that a Protestant (and in particular, an ordained Protestant minister) will be accepted in any Protestant church. By and large, it must be said that Protestants find the church's claim to "catholicity" puzzling and do not know how to interpret it. The result is that it is either ignored in practice or identified as something that belongs to the Roman communion and must therefore be rejected as alien to their own beliefs, whatever their official confessional statements may say to the contrary.

The Apostolic Succession

It is the fourth mark of the church that has had the greatest ramifications for the post-Reformation church and that brings out more clearly than the others what the differences among the major Christian bodies are today. Broadly speaking, the church's apostolicity has been defined in one of two ways. The first interprets it as a historical succession from the apostles down through the generations, symbolized by a laying on of hands that can be traced back to the New Testament. The second understands it as being primarily doctrinal fidelity to the teaching of the apostles, preserved for us in the New Testament and the creeds of the early church. Virtually all Christian bodies accept the second of these definitions, even if some of the more radical Protestant bodies reject or hesitate to accept the ancient creeds as doctrinal standards. It is the first definition that has caused the greatest difficulties, even among those churches that accept it in principle.

The Eastern churches generally believe that their ministry descends by the laying on of hands from the apostles and are even willing to grant a primacy to Peter and the see of Rome, which they accept is of Petrine origin. What they argue is that the Roman pope has exceeded his authority and has tried to impose his jurisdiction on the other churches without their consent. To their minds, this has caused Rome to fall into error and to forfeit its place of prominence in the worldwide church. By default, that position is now occupied by the patriarch of Constantinople, who, although he is not himself the occupier of a see founded by an apostle, was recognized by the First Council of Constantinople (381) as second in the hierarchy. If ever the papacy renounces its claims to universal jurisdiction over the entire Christian world, the Eastern churches would welcome it back into the fold and grant it the place of honor that belongs to it by tradition. That, at least, is the theory. In practice, the Easterners know full well that Rome cannot do what they want without surrendering its own principles and identity, so there is no chance that the present situation will ever change. That suits most Easterners perfectly well, not least because many of them have a visceral hatred of Rome that makes that associated with Protestant fundamentalism pale by comparison.

In pure theological terms, the Roman Catholic Church holds much the same view as the Eastern churches about the nature of apostolicity, but with the all-important difference that it claims that the primacy of Peter entitles it to a position of authority that the others refuse to accept. It is essential to grasp that Rome does not believe in a merely historical succession from one generation to the next. The present pope is not the descendant of Peter in the way that Queen Elizabeth II is the descendant of William the Conqueror, or that the current president of the United States is the successor to George Washington. Unlike them, the pope enjoys all the power that the founder of his office had, which means that he can proclaim new doctrines with apostolic (and thus infallible) authority. This claim is rejected by the Eastern churches, as it also is by Protestants, who do not believe that there is anyone in the church today who possesses the kind of divine authority that was given to the New Testament apostles.

Within the Protestant world, claims to historic apostolicity are heard most often among Anglicans and Lutherans, though it must be said that both those communions are divided over it. There can be little doubt that the churches of England and Sweden (to go no further) have preserved an apostolic succession in the purely historical sense, even though this claim has been disputed by Rome.[31] But in 1536 the Lutheran church of Denmark broke deliberately with apostolic succession by the laying on of hands and has hesitated to enter into agreements, even with other Lutherans, because of their sensitivity on this subject. Of course there is a strong political element here: Denmark and Sweden have been rivals for centuries, and if they can find a respectable theological reason to justify staying apart from one another, they will do so.[32] Anglicans, on the other hand, seldom worry about this as a matter of internal church order, but it has been a factor hindering ecumenical projects, such as

31. Anglican orders were declared "null and void" by the papacy in 1896, on the ground of "defect of intention." This means that Anglican bishops, priests, and deacons are not genuine because those who ordain and/or consecrate them do not *intend* to make them bishops, priests, and deacons in the Roman Catholic sense. See R. W. Franklin, ed., *Anglican Orders: Essays on the Centenary of* Apostolicae Curae, *1896–1996* (Harrisburg, PA: Morehouse, 1996). Needless to say, the recent decision of many Anglican and Lutheran churches to ordain women and to consecrate them as bishops has ended any chance that Rome will change its mind in the foreseeable future. Much the same can be said for the Eastern churches, though (characteristically) they have been more reticent to state their position publicly.

32. Until recently, Swedish bishops were not allowed to lay hands on Danish ones at their consecration, because of the fear that the latter would then acquire apostolic succession by stealth.

the union of the main Protestant bodies in India that has taken place there since 1947. In the eyes of high-church Anglicans, only when all the bishops of the Church of South India had been consecrated by someone who stood in the apostolic succession as they conceived of it could that church finally be accepted as part of the worldwide Anglican Communion.

Most other Protestants have little time for these historical arguments, preferring to base their claims to apostolicity on their faithfulness to the apostolic doctrine contained in the Scriptures, a criterion that they usually find lacking in bodies that make much of the historic episcopate. There are, however, some exceptions to this within the Protestant world, which (given its variety) is not surprising. Bodies that have a charismatic nature may claim that apostles still exist in the church today and that the church must be governed by their authority. This was the position held by Edward Irving (1792–1834), who founded the Catholic Apostolic Church, a small but surprisingly active and influential Protestant denomination. Their claim is denied (or at least ignored) by virtually every other church, but the fact that it can be made at all is a reminder that it is not absolutely clear that the New Testament envisaged the cessation of the apostolic ministry after the first generation. It is true that everyone since that time has agreed that it did in fact cease, whether that was foreseen or not, but of course, until quite recently, the same was also true of speaking in tongues. If that can reappear in the modern world, why not the apostleship?

Churches that claim a living apostleship are few in number, but they clearly belong to the radical tradition of the Reformation, which asserted that a true church needed to be started from scratch, whether or not it was headed by an "apostle" designated as such. These churches, which have multiplied over time and are now a common feature of the Evangelical scene, seldom bother much with traditional structures or confessions of faith. They are usually orthodox in intention, which is to say that they accept the doctrines expressed in the creeds of the early church (if not the creeds themselves) and have a generally Evangelical understanding of Protestantism. It is in light of this that, consciously or unconsciously, their pastors and preachers interpret the Bible, which remains central to their worship and teaching. Over time, some of their leaders may seek formal theological training, which will normally be conservative, Evangelical, and Protestant, often with a charismatic tinge, but their congregations remain outside any denominational structure. For them, apostolicity is basically the teaching of the New Testament, which the apostles either gave themselves or authorized others to give on their behalf, and they believe that if they are faithful to that, their claim to be apostolic is as good as (if not better than) anyone else's.

This radical position on the apostolicity of the church is usually shared by Evangelical congregations in mainline Protestant denominations, even though they may be reluctant to admit it openly. Historical antecedents are of little significance to them, and they would certainly be suspicious of anyone who insisted on them if it was clear that these claimants' own beliefs and practices did not conform to the claims they were making. In other words, a pastor or congregation that said it stood in the historic apostolic succession would not be recognized if their teaching and spiritual life did not conform to the principles laid down in the New Testament. This position, which may seem radical, is in fact generic to Protestantism of all kinds. The Reformation would never have occurred if the late medieval church were living according to its traditional principles, and Protestants have always maintained that the Roman Catholic and Eastern Orthodox communions, which make the most of this historic succession, have departed from it to a greater or lesser degree. In recent years, conservative Protestants (including virtually all Evangelicals) have extended this judgment to cover those Protestant churches that say that they stand in the apostolic succession but deny fundamental Christian beliefs and tolerate behavior that is inconsistent with a conservative Evangelical inter- pretation of the gospel. In the eyes of these conservatives, a man who denies the doctrine of the Trinity or contracts a homosexual marriage cannot hide behind the traditional rites and structures of the church, as if they give him a legitimacy that his faith and practice do not support. Apostolicity, if it exists at all, must reflect the teaching and behavior of the apostles; otherwise it is an empty concept with no meaning or application to the life of the church.

A New Kind of Church

Until the Reformation there had been very little discussion about the nature of the church. Some people were aware of the ancient differences between East and West, especially if they lived in borderlands where the two tradi- tions competed for influence, but those divisions were rooted in quarrels over jurisdiction. Did the bishop of Rome have the right to impose his will on the other churches? Were the practices followed by one church obligatory for all? Some of the questions, such as whether clergy should be married or celibate, were far from trivial, but none was serious enough to touch on the nature of the church itself. All agreed that the church had been founded by the apostles and that the later congregations descended directly from them, complete with a hierarchy of bishops, priests, and deacons. They agreed that the adminis- tration of the sacraments, in particular baptism and Holy Communion, was primarily the responsibility of this hierarchy, and that whatever the clergy did was valid in all times and places. Other things might be added to the list, and in most places the church was the central institution of social life, but the hierarchy and the sacraments were fundamental to its very nature.

It was also important that the church should have a common confession of faith. This was contained in the Scriptures and summarized in the Niceno-Constantinopolitan Creed. The Western addition of the *filioque* clause was controversial and regarded by many as a barrier to full communion between the two halves of Christendom, but it was a matter for discussion, and until the fifteenth century most people believed that a solution could be found, as long as there was sufficient goodwill on both sides. The church was divided, but people on both sides recognized its presence in the other and hoped that the schism could somehow be brought to an end.

Protestantism was another thing altogether. The Reformers were not particularly interested in jurisdictional disputes between popes and patriarchs, nor did they lose much sleep over the *filioque* dispute. They all accepted the Western position on that question when the matter was raised, but they did not think that it was something worth dividing the church over. Their focus was somewhere else altogether. Fundamental to their understanding of the church was the preaching of the Word of God. In one sense this was nothing new. There had always been great preachers in the church, and many of the Reformers were inspired by the homilies of John Chrysostom, patriarch of Constantinople, whose works had been unknown in Western Europe for most of the Middle Ages but had recently been rediscovered and published. Chrysostom combined biblical exposition with practical application, and it was that formula that guided the Reformers. The sermon became the central element of public worship, and the clergy were expected to be able to preach in a responsible and edifying manner.

That was not easy to achieve. For a university lecturer like Martin Luther, preparing a sermon would not have been too difficult, but people like him were exceptional. The vast majority of priests had received no formal training in biblical exegesis or in sermon preparation, and what little doctrine they may have absorbed was closely tied to the sacraments, in particular, to the celebration of the Mass. What the Reformers were asking for was a radical transformation of the church's ministry, which they had to achieve as far as possible by using the men and resources available to them. If they were to have any hope of succeeding in this, the Reformers had to embark on a massive program to educate the clergy—and to prepare the laity to receive their teaching. People who had gone to church all their lives primarily to receive the consecrated body of Christ now had to be told that it was more important to hear and receive the preached Word of God, whether that was accompanied by the sacrament or not. In fact, the ministry of the sacrament was subordinated to the ministry of the Word; baptism and Holy Communion were seen as extensions of preaching and applications of preaching to the lives of individual church members, not as rites that could somehow impart and sustain faith of their own accord.

To make matters even more upsetting for the traditionally minded, the number of sacraments was reduced from seven to two, and the devotions that surrounded the Mass were severely curtailed, if not abolished outright. Explanations for these changes were given, to be sure, and congregations were instructed in what they meant, but the habits of a lifetime are not easily abandoned, and it is hardly surprising that the Reformers encountered opposition. What is really astonishing is how limited most of the opposition was. Within a few years, the churches of northern Europe had adopted a Reformation that made what had gone before seem alien and even pagan. Despite a few half-hearted attempts at reunion, everybody knew that there could be no going back, because a new form of Christianity had appeared that was as different from the old as the computer is from the abacus.

The reality of the new faith was apparent from the very beginning of the Christian's life. As the Reformers understood it, to be baptized was to receive the promise of God in the gospel, which was that all who believed in Christ would be saved. It did not mean that the rite itself produced a saved person; the physical act of sprinkling water on someone, or immersing him or her in it, could not have such a spiritual effect. This emphasis on faith led to a debate about whether it was right to baptize infants, who could not understand what was happening to them. But what difference would baptism make if an unbaptized person made a profession of faith, and that was all that was needed to get to heaven? The issues involved in these debates are complex and need to be thought through carefully, especially in the modern world, where individualism is so rampant that there are even cases of people who want to be "unbaptized." This curious phenomenon has occurred in some European countries, where people who were baptized in infancy (usually as Roman Catholics or Eastern Orthodox) have asked for their names to be erased from the church's baptismal registers because as adults they are not believers.[33] That may be taking things to an extreme, but the fact remains that the Reformation opened up the question of baptism in a way that had never happened in the previous history of the church since the ancient

33. The churches concerned refuse to do this on the ground that the people making the demand were not baptized on profession of faith, so lack of it makes no difference one way or the other.

rebaptism controversies, and the debate about it continues to this day with no resolution in sight.[34]

Martin Luther argued that there was such a thing as "infant faith," a concept that he needed in order to explain how even a baby could be saved by trusting in God. Few others followed him in this, if only because the idea was difficult to explain and impossible to verify.[35] More coherent was the notion of a covenant promise, made originally to Abraham and sealed with the sign of circumcision. Circumcision had been abolished in the church, but the faith of Abraham remained fundamental. This led people such as John Calvin to transfer what had previously applied to circumcision to the rite of baptism, which seemed to fulfill the same role for Christians as circumcision had for Jews. Using the argument that the church had broken down the barriers that existed in Judaism, where circumcision had been administered to males only, Calvin and his colleagues claimed that baptism could (and should) be administered more generously. Women were included in it, as were gentiles. How could it be, therefore, that children should be *excluded* from something that young boys had enjoyed under the old dispensation? That made no sense. If the doors of the church were flung wide open, children must also be included because they too are heirs of the promises made to Abraham.[36]

This did not guarantee that they were saved, however. Just as circumcision was no guarantee that a Jewish boy would claim the promises as an adult, so baptism could not ensure that recipients would profess the faith that was assumed on their behalf. It did, however, mean that baptized children came under the umbrella of the church and ought to be brought up as Christians. If they then rejected the faith as adults, that was their responsibility—as with the parable of the sower, some of the seed would fall on stony ground. But that was no reason for the sower not to sow, and that is what baptism was. It was the duty of every minister to seek out children and have them baptized so that they could become heirs to the promises and be brought up in the faith, whether they accepted it in the end or not.

Another important theological consideration was that all children came into the world as sinners. It is important to remember that the early Anabaptists were (wrongly) accused of Pelagianism, the heresy that said that human

---

34. See D. Bridge and D. Phypers, *The Water That Divides* (Leicester: Inter-Varsity, 1977); M. Root and R. Saarinen, *Baptism and the Unity of the Church* (Grand Rapids: Eerdmans, 1998).

35. Luther developed his thinking in response to the Anabaptists. See his "Concerning Rebaptism," written in 1528 and published in English translation in J. Pelikan and H. T. Lehmann, eds., *Luther's Works*, 55 vols. (St. Louis: Concordia, 1955–86), 40:229–62. Also published in T. F. Lull, ed., *Martin Luther's Basic Theological Writings*, 2nd ed. (Minneapolis: Fortress, 2005), 239–58.

36. John Calvin, *Institutes of the Christian Religion* 4.16.5–6.

beings are not completely sinful and can cooperate with God in achieving their own salvation. According to this argument, if a baby could not be baptized, it meant that he or she was not sinful. Of course, babies have not had the opportunity to commit actual sins themselves, but they have nevertheless inherited an innate sinfulness from Adam. There is no point in human life at which a child repeats the original fall. Everybody is in need of a Savior, and in a world where a high proportion of babies died in infancy, people were much more aware of that than we are today.

The Reformers also had to live with the fact that most ordinary people continued to believe that baptism saved a child, because that is what they had been taught by the medieval church. A great deal of superstition surrounded the rite, and everyone agreed that false teaching had to be attacked and removed as much as possible. By denying baptism to infants and insisting that only professing believers could be baptized, the Anabaptists hoped that superstition and false confidence in the power of an external rite could be effectively countered. Those who practiced believers' baptism did not believe that it saved the recipients, for the simple reason that they had been saved already; baptism was merely an outward sign and testimony of a spiritual regeneration that had already taken place. They also argued that while the New Testament offers plenty of examples of adults who were baptized on profession of faith, there are none of children, although infant baptism is nowhere excluded either. As far as the biblical evidence was concerned, the debate over infant baptism was therefore more about what the text did not say than about what it did, and so it has remained to this day.

For good measure, the Anabaptists also insisted on total immersion as the only biblical mode of baptism, though most Baptists today would probably agree that this is of secondary importance. If a believer is baptized on profession of faith, it is hard to see that the amount of water used could make any difference, and strict insistence on this is a form of legalism that is at odds with other, more fundamental, principles that Baptists are concerned to uphold.

Unfortunately, disagreement over the proper administration of baptism was enough to divide the Protestant movement, and to this day not only Baptist churches but also many others reject infant baptism. The question has proved divisive among the Reformed as well.[37] Compare this with the fact that there are no Protestant churches specifically dedicated to a particular view of Holy Communion—though there are certainly differences of

37. For the debate within the Reformed tradition, see P. Marcel, *The Biblical Doctrine of Infant Baptism* (London: James Clarke, 1953), and D. F. Wright, *Infant Baptism in Historical Perspective* (Milton Keynes: Paternoster, 2007).

opinion among Protestants on that subject also—and baptism's particular significance for the doctrine of the church becomes apparent. Baptism remains fundamental to ecclesiology because it is the sacrament of initiation. A baptized child belongs to the church in a way that an unbaptized one does not. We might compare this to secular citizenship. Children are citizens of the country to which they belong even though they do not possess the full rights of adults, which they must claim for themselves when they reach the age of majority. This comparison is not far-fetched, because until the nineteenth century (and in some places even later) baptism was the standard way in which births were registered in most traditionally Christian countries and was therefore in effect a claim to citizenship, since there was often no other way of proving it.

Just as almost all children are trained in the responsibilities of citizenship, and hardly any want to reject it when they reach adulthood, so it was assumed that children trained in the responsibilities of church membership would accept it for themselves when they reached the age of discretion. In practice, of course, Anabaptists (and later, Baptists) work on the same principles, even if they analyze the process differently. Their children are not neutral but are brought up in the church just as baptized children are, and both are required to make a profession of faith before assuming adult responsibilities in the congregation, so the differences between them, though theoretically significant, amount to much less in practice than they appear to on the surface.

Most churches that baptize infants do not automatically admit them to Holy Communion, though the logic of this has been questioned in recent years. The Eastern churches have always given Communion to newly baptized infants, but this is less important than it might seem because Communion in the East is infrequent. Very few adults are regular communicants, so the question of the children does not often arise. It is different in the West, where confirmation, either as a distinct sacrament or as the completion of baptism, has been the norm since well before the Reformation. In episcopally ordered churches it is normally reserved to the bishop, whose ministry in this respect is seen as one of uniting the church in a common faith. In other churches it is usually administered by the pastor, acting on the advice of a group of elders who have examined the candidates and approved them for confirmation. Baptist practice is similar to this, with the difference that it is baptism, not confirmation, that the candidate receives.

In recent years there has been a sacramental movement among Protestants that has tried to tie baptism and Holy Communion more closely together. For Baptists this is not a problem, since no unbaptized person can be admitted to the Lord's Table and children are thus automatically excluded. But for other churches it is more difficult. The Roman Catholic Church long confirmed children at a very young age (six or seven), so that they had little conscious memory of a time when they could not participate. But the mainline Protestant churches have usually deferred confirmation to the teenage years, not least because of the stronger emphasis they have placed on instruction before admission to full membership of the church. This is necessary for them, because Protestant churches almost always have much greater lay participation than Roman Catholic ones. Laypeople are involved in the conduct of worship, in the discipline of the congregation, and in decision making at national synods to an extent that is unknown in Rome, so it is essential that they should be better educated and aware of their responsibilities. It is also a sign that Protestants value the personal profession of faith more highly, and in this respect, those who baptize infants and those who do not are closer to each other than either are to Roman Catholics or the Eastern Orthodox.

Does the deferral of confirmation to the teenage or later years mean that an unconfirmed person should be denied admission to the Lord's Supper? Here things are more complicated. Anglican churches have often practiced exclusion, but there is a formal provision that anyone "desirous of being confirmed" may receive Communion. In other words, somebody who understands what is going on and wants to be part of it can be; confirmation is not, by itself, the only gateway to Communion. There have been times, indeed, when this provision has been of particular relevance. In the American colonies before the revolution, for example, there were no Anglican bishops and therefore very few confirmed adults, so virtually everyone who took Communion would have come into this category. Nowadays, this is less of a problem in most places, but the provision does allow Anglicans to open the Supper to all who profess the name of Christ and are loyal members of their own churches, whether they have received episcopal confirmation or not.

Many other Protestant denominations are equally generous, but this is not true of them all. In the English-speaking world, there has been a tendency for some smaller groups to practice what is known as "closed Communion"; that is to say, participation in the Lord's Supper is reserved for those who are members in good standing of that particular denomination, or even that local congregation. The motive for this is largely disciplinary. If the pastor or elders administering the sacrament do not know who is receiving it, they have no way of determining whether the recipients are worthy. In one sense, of course, no recipient is "worthy" because no one is perfect, but certain criteria are laid down in the New Testament for those who would approach the Lord's Table, and some Protestants feel that they must do what they can to implement them. This requires a form of examination before reception, which is difficult to administer on a large scale. Presbyterians (and indeed Anglicans) traditionally prepared people to receive the sacrament, but with the growth of frequent Communion that practice has now largely fallen into abeyance. Even so, some conservative congregations still continue to maintain it as best they can, and they can claim both scriptural and denominational precedent for their approach.

Closed Communion is more prevalent in Lutheran churches, particularly in conservative ones like the Missouri Synod. Here, though, the motives are theological as well as disciplinary. For conservative Lutherans, it is not enough that persons confess their sins and be "in love and charity with their neighbors and intend to lead a new life"; participants must also confess that the body of Christ is present "in, with, and under" the sacramental elements of bread and wine. This is not transubstantiation in the Roman Catholic sense, but neither is it quite what the Reformed churches (including Anglicans) teach. It is in fact very difficult to define precisely, and in the nineteenth century, Anglican observers took to calling it a doctrine of "consubstantiation," although this term is seldom (if ever) used by Lutherans themselves.

What it means is that the body and blood of Christ are present in the sacramental elements "in a heavenly and spiritual manner," so that those who receive the material bread and wine also receive the spiritual body and blood of Christ, whether they are believers or not. Other Protestants prefer to say that those who receive the sacrament unworthily do not consume the body and blood of Christ in any form, because only those who are spiritually alive can receive him, but as Lutherans do not hesitate to point out, this "receptionist" view has its own problems. Those who hold it tend to adopt a purely symbolic understanding of the bread and the cup, which obviously calls into question the need for the rite in the first place. If the spiritually minded can commune with Christ independently of the sacrament, and the sacrament cannot affect that spiritual communion in any way, why bother with it? This approach disturbs the Lutherans (and many Anglicans as well), but in a curious way it resembles the attitude of the desert fathers of the Eastern church. As hermits, they seldom received Communion, but they did not feel that they were missing anything, because their spiritual warfare was on a higher plane and their mystical experience of God surpassed anything that the sacrament had to offer them.[38] Protestants would not express themselves in that way, but their devotional fervor seldom if ever finds an outlet in increased sacramental

---

38. This does not mean that they abandoned the sacrament entirely, but they received it only infrequently, a custom that is still the norm in the Eastern churches. See D. J. Chitty, *The Desert a City* (London: Mowbrays, 1966), for examples of the practice.

observance, which most of them would consider an extremely strange way of demonstrating their personal commitment to Christ.

As for the other sacraments of the medieval church, Protestant bodies either dismiss them entirely or relegate them to a different and less important category of "church ordinances." Protestants generally restrict the term "sacrament" to what may be called the "sacraments of the gospel," that is to say, those rites that were authorized by Christ and that specifically proclaim the gospel message.[39] Baptism does this, of course, and so does Holy Communion, but the others do not. Confirmation may be retained by Protestant churches as a kind of completion of baptism, but it is not regarded as a sacrament in its own right. Penance and extreme unction are usually rejected as being corruptions of what the New Testament teaches. Confession of sin and the anointing of the sick may be practiced by some, but they are not integrated into the sacramental life of the church in the way that they are by Roman Catholics.

Ordination is practiced by most Protestant churches in some form, but it is not regarded as a sacrament either, except by some extremely high-church people who have been influenced by Roman Catholicism. The form it takes differs from one denomination to another. Anglicans, and many other episcopally ordered churches, retain the traditional threefold order of bishops, priests (presbyters), and deacons, originally on the ground that all three were present in the New Testament church. Modern scholarship has forced them to revise this assessment, but they continue to maintain that the monarchical (or "historic") episcopate developed at a very early date and ought to be retained in the church today. Presbyterians and many other Reformed Protestants reject this "historic episcopate" and claim that it is manifested by the presbyterate instead. Not all presbyters are "teaching elders," but every congregation has a body of them, who operate as a church council that exercises collective leadership in the local congregation. All the elders are ordained to their office, but only the "teaching elder" is expected to have received formal theological training and is paid by the congregation as a full-time minister, making his or her role the functional equivalent of the Anglican priest. Other Protestants use different names for these roles, but in practice almost all have a pastor who leads the congregation and a council of some kind that is responsible for the running of the church.

How these officials are chosen varies from one denomination to another, but usually there is some form of election for the church council, and pastors

39. The distinction is very concisely expressed in Article 25 of the Thirty-Nine Articles of the Church of England. Most other Protestant churches agree with this, implicitly if not always explicitly.

will normally be selected by them, often with a vote taken among the wider membership. In connectional churches like the Anglican, Lutheran, and Presbyterian ones, the choice of a minister will involve approval from someone outside the local congregation, either the bishop (for Anglicans and Lutherans) or the presbytery, by which is meant an association of local churches, for the Presbyterians. In some cases, especially if there is a problem in a local congregation, the bishop or presbytery may appoint or suspend a local minister, thereby exercising the oversight that is entrusted to them. The strength of this system is obvious, but it has weaknesses, too, the most serious being that these external authorities can prevent a congregation from hiring a pastor whom they want to have. This problem is particularly acute when a local church wants to hire a minister whose theological convictions put him or her at odds with the bishop or the presbytery. In recent years, Evangelical and charismatic ministers, who are often resented by more liberal church authorities, have occasionally been shut out from pastorates for that reason, and it must be admitted that the system of collective responsibility has often been used as a means of stifling diversity within the church's official ministry.

Other Protestant bodies may follow a similar pattern but without the connectional element. These are congregational, or independent, churches, of which the Baptists are an outstanding example. Their congregations are free to order their own internal life, not merely on the ordination of ministers but on the forms of worship and even the doctrine that they will espouse, although if they depart too obviously from the general norm they may be "disfellowshipped" by the wider body with which they have chosen to associate. At the same time, a Baptist church (for example) may belong to more than one regional association or to none at all.

In practice, it must be said that Protestant churches are more like one another than their official differences might suggest. Protestant ministers, despite every effort on their part to disclaim the role, are still regarded by most of their congregations in much the same way as Roman Catholic priests are, the most obvious difference between them being that the pastors are usually married whereas the priests are not. Abolition of compulsory clerical celibacy was a major plank in the sixteenth-century Reformers' platform, and it has never been seriously challenged or reversed in Protestant churches. Even the highest Anglo-Catholics are likely to be married and not celibate, as their Roman counterparts have to be. Indeed, so far has the pendulum swung away from compulsory celibacy that it can be extremely difficult for a single person to be accepted in Protestant ministry, even though there is no formal prohibition against it. This situation persists, even though it is explicitly contradicted by the New Testament, and it has to be said that the main reason is popular prejudice. Many people think that pastors who are single are unable to lead congregations, partly because they are inexperienced in what to the critics is a vital part of life and partly because they may be susceptible to temptations to which married persons are supposed to be less exposed. These beliefs are seldom, if ever, put to the test; they are just assumed to be the case, even though there is plenty of evidence of sexual failure on the part of married pastors and an increasingly high rate of divorce among them. Single women have a slightly easier time than unmarried men, but since they are often more restricted in the kinds of ministry open to them, it makes little difference in the end.

The fact is that the Reformation created a new kind of clergy. Priests who were previously cut off from normal society by their celibacy were integrated into the social structure, where they soon acquired a particular place of their own. Protestant pastors were supposed to be university graduates in theology, a qualification that immediately lifted them out of the working class. For many centuries only a small number of young men could go to university, and these were almost all from families with the means to pay for such an education, so the clergy were almost invariably "middle class" by this informal process of self-selection. It was, of course, possible for sons of the aristocracy to enter the ranks of the clergy, and some did, but they were exceptional. On the whole, clergymen were put in the same category as doctors and teachers: men with a professional qualification that gave them a particular identity without cutting them off from the wider society.

It is only in modern times that this form of clerical professionalism has been questioned, with ambiguous results. On the one hand, there has been a certain push to encourage people with different social backgrounds and experience to enter the ranks of the ordained ministry, so as to break down the sense of class barrier that the traditional pattern encouraged. But on the other hand, there has also been a growing movement to encourage serious academic preparation, especially among Evangelical and revivalist groups that in earlier times would have ordained almost anyone who appeared to have the gift of preaching, whether theologically trained or not. Now that university entrance is much more democratic than it used to be, the old class barriers have faded, but there are still complaints that the ministry produced in this way is too intellectual and often not fit for its purposes. At the same time, there are more opportunities for laypeople to get some basic theological training, and this has often led to an expansion of lay preaching and other forms of ministry being recognized even by churches that normally rely on traditional Protestant ordination.

This brings us finally to matrimony, which was a sacrament in the medieval church but is no longer recognized as such by most Protestants. Until fairly recently, most Protestant churches agreed that heterosexual monogamy was the only permissible form of marriage and that divorce was to be strongly discouraged. It would have been unthinkable, for example, for a man who had divorced and remarried to occupy a position of pastoral or teaching authority in any church. That position has now been greatly eroded, though in varying degrees across denominations, largely depending on how liberal a particular body has become. At one end of the spectrum are those who have maintained the traditional standards, and these include Evangelicals on the whole, though tolerance of divorce and remarriage has also been growing among them in recent years. Homosexual marriage, on the other hand, is still rejected by most Protestants, though some liberal denominations (especially in the United States) have been in the forefront of promoting it.

Protestant state churches are in a particularly difficult position, because they have traditionally acted as marriage registrars for the entire population, whether regular churchgoers or not. Scandinavian Lutherans have often been given no choice in the matter; they have had to follow the laws of the state whatever they may think of them, and if the state has approved of remarriage after divorce and of homosexual marriage, the church has to comply with its decisions. The Church of England, by contrast, has the freedom not to employ people who have been divorced and remarried, though this discipline appears to be breaking down in some places. More recently it has been legally forbidden to perform same-sex marriages, and its bishops are at least attempting to ensure that the clergy do not contract them themselves, despite the fact that they have now been legalized by the state.

Other Protestant churches are free to establish their own matrimonial discipline, but they often face practical difficulties if they try to enforce it. Popular demand for a church wedding, even among nonchurchgoers, is still high enough to put considerable pressure on particular churches, especially those that look good in photographs, to make exceptions to their rules, and the same applies to the remarriage of divorced people who may belong, or have close relatives who belong, to a church that would normally not perform such a ceremony. The existence of "wedding chapels" in places like Las Vegas, where couples can marry in a matter of minutes, is sufficient reminder of the problems that the traditional association of the church with matrimony still causes.

Perhaps the fairest thing to say about this is that the discipline practiced in previous generations has now largely broken down, and the understanding of matrimony among Protestants is weaker today than it has ever been. The churches are caught in a dilemma: Should they tolerate a wider range of marital situations than they officially approve? Should they try to enforce a stricter standard for the clergy than for laypeople? And what can they do when individuals break the rules in order to get their way, as they sometimes do? The trends of modern life encourage people to think that the official teaching of the church will eventually catch up with the more "advanced" behavior of a substantial number of its members, which in turn promotes laxity and indiscipline in practice.

In conclusion, Protestant churches, however varied on the surface, tend to be more like one another than like Roman Catholic or Eastern Orthodox churches. This has allowed for the spectacular growth of interdenominational and parachurch ministries, not least among young people and on university campuses, that have produced generations of believers who have no particular attachment to any local church. One result of this phenomenon is that denominational "distinctives" are far less important than they used to be and tend to be of interest mainly to the clergy and other religious professionals. Relatively few laypeople now choose a church mainly because it is Methodist or Presbyterian; it is usually far more important to them that it should have a good youth group or daycare facilities than that it should be governed by bishops or elders. Some people look for good preaching and a style of worship that suits their tastes, but those who do so are liable to be particularly well aware that they cannot depend on a denominational label to guarantee that they will get what they want. As society urbanizes, individuals have more choices, and the churches find themselves in a consumer's market; they are expected to adapt their activities and policies to attract new members, an impulse that is unlikely to encourage them to put much emphasis on their historic traditions. New suburbs tend to have a "community church" that may be independent or a cooperative venture sponsored by more than one denomination, which also tends to reduce the average person's awareness of the formal differences that might exist behind the scenes or in the mind of the minister.

The current scene is a fluid one, and it would be rash to make predictions of where it will lead. So far, it is safe to say that the mainline churches are in decline, partly because "brand loyalty" is not what it once was and partly because in some cases, liberal theology and a somewhat mindless conservatism imposed by elderly or wealthy members who want to keep things the way they are have ensured that new people do not often join them. Independent congregations and "storefront" churches, with few liabilities and no baggage from the past, are booming, but what will become of them in the longer term is uncertain. Will they institutionalize, as their predecessors have done, and lose their novelty, or will they simply disband as their enthusiastic members age or move away and join more sedate congregations? If that happens, will they be replaced, as they always have been in the past, by new independent and breakaway groups that cater to the next rising generation? Whatever happens next, it is clear that Protestantism is undergoing a metamorphosis that has no real counterpart in the Roman or Eastern churches, although they too have to deal with the stresses that the modern world creates. As always, "the wind blows where it wishes, and you hear its sound, but you do not know where it comes from or where it goes. So it is with everyone who is born of the Spirit."[40] And the church, whatever else it may be, is still at heart the community of those who have been born of the Spirit of God.

40. John 3:8.

7

What Should the Church Be?

Theory versus Practice

So far we have been considering the church as it has developed over nearly two thousand years, and as it now is, in all its variegated glory. Individual churches all want to believe that they reflect the body of Christ, but a fair-minded analysis cannot accept that what they claim for themselves is an accurate picture of what the church as a whole ought to be. Roman Catholics, for example, insist that theirs is the one and only true church, but even they have to admit that other Christians exist and that they form "ecclesial communities" of their own, which Rome now officially regards not as heresies or schisms but as groups of "separated brethren." The Eastern Orthodox churches also have to come to terms with the rest of the Christian world, even if their doctrine of the church is just as exclusive as the Roman one. Protestants are usually more prepared to accept the legitimacy of other churches, however much they may dislike or disagree with them, but the challenge they face from both the Catholics and the Orthodox forces them to think through their own raison d'être. One way or another, they have had to justify their existence as bodies faithful to the teaching of Jesus Christ even though they could not accept the authority of Rome or recognize Rome as the true successor of the New Testament church. In fact, the early Protestants argued that it was *because* they were being faithful to Christ that they had no option but to reject the

Roman claims, which they believed represented the usurpation of the "crown rights of the Redeemer" by a human authority set up in his place.

The result of this defense was the birth of ecclesiology, or the doctrine of the church, as a subset of theology. For the first time, theologians (and apologists for different denominations) were obliged to describe the church not merely as it was in practice but as it ought to be in principle. The churches were confronted with a challenge: Should they continue as they were and seek to justify their existing traditions, or should they reform themselves according to a theoretical scheme proposed by a particular ecclesiology? Over time, those who began as radical critics of the medieval order settled into traditions of their own, but the basic questions that prompted the Reformation kept coming back. The history of Protestantism has shown that new formations calling themselves "churches" continue to emerge; each generation finds itself having to address ecclesiological issues over again, much as their sixteenth-century predecessors did.

The first and perhaps most fundamental point that must be made is that the Protestants started with the assumption that the church they knew was not what it was supposed to be. Their Catholic opponents often conceded that the traditional church was corrupt, that many in the hierarchy were unworthy of their positions, and even that some doctrines might need to be revised and clarified in order to avoid popular misunderstanding and superstition. But these were the problems that any human organization is bound to encounter sooner or later—Protestant churches have certainly not been immune. What Catholics could not accept, and what Protestants insisted on, was that a more fundamental change was required, one that would remake the image of the church that had become dominant in the Middle Ages.

Anyone ambitious enough to want to remake the church has to have a plan for doing it, but to begin with at least, the Reformers did not find this a problem. As far as they were concerned, the doctrine of the church was set out in the Bible, and particularly in the New Testament. As they saw it, the main principles laid down in Scripture were the following:

1. Jesus Christ is the head of the church, which is his body. This was agreed on in principle by everyone, including Catholics. The problem was knowing how to implement it. In the Roman church the solution was relatively simple. The pope was the "vicar of Christ," the man who stood in for him on earth and who therefore exercised a comparable (though delegated) authority. This was anathema to Protestants. As far as they were concerned, no earthly person or body could play such a role. Individuals might be appointed to different offices or functions

within the church, but none of these could claim absolute authority over it. Power in the church was necessarily shared among different people, and there had to be a system of "checks and balances" to ensure that no single person could arrogate to himself the kind of dictatorial role that many believed the pope had seized.

2. The church must be subject in all things to the Word of God, that is to say, to the teaching of Holy Scripture. Whatever was not taught in the Bible could not be imposed by the church as a matter of faith. How (and to what extent) a church ought to make its worship, doctrine, and government conform to the New Testament pattern was a matter of dispute. Everyone agreed in theory that it should be done, but deciding how to proceed and then putting it into practice was more difficult. In some cases there were genuine differences of opinion among the Reformers that caused them to go their separate ways. In other cases, external factors (above all, state control) limited the freedom of the church authorities to decide how they should be governed, and those who resented this broke away to form their own churches where they could do as they pleased.

3. The church must preach the Word of God and administer the sacraments in a way that is faithful to the New Testament's teaching. This again was broadly agreed on by everyone, but putting it into practice was not so easy. In theory everybody agreed that the Holy Spirit had been given to the church to preserve it from error and to protect it as it sought to spread the gospel. But how was this supposed to operate in practice? For the Roman Catholic Church the answer was relatively simple. Any bishop or priest who had received the laying on of hands from a bishop who stood in the apostolic succession had what was required and could dispense the gifts of the Spirit to the church according to the rules and regulations that the popes and councils had laid down. Protestants objected to this. Whether they were conservative traditionalists or radicals, they believed that a ministry was valid only insofar as it bore fruit in the Spirit. The outward signs and ceremonies were aids to this ministry, and although some argued that they were valuable (and even indispensable), they were no substitute for the action of the Holy Spirit himself. That action could not be guaranteed, controlled, or manipulated by any human authority, though the church had the promise that when its members acted in faith, God would honor them by granting their requests.

The sacraments were a particular area of disagreement among Protestants and between Protestants and Catholics, but practices varied widely. Generally speaking, Protestants who practiced infant baptism were prepared to accept baptisms performed by a Catholic (or Orthodox) priest as valid, not least because the first generation of Reformers had been baptized in that way. Only the Anabaptists objected to this, but as they refused to accept even the baptisms of other Protestants, they were anathematized and excluded by virtually everyone. Protestants were also more inclined than others to allow members of other churches to receive Communion in their congregations, though there were exceptions to this, especially among Lutherans. Nevertheless, in modern times it has generally proved easier for Protestants to practice intercommunion than for Baptists to accept the validity of infant baptism, and most would be prepared to allow Catholics and Orthodox to participate if they wish to—though reciprocal hospitality is not offered and both Catholics and Orthodox are expected to refuse Protestant invitations to intercommunion.[1]

4. The church must discipline its members and protect its purity as best it can. Here again, there was widespread agreement among the Protestant Reformers in principle, but there was also a recognition that effective discipline was often impossible in practice. To carry it out fairly and on a universal scale would have required a full-time police force and was only practicable in small communities like those of the Mennonites and the New England Puritans. Those experiences were not always happy ones, however, and many Protestants thought that ecclesiastical discipline of any kind was tyrannical. This feeling grew stronger as Protestants realized that their churches could (and sometimes did) exercise it against fellow Protestants, with whom they might have been in agreement on the essential points of doctrine but from whom they dissented on other matters, which to many must have seemed of secondary and even trivial significance. In England, for example, Puritan ministers were disciplined by the state church for not wearing the right clerical dress or using the precise words of the officially approved liturgy. To put such details on a par with the denial of the Trinity or of the deity of Christ was to distort the nature of Christian truth and harm the church, but that is what happened, and it was often impossible to persuade the authorities of the error of their ways. Unfortunately, it must be said that those who suffered this kind of persecution also believed in exercising discipline,

1. There are some curious exceptions, however. In France, for example, the Roman Catholic Church allows Anglicans to receive Communion, even though this goes against the official policy of the church, which is supposed to be the same the world over.

even over such secondary matters, and when they had the chance to impose their views on others, they did so. This was apparent in New England, where Congregationalists, who were discriminated against in the mother country, set up their own church establishment and started harassing those who failed to conform to it.[2]

5. The church must have an organization in which people can exercise their spiritual gifts, which include those of teaching, preaching, and pastoring. For the sake of decency and order, these gifts have to receive some kind of public recognition, and times must be set aside when the congregation can come together to share them. Normally this will involve some kind of theological training for ministers and a system whereby they can be employed and paid. It will also involve set times for public worship, which may vary from place to place but will almost always occur on Sundays (at least). In England and Scotland there developed a strong sabbatarianism, reminiscent of Judaism, and laws were passed to ensure that as few people as possible worked on Sundays. That strictness has largely broken down in the face of modern pressures, but remnants of it survive, and in most traditionally Protestant countries Sunday is still noticeably different from the rest of the week.

6. Public worship will involve prayer to God, the reading of parts of the Bible, preaching, and the administration of the sacrament of Holy Communion. It may be assumed that the first two of these will take place on every occasion, and the third on most, but the frequency of the fourth is much debated. The singing of hymns, a New Testament practice, is now very common, but it did not become so until the Evangelical revival of the eighteenth century. The Reformers were ambivalent about the place of music in worship, and even today it is not unknown for services to be held without it. A few denominations reject the use of musical instruments, but most Protestants regard this as extreme, and there are signs that things may be changing—slowly.[3]

7. Individual congregations must recognize that they belong to a universal fellowship. Traditionally this has been done by various forms of connectionalism, such as episcopacy or synodical government by presbyteries,

---

2. Few people realize that although the First Amendment to the United States Constitution forbids the establishment of religion at the federal level, state establishments were initially left untouched. Connecticut was therefore able to retain its state church until 1818, and Massachusetts until 1833.

3. For example, in 2011 the Free Church of Scotland agreed to let individual congregations decide for themselves whether they would sing modern hymns and use musical instruments. As might be expected, the church split as a result, though the breakaway groups were not numerous.

but if these are rejected or not present, some other form of establishing fellowship must be devised. No Christian congregation can alter the fundamentals of the faith by itself; if it does so, it will cease to be regarded as Christian by the rest of the worldwide church.

In practice, of course, perfection is unattainable, so churches that started with an ideal model of what ought to exist were always liable to be challenged from within by those who perceived that they had failed to live up to their principles. Thus we find that there has been a constant pattern of breakaways from breakaways, each new group claiming to be purer than the one it has left behind. The root of the problem lies in the fact that while Protestants believe that their doctrine should be based on Scripture alone (*sola Scriptura*), no church today can aspire to re-create the New Testament situation with any credibility. There are several reasons for this:

1. The New Testament does not give us enough details about how particular congregations were organized. Did they have elders? Was one person in charge of the others? How often did they meet and what did they do when they assembled? We have indications that help us to appreciate that these questions were considered and dealt with, but we do not know precisely how. Was the Corinthian church, for example, about which we know more than most, typical of the others? Or was it exceptional, at least in some respects, and therefore in need of more guidance? Given that the apostle Paul normally wrote to a church in order to put right something that was not functioning properly, it is extremely dangerous to draw conclusions from the evidence he gives us. We simply do not have enough information to be able to reconstruct the inner life of any New Testament congregation, let alone make rules that would be valid for the universal church.

2. The apostles are no longer with us. However the churches governed themselves in New Testament times, they were always subject to being overruled by the apostles, who had some kind of roving commission over them. Paul, for example, did not hesitate to write at length to the Romans, even though he had not visited their church, let alone founded it. For their part, the churches could always appeal to an apostle for his advice about what they should do in a particular circumstance, something that we cannot do today. There is therefore a missing level of governance that cannot be replaced, and this is bound to influence both how we organize our churches today and what we do about the New Testament evidence.

3. Two thousand years of history have left their mark. When Paul went to Athens, he and his companions were the only people in the city who knew anything about Jesus and the gospel; Paul was proclaiming the unknown God. That is not true today, with the possible exception of remote tribal peoples who have no idea of what Christianity is. Like it or not, modern church planters have to take this tradition into consideration because they depend on it to a large extent, even if they do not admit it. The Bibles they read, the hymns they sing, and much of what they say and do have been inherited from elsewhere. They may reject the corruption and inadequacy of other church bodies, but they have to deal with them, if only because they have worked out their own positions in reaction to what they have found or experienced in other places. Sooner or later they will have to explain and defend themselves in relation to other Christian bodies, something that the New Testament church did not have to do.

4. The church is now a worldwide phenomenon with a great deal of diversity. A congregation that sets itself up and claims to be *the* New Testament church, to the exclusion of all others, simply finds itself becoming one more sectarian body. Its own members might be persuaded to accept such a claim, but nobody else would, and it is unlikely that such a group could exist for long on its own. Sooner or later it would have to admit that other Christians exist, that it did not spring out of nowhere, and that in fact it is highly dependent on the rest of the Christian world for the content of its faith and even for its identity.

In practice, few churches today go to the kind of extreme portrayed here. Even independent congregations usually recognize that they have to be pragmatic in the way they organize their affairs, and most of them follow a pattern that in traditional Protestant terms would be regarded as "congregationalist." The extent to which they enter into fellowship with other bodies varies from one situation to another; in the nature of things, it can hardly be otherwise. Some may evolve into connectional denominations, though most of these tend to be breakaways from ones that already exist—dissenting Anglicans, for example, or Presbyterians. Because of the essentially connectional nature of a denomination, these dissenters often find starting a new one more difficult, not least because they have to establish the connection first before deciding which individual congregations will be permitted to join it. Protestantism exhibits enormous variety at the ecclesiastical level, but behind the apparent diversity there are a few basic patterns that can be found almost everywhere, either on their own or in combination. Among the connectional types of church, some are episcopal, but most are not. However, when an episcopal church unites with others that do not share its polity, it usually insists that the new body should be episcopal in structure, even if that is combined with elements of presbyterianism or congregationalism.[4]

Most independent Protestant churches are not episcopal, at least in the traditional sense. If they have a "bishop," their basic independency will mean that he or she will be no more than the chief minister in that congregation, not the representative or overseer of a group of like-minded churches. Given this variety, it is extremely unlikely that Protestants will ever be able to form a single institutional church, and most of them probably believe that it would be unwise to try to do so. What they would prefer to see is "mutual recognition," so that it would be possible for people to go from one congregation to another and be accepted without having their previous church allegiance called into question. There is some hope of achieving this, though opposition would still have to be expected from conservative baptistic and Lutheran churches, which would probably insist on the exclusive nature of their own sacramental practices.

Christian Unity

Any discussion of the oneness of the church today must begin with the question of Christian unity. From at least the beginning of the twentieth century, missionary organizations and others have become increasingly aware of the limitations of denominationalism and the need for Christians of different allegiances to work together. The Edinburgh Missionary Conference in 1910 is often held up as the founding moment of the ecumenical movement, which, despite many setbacks and disillusions, has been one of the key markers of modern times. The initial motivation of ecumenism was to prevent unnecessary duplication and competition on the mission field. Unevangelized tribes and regions were assigned to different groups so that they would be able to work unhindered and bring non-Christians a single gospel message, without divisions and quarrels that made sense only in a sixteenth-century European context. Once that was achieved, the hope was that different denominations might eventually merge into a single native church, as in fact happened in South India in 1947 and in North India in 1970. It is true that not every Christian group took part in these unions and that a case can be made for saying that the result has not been as successful as originally hoped, but despite all

4. The churches of North and South India are examples of this.

the hesitations, the fact remains that well-entrenched denominations were persuaded to sacrifice their particular identities in search of a greater unity. Similar unions have also taken place in traditionally Christian countries like Canada, the United Kingdom, and Australia, though with uneven impact.

On the whole, it has to be said that these mergers have favored liberal elements within the participating denominations, which have seized control of the enlarged ecclesiastical structures but done little to promote evangelism. It is also true that more conservative elements have resisted the loss of their particular identity, and that in going against the grain they have been forced to develop firmer convictions about what it is that they believe, making them generally stronger and more internally united than they were before. The Presbyterian Church in Australia, for example, was once a mixed denomination in which liberals and conservatives vied for influence, but with the departure of most of the former, it is now more carefully defined and more active in preaching and evangelism than the larger denomination previously was.

Today it is widely recognized that institutional unity has not worked very well in most places, and the emphasis has shifted to cooperation instead of outright merger. Cooperation has been most successful in the academic world, where theologians and biblical scholars now work across the entire Christian spectrum. Even denominational seminaries no longer ignore what is written by others, and it is normal for any serious theological writer to engage with the full range of Christianity, from Eastern Orthodox to Evangelical Protestant. The result has been a major reconfiguration of the academic theological scene, where confessional allegiances have largely given way to conservative and liberal tendencies that cut across all denominations. As a result, conservative Evangelicals are more likely to appreciate equally conservative Roman Catholics, while liberals who hold loosely to their own tradition tend to move freely from one church to another without noticing the difference. Today, all churches experience this cleavage, which is often more important than the formal divisions that continue to separate them institutionally.

The allegiance of laypeople is another way in which ecumenism has made considerable progress. Those who are not officially committed to any particular church structure are often quite prepared to migrate across denominational lines. They intermarry more freely than they once did and may choose to worship with whatever congregation suits them, regardless of its confessional label. They are also often ready to start new churches that have no denominational affiliation, with the result that whereas a century ago most nondenominational congregations would have begun as breakaways from an established church, today they are often independent formations with no history of conflict with anyone else. In some ways that should make it easier for them to cooperate with others, but it might also increase their sense of self-sufficiency and therefore isolate them from the wider church. In the nature of things, each case has to be examined on its own merits.

Where Christian unity is least in evidence is at the level of denominational structures and ministry. People ordained by one denomination are much less likely to be able to move freely across the spectrum of churches than laypeople are. A minister who wants to change from one church to another is likely to meet with opposition—often from the church he or she is trying to join. Almost all denominations impose some kind of acceptance test for these "converts," largely (so they would claim) to protect the integrity of their own tradition. After all, they would say, how can someone who has trained for Presbyterian ministry be a good Lutheran without having at least some form of reeducation? It is also the case that many denominations insist that ministerial candidates who have done their basic theological training at an inter- or nondenominational seminary must complete it in an institution that they control or (at the very least) take examinations that they set. Again, protecting the integrity of the brand name is the excuse given, though how valid that is in a denomination that already embraces a wide range of theological views may be questioned.

It is when we turn to cooperation among existing congregations and denominations that theological cleavages tend to come to the fore. For example, the Roman Catholic Church pursues a steady campaign against abortion, but few Protestant denominations support Catholics wholeheartedly in this. Some individual congregations do, whether the denomination they belong to approves or not, but on such an issue, consensus within a theologically mixed denomination is almost impossible. The same can be said for evangelistic campaigns, which will usually attract widespread Evangelical support, regardless of denominational affiliation, but not extend their appeal much further. In this case, there may even be outright hostility *within* denominations, especially if non-Evangelical congregations and ministers feel threatened. When this happens, a very real question comes to the fore: Why would anybody object to someone who preaches the gospel, just because the preacher is not one of them? It is at this point, ironically, that liberals who would otherwise be inclined to ignore denominational distinctions tend to pull up the drawbridge and insist that they cannot cooperate across theological lines. Conservatives, on the other hand, may criticize a man like Billy Graham for his open-minded approach to Roman Catholics, but usually they swallow whatever reservations they may have about this because they realize that bringing people to Christ is what counts, and they do not want to be distracted by controversies that are better left for another time and place.

At the local level, Christian unity among Protestants is often best exemplified by networks of personal relationships that lead to cooperation, especially in unusual circumstances. Most local communities now have ministers' organizations or alliances, where the clergy of different churches meet to discuss their common problems. Out of these can come practical forms of charity, as (for example) when an Anglican church burns down and the local Baptists let the congregation use their fellowship hall until a new church can be built. This may not be the ecumenism envisaged back in 1910, but it is a good deal better than the sort of interdenominational rivalry (and often hostility) that marked so much of the nineteenth century. At this level, pan-Protestant unity often reaches out to include Roman Catholics and Eastern Orthodox clergy, at least to the extent that they are willing and permitted by their superiors to participate. In their cases, practical cooperation is necessarily more limited, but priests and pastors often find that their problems and experiences are similar, if not identical, and this creates a bond between them that their formal church commitments do not provide. Here again, the current situation, though less than ideal, is far better than what was the case up to a generation ago, and is probably the best that can be achieved at the present time.

A Distinctive Witness

In the modern world, the traditional emphasis on the holiness of the church often expresses itself as the need to create a distinctive witness in our increasingly secular society. Non-Christians seldom bother to think in denominational terms, and even the divide between Protestants and Roman Catholics is often overlooked. To them, the "church" embraces every denomination, so that what takes place in one affects them all. This is seen at its clearest—and cruelest—in the public reaction to scandal. When a minister is arrested for some crime or other, the entire church is tarred with the same brush. Sexual scandals among the Roman Catholic priesthood may be regarded by many Protestants as peculiar to that church (and probably due in part to the requirement of clerical celibacy, though few venture to say that aloud), but every denomination is affected by them. A silent but telling sign that this is recognized among Protestants is the fact that they have not taken advantage of the situation in the Catholic Church to condemn its teachings or to seek to win converts. If there are Catholics who become Protestants because of these problems, this is almost always their own decision, not something that they have been encouraged to do by firebrand Protestant preachers denouncing the evils of Rome.

Solidarity at this level is encouraging, but it is not always met in other areas of church life. It is relatively easy to get wide backing for campaigns against racial discrimination, child pornography, or religious persecution in third-world countries, but these campaigns promote general principles that seldom impinge directly on the behavior of individuals and often are not specifically Christian. Buying fair-trade coffee, for example, is something anyone can do, and Christians are by no means the only people to advocate it. That does not make it wrong, of course, and such initiatives must be encouraged, but by their nature they are less conducive to the unity and growth of the church than they might appear.

Traditional divisions between denominations over such questions as the use of alcohol or gambling, activities once widely regarded as social evils, may be less in evidence now that these things are more often seen as personal addictions, but such divisions have not completely disappeared and may still make practical cooperation between churches at the local level difficult. Almost all Christians are opposed to drunkenness and are happy to do what they can to prevent it, but there is a wide gap between denominations that permit the moderate use of alcohol and those that ban it altogether. There is also a gap between churches that are prepared to receive lottery money to help with building repairs and those that are not.[5]

More important are the policies that churches have adopted toward changing social mores, especially with relation to marriage and divorce. In 1900, despite the deep divisions that then existed among the different denominations, almost all agreed that marriage was a lifelong heterosexual union. Divorce was strongly discouraged, if not banned, and homosexuality was universally condemned. Today, despite increasing cooperation and friendliness among the different churches, issues like these have become contentious in ways that were never the case previously. The sad truth is that non-Christian standards of behavior have been allowed to infiltrate the church to a degree that would have been unthinkable a generation ago, and this is now the greatest single challenge to its holiness. Once biblical standards are abandoned, it is very difficult to get them back, and the fact that different congregations and denominations operate by different standards in these matters makes real cooperation harder than ever.

Another area of contention is the degree to which the church is, or ought to be, involved in secular affairs. There has always been an element in the

5. This is a particularly contentious issue in countries like the United Kingdom, where the state operates a lottery and uses the proceeds to fund cultural and sporting causes of different kinds. Many Christians dislike this but argue that if they do not take the money, others will, and those others might use it for purposes that most churches would disapprove of even more strongly.

church that has resisted the temptation to acquire worldly goods. The medieval monasteries, and later the friars, were examples of this. So, in a somewhat different way, was the Salvation Army in the nineteenth century. Today, there are house churches and Christian communes that promote an alternative lifestyle, though these are fringe movements that do not affect the main denominations in any serious way, except perhaps to encourage things like recycling. More significant is the way in which church property and investments are managed. What activities should be permitted on church property? This may seem like a simple question, but it can get complicated when church buildings are used as community centers. Should a church hall be used for dances, or for an event such as a Hindu wedding? Here again, standards differ from one place to another, and a common policy may be difficult to achieve in any one community. Yet a congregation ought to consider how its activities are perceived by others. Once a building is being used for something unrelated to the church itself, questions are bound to be asked sooner or later, and people should be more aware of the implications of this than they sometimes appear to be.

As for investments, should a church keep its funds in tobacco stocks? What about supporting companies that outsource production to third-world countries where people work in conditions approaching slave labor? Some people call for boycotts of countries whose behavior strikes them as unacceptable. Can a church do anything about that? The complexities of the modern world are such that it is very difficult to engage consistently in what has been called "ethical investment," because most banks and other financial institutions are involved in a number of projects that cannot easily be disentangled. Often it is virtually impossible to know for sure what they have invested in or to find viable alternatives. How far should churches try to do so? How much influence over company policies can they ever hope to have? These questions matter, because a church is expected to practice what it preaches and can easily find itself embarrassed by activities that make use of its money but over which it has no control. There is no simple answer here, but the churches must at least consider the questions, and they have a duty to do what they can to be responsible stewards of their resources in a fallen world.

In some places, churches can also find themselves involved in politics, often against their will. This is a particular problem in Eastern Orthodox countries, where the identification of church and nation (if not state) is such that separating them is practically impossible. For example, to what extent is the antipathy between Serbs and Croats in the former Yugoslavia a reflection of Catholic-Orthodox enmity? Can the churches do anything to overcome this? A similar situation obtains in Northern Ireland, where Catholics and Protestants do battle under various surrogate political labels that most people ignore because they sense that the religious divide is deeper and more important. The churches have made some effort to overcome this, but it cannot be said that they have been very successful, and the credibility of the gospel suffers as a result. It is not without reason that some commentators have suggested that secularization is the best hope for such places, but what an admission of defeat that is for the churches involved. If the message of Christ, which they all claim to share, cannot bring peace, their witness is fatally compromised, and we must not be surprised if a cynical world shakes its head and turns away.

Universally Welcoming

Today the catholicity of the church can really mean only that it welcomes everybody without distinction of language, race, or social background and that it is ready to reach out to the entire world. This does not mean that a church should believe that everybody will be saved, or that those who profess other religions are really "anonymous Christians," doing what they think is right but unaware of the higher truth revealed in Jesus Christ. To think like that would be a betrayal of the message with which the church has been entrusted. What it means is that the gospel must be preached to everyone in the world, without fear or favor, and that those who receive Christ into their hearts and lives must be accepted into the church as equal members.

In terms of worldwide mission, the church today has been more successful than ever before in its history. Virtually every country in the world now has an indigenous Christian church, even if it is persecuted in places like North Korea and Saudi Arabia. The Bible has been translated and is readily available in every major world language, and less than 1 percent of the human race is still unable to access the Scriptures in their mother tongue. It is estimated that in China there may be more than 100 million Christians after nearly two generations of communism, and the numbers seem to be multiplying exponentially. On paper, it is estimated that about a third of the world's population is at least nominally Christian. Of those, about two-thirds are Roman Catholics, another 10 percent or so are Eastern Orthodox, and the rest are Protestant. Of course, these are inflated figures and do not reflect genuine faith or real commitment to a church. By those criteria, both the Roman Catholic and the Eastern Orthodox figures would have to be slashed dramatically, and the Protestant one would also go down, though not as much because Protestants are less inclined to count nominal adherents as church members.

Against this apparent progress has to be balanced the de-Christianization of much of Europe and North America, in traditionally Christian countries where it is becoming increasingly difficult for believers to maintain a public presence. The churches in these places have proved to be incapable of resisting the secular tide, and none of them exercises influence even approaching that of a century ago. Their internal integrity is also under serious attack, as the mainline denominations succumb to theological liberalism and many conservative ones retreat into an individualistic piety as an escape from the unpleasant reality of the outside world. It is symptomatic of this that a word such as "fundamentalism," which was coined in the early twentieth century to describe conservative American Protestants and was used almost exclusively in that sense for two generations, has now been transferred to Islamist jihadists, who appear to the secular media to represent a religious threat greater than any to be found in the Christian world.

This public retreat of the churches in their traditional homelands may turn out to be only temporary, but there can be no doubt that the most lively Christian countries today are in the third or "majority" world. Whether this will continue to be the case is impossible to say. There may be a revival in traditionally Western countries, or the third world may become secularized. In many places today, Christians are persecuted, most often by Islamic extremists, and there is a real danger that the church will be wiped out in its ancient Middle Eastern homelands.[6] On the other hand, the blood of martyrs is the seed of the church, and it may be that the terrible sacrifice that so many believers there are being forced to pay will rebound to the glory of Christ and the gospel.

How welcoming churches are of new spiritual movements is hard to say. Institutions are innately conservative, and historically those who have preached or promoted revival have had a hard time. We have only to think of the difficulties that John Wesley (1703–91) had in the Church of England, to which he was personally devoted, to realize how easily an establishment can make a historic error and virtually expel people who ought to be its lifeblood. In our own time, this problem has been most evident with respect to the charismatic movement, which has been fully accepted in some places, not at all in others, and with reservations by many. Aside from the Pentecostal churches, which have obviously accepted the continuing practice of the charismatic gifts, few denominations have made an official pronouncement about them one way or the other, but tolerance of charismatics tends to be at a congregational, rather than denominational, level. Even the Roman Catholic Church has been open to the movement to some extent, though it could hardly be said to have embraced it wholeheartedly. This is not to say that charismatics are above criticism. Many of them have a naive faith that is all too willing to be seduced

6. R. Shortt, *Christianophobia* (London: Rider, 2012).

by strange phenomena, and they often seem resistant to self-criticism, but their desire for a deeper spiritual experience is consonant with the deepest instincts of the church and ought to be honored accordingly.

The main problem for catholicity today is the degree to which a church can (or should) accept differences of doctrine as legitimate. Traditional churches with a highly developed confessional theology naturally find this more difficult than others do, and this is reflected in their behavior. The Roman Catholic and the Eastern Orthodox churches both have a comprehensive theology that they insist must be accepted in full by all their members. It is obviously very difficult to enforce this on laypeople, but the clergy, and especially theological teachers, are held to the standard, even when the doctrine in question is controversial and not accepted by other churches. The obvious case in point is the Roman insistence on papal infallibility, with which no other church agrees, but which is strictly imposed on all who want to call themselves Catholic theologians. The Eastern Orthodox are less dogmatically inclined and more prepared to relegate controversial questions to the realm of "mystery," but within the parameters they set for themselves they are just as strict as the Roman Catholics, and perhaps even more so. They may not have a pope, but disobedience to the hierarchy is frowned upon every bit as much as in Rome.

As we would expect, Protestant churches present a much greater variety of responses to this theological challenge. A few are just as strictly orthodox as the Roman Catholic Church and insist on total conformity to their confession of faith. Others permit a much greater latitude, particularly if (as in the Anglican Communion) their confession of faith is several hundred years old and has not been updated. In most mainline Protestant churches today, the place of their historic confessional statements is a matter of controversy, with some members of the church arguing that they should be sidelined while others insist that they must remain valid and important for defining the boundaries of acceptable belief within the church in question. In such a situation, prosecutions for heresy are liable to cause more trouble than they are worth and so are virtually unknown. To the chagrin of the orthodox, renegade individuals can often get away with a wide range of beliefs, some of which might well contradict the most fundamental doctrines enshrined in the ancient creeds.

But although this tolerance might easily be extended to individuals, it is seldom evident in the church's official statements, which usually remain within the framework established by its traditional doctrinal standards. In dealing with other denominations, of course, there is greater latitude, and often ministers from different churches will be invited to preach or teach without the imposition of any specific doctrinal test. It will normally be assumed by the host church that if the guests are in good standing with their own denomination, they will be acceptable to the host also, and well-mannered guests usually take care not to cause offense when they are invited elsewhere.

The question of women ministers is more problematic, because some denominations accept them and others do not, and the conditions of their acceptance can vary enormously. Some churches that have agreed to ordain women insist that all ministers in the church must accept them, and those who cannot do so on grounds of conscience are dismissed or asked to resign. Other churches tolerate existing ministers who have scruples about this, but do not ordain new ones if they cannot accept the change. It even happens, as in the Anglican Communion, that some member churches ordain women while others do not and that different policies are adopted with respect to those who cannot agree with the majority. In those cases, an ordained woman may have to accept that she will not be accepted as a preacher or teacher in a place where women's ordination is not practiced, regardless of what her theological convictions may be. In the Anglican case, this has led to what is called "impaired communion," a situation in which members of the same church do not accept each other's orders and are therefore unable to receive the sacrament from those whom they do not believe have been validly ordained. Here perhaps more than anywhere, we can see how a change of practice can divide a church internally, and how it can set limits to catholicity for reasons that may have more to do with church discipline than with any specific doctrine.

Independent churches have much greater freedom in such matters, of course, and for that reason they cannot be categorized as easily as traditional denominations. Most of them subscribe to a broadly defined Protestant and Evangelical faith, though as often as not, this will be implied rather than officially stated. There is an obvious danger that a preacher or teacher might deviate from historic Christianity and not be subject to discipline, but although this sometimes happens, it must be said that unsound teaching is often detected by such churches, which will do their best to ensure that their ministers stay within the bounds of generally recognized orthodoxy, whether the church has a defined confession of faith or not.

It is probably true to say that baptistic congregations are disproportionately highly represented among independent churches, but the fluidity of their structures may mean that different convictions are respected to a degree that they would not be elsewhere. For example, an independent church that does not baptize children may nevertheless accept people who were baptized as infants into membership, in a way that most Baptist churches would not. But in the nature of the case, it is impossible to generalize about this, because each congregation is a law unto itself. What can be said, however, is that independent churches, which formally deny the catholicity that is expressed by being part of a network of denominational structures, may turn out to be more flexible than many denominations when it comes to dealing with specific cases and are therefore more catholic in practice than their lack of institutional form would suggest.

A major challenge to the catholicity of a church comes when a significant number of its members leave to join another denomination on the ground that it is the "true church" in a way that the one they are leaving is not. This is almost invariably the case when people leave a Protestant church to become Roman Catholics or Eastern Orthodox. Before the nineteenth century, conversions of this kind were relatively rare and often due to special circumstances. Protestant women who married Catholic or Orthodox men might be expected to take on their husband's religion, particularly if they were nobles or members of royal families. Sometimes there were forced conversions, as when French and Austrian Protestants were given the choice of becoming Catholics or going into exile. But neither of these can be regarded as a genuine act of faith on the part of the converts—a defect that was well understood at the time.

It was only in the nineteenth century, as religious faith became more of a personal choice, that converts from Protestantism to Catholicism became a serious theological problem for the churches they were leaving. Here it must be remembered that virtually all Protestants in the early nineteenth century were convinced that their churches were in the vanguard of social and intellectual progress and that Roman Catholic countries were backward and in the thrall of a spiritual tyranny. A classic work that enjoyed immense popularity and is still in print today is the memoir of George Borrow (1803–81), a colporteur for the British and Foreign Bible Society who went to Spain in the 1830s and tried to distribute copies of the Bible there. His account, which is highly valued as a description of Spanish society at that time, pictures a country that was wallowing in a darkness induced by the Catholic Church, and it must be admitted that he was not far wrong. After the French Revolution, the church set itself against any form of liberalism, and in Spain it was to play a leading role in combating progress of any kind for the better part of 150 years.[7]

Given that context, it came as a shock that a few highly educated British and American intellectuals chose to convert to Rome of their own free will.[8] Their motives were varied, ranging from romanticism to sympathy for Catho-

7. G. Borrow, *The Bible in Spain: The Journeys, Adventures, and Imprisonments of an Englishman, in an Attempt to Circulate the Scriptures in the Peninsula* (London: John Murray, 1843). The grip of the Catholic Church on the country was not relaxed until after the end of the Franco dictatorship in 1975.

8. See P. Allitt, *Catholic Converts: British and American Intellectuals Turn to Rome* (Ithaca, NY: Cornell University Press, 1997).

lics who had suffered persecution during the French Revolution to a feeling that industrialization was destroying society by replacing spiritual values with purely material ones. The Catholic Church represented the old order. It was the living embodiment of the Middle Ages, which were now recast as an "age of faith" complete with Gothic cathedrals, crusader knights, and holy virgins who sacrificed their lives for the church.

In England, conversion to Rome was partially thwarted by a group of high-church Anglicans who insisted that the Church of England was fully Catholic and that no Protestant Reformation had ever occurred in the country. In 1841 the leading exponent of this view, John Henry Newman (1801–90), published *Tract XC*, in which he tried to demonstrate that the Thirty-Nine Articles were susceptible of a Catholic interpretation and had little or nothing to do with Protestantism.[9] Newman's eccentric thesis provoked a huge backlash and helped spur him to seek his own personal rapprochement with Rome. He knew that the Catholic Church of his day was quite different from anything that could be found in the New Testament or the early church, but he overcame this difficulty by coming up with a theory of development. According to this idea, the church had evolved over the centuries by a Spirit-guided process that had seen the emergence of a worldwide body centered on the papacy. He published his thesis in 1845, at the same time as his conversion to Roman Catholicism.[10]

Newman's submission to the papacy caused a considerable stir at the time, and some (though by no means all) of his Anglo-Catholic supporters followed suit. Newman's understanding of the Roman church was external and superficial, and modern research has shown that his analysis of the Protestantism he rejected was faulty.[11] His subsequent experience of Catholicism was also far from happy, as he came to appreciate that the church he had joined was rather different in practice from the one that had attracted him in theory. He lived to see the declaration of papal infallibility in matters of faith and morals, which was proclaimed in the face of considerable opposition at the First Vatican Council in 1870.[12] Newman was appalled, but he submitted, since the logic of his doctrine of development left him with little alternative.

9. A. W. Evans, *Tract Ninety, or Remarks on Certain Passages in the Thirty-Nine Articles by John Henry Newman, with an Historical Commentary* (London: Constable, 1933).

10. Reprinted as J. H. Newman, *An Essay on the Development of Christian Doctrine*, with an introduction by J. M. Cameron (London: Pelican, 1974).

11. See F. M. Turner, *John Henry Newman: The Challenge to Evangelical Religion* (New Haven: Yale University Press, 2002).

12. A number of prominent Catholic theologians refused to accept the new dogma and seceded to form what has become known as the Old Catholic Church, a small body but one that has managed to preserve its independent existence ever since.

Since Newman's time, there has been a steady trickle of converts from An-glicanism to Rome, usually through the halfway house of Anglo-Catholicism, and in recent years that has been augmented by a number of individual conver-sions from other Protestant denominations. Lutherans have been especially prominent, but a fair number of Evangelicals have also "swum the Tiber," as the expression is, and some have aggressively sought to persuade their former coreligionists to join them.[13] More recently, a certain number of such people have preferred to join one of the Eastern Orthodox churches, probably because those churches' mystical tradition and unwillingness to define certain doc-trines too closely have proved more attractive than the dogmatism of Rome.[14]

Common to all these accounts is a repudiation of Protestantism in favor of one of the historic pre-Reformation churches. In most cases, these converts have turned away from their Protestant background because they are dissatis-fied with the weaknesses they perceive in the church or churches to which they belonged. Often they deplore the theological liberalism that has invaded most of the mainline Protestant churches, and they have been alienated by those churches' apparent inability to counteract its influence. Sometimes they have also rebelled against the superficiality of so much popular Evangelicalism, with its exaggerated emphasis on individual religious experience and apparent indifference to history and tradition. They are attracted to Rome (and to a lesser extent, the Eastern churches) because they see in them a determination to resist modern trends and an ability to transcend a purely personal spiritual-ity in what appears to be the unity of a worldwide church.

One way or another, it is the doctrine of the church that has captured the converts' interest and attracted their allegiance. This is all the more interesting in that it has come at a time when many members of these ancient churches are increasingly dissatisfied and either reducing their commitment or leaving altogether. The intense Catholicism of Spain, Ireland, and Poland, to name but three obvious examples, has greatly declined in the past generation, and everywhere many priests, monks, and nuns have abandoned their vocations. Seminaries have closed, schools and universities have been secularized (or else laicized to the point where it makes little difference), and the revived Ortho-doxy of Russia seems to have become a tool of the state in much the same way as it was under the tsars. Intellectual Protestant converts either ignore

13. See, for example, S. Hahn and K. Hahn, *Rome Sweet Home: Our Journey to Catholicism* (San Francisco: Ignatius Press, 1993).

14. See M. L. Mattox and A. G. Roeber, *Changing Churches: An Orthodox, Catholic, and Lutheran Theological Conversation* (Grand Rapids: Eerdmans, 2012). Mattox has gone from the Southern Baptists to the Lutherans and now to Rome; Roeber from Roman Catholicism to the Lutherans and now to the Eastern Orthodox (in their American form).

these unpleasant facts or make excuses for them in a way that they would never do for the Protestant denominations they have left.

It is tempting for Protestants who observe this pattern to conclude that it is further evidence of the ability of human beings to create a fantasy and believe it in the teeth of the evidence, but while this may be true to some extent, it cannot be the final answer to the challenge posed by the claims of the pre-Reformation churches. Those who have converted to them are often right in their unfavorable analysis of current Protestantism. The mainline Protestant churches often seem to be on the verge of institutional collapse, and concessions to liberal tendencies in the hope that their fortunes will be reversed have only made the catastrophe more likely. Since the 1960s, Protestants have been told that new translations of the Bible, new forms of worship, and the opening of the ministry to women (and to men who are inadequately trained and who work on a part-time basis) will restore their fortunes, but the long-term decline has continued and shows no sign of abating.

Evangelical churches have resisted the trend to some extent, but although they are good at winning people to Christ, they are less successful at keeping them in the fold, and many of their churches suffer from the "revolving door"—those who come easily also go easily, and steady commitment to a coherent theological vision is at a premium. Conservative Protestant theologians, meanwhile, have all too often taken refuge in an exaggerated denominationalism that artificially revives sixteenth- and seventeenth-century debates or indulged in hair-splitting controversies that merely convince most people of theology's abiding irrelevance to the problems and challenges of real life.

Whether Protestants, and especially Evangelicals, can rise above these difficulties and find a new and deeper understanding of the catholicity of the gospel that embraces a complete theological and social vision is uncertain, but as the flight to Rome and the East reminds us, it is the most urgent test that they currently face. Catholicity has been neglected, derided, and ignored by Protestants in the past, but if they are ever to recover their traditional position at the cutting-edge of Christian witness to the contemporary world, they must rediscover it and produce a version that is both coherent and compelling to the present generation.

The Faith Once Delivered

The classical mark of a church's apostolicity is seen most clearly in the way it adheres to the New Testament as its supreme guide in matters of faith and practice. At one extreme are those charismatic churches that claim to have "apostles" and, of course, the Roman Catholic Church, which regards the pope as the living Peter, with his apostolic authority to make further additions to the church's official doctrine. Of course it is true that most of the charismatic groups would not expect their "apostles" to deviate from biblical teaching. As they see it, the duty of these apostles is to proclaim the ancient faith afresh, and this belief is widely shared by people who would not accept the idea that there can be living apostles today. Even in the Roman Catholic Church, the apostolic authority granted to the pope (speaking *ex cathedra*, or in his official capacity) is regarded not as superseding Holy Scripture but as supplementing it in matters that the sacred text does not itself clarify. Thus, for example, a pope can and has decreed that the Virgin Mary was taken up into heaven like the prophet Elijah, because nothing is said about this in the New Testament and he has the authority to canonize the tradition that claims this. But he cannot rule out the second coming of Christ, because that is clearly affirmed by the Bible and the ancient creeds of the church, whose authority he is bound to respect.

All Christians agree that the apostolic deposit in the church today is contained primarily in the New Testament. Whether there is anything else that can be traced back to the first generation is uncertain, though the possibility cannot be completely ruled out. There is even a remote chance that a genuinely apostolic letter might one day turn up in the sands of Egypt, as other documents from that time have done, but if that were ever to happen, it would not be added to our New Testament. One of the reasons is that it would be impossible to prove the authenticity of such a letter. Another is that it would be impossible to get the entire Christian world to agree to the addition. But the third, and in the end most important, reason it would not happen is that the church has survived for two thousand years without this letter. A newly discovered apostolic letter would not be part of the faith once delivered to the saints and therefore would have no place in the New Testament canon.[15] Like the *Didache* and other texts that may go back to the first century, the letter could be used as evidence of what the early church was like, but it could not claim any authority to inform the modern church about what it should do.

This distinction between the New Testament as evidence and the New Testament as authority is one that is not often explicitly made, but it is crucial to our understanding of apostolicity. Everybody, including people who have no faith at all, agrees that the New Testament is evidence for the life and beliefs of the early church. Most people also accept that there is nothing that can be compared to it; the numerous nonbiblical texts that purport to

15. Jude 3.

come from an apostle or from one of their associates are all regarded as both spurious in origin and relatively late in date. Some of their contents may be historically accurate, but it is impossible to know for sure what is authentic, and most scholars are rightly cautious in their assessments. Occasionally somebody claims that a text represents a suppressed tradition and ought to be taken seriously as evidence of what the apostles believed and taught, but most people recognize that this is at best a very dubious proposition and discount such claims as a form of special pleading.[16]

The big difference between the academic world and the church is that while both read the New Testament as evidence, the latter also uses it as the chief authority for its doctrine and practice. Indeed, it is not too much to say that the degree to which a particular denomination remains faithful to the teaching of the New Testament is the main test of its claim to apostolicity. Some radical Protestant groups claim that they do this fully and exclusively. The Churches of Christ, for example, say that they do what the New Testament commands and refrain from doing what the New Testament either forbids or does not mention—an admirable principle in theory, but one that is practically impossible to apply with any consistency. For example, the New Testament has no clear examples of infant baptism, so the Churches of Christ do not practice it. But the New Testament also has no indication that women participated in the Lord's Supper, an omission that the same churches ignore. This example is not as trivial as it may seem, because in ancient times it was normal for men to eat together without women and children present; that was certainly the case at the Last Supper, and for all we know, it may have been the practice followed in the early church. Nor, of course, do the Churches of Christ normally meet in people's houses, which is what the earliest churches were forced to do. They erect buildings for public worship and generally operate much as other denominations of their type. They conform to New Testament practice in a few selected ways that allow them to make their claim to be adhering to it exclusively, but the truth is that if the apostles were to come back today, they would be just as puzzled by what goes on in those churches as they would be everywhere else.

A literalistic adherence to the New Testament in every detail is impossible for any church today, if only because times have changed so much that we can no longer re-create anything resembling the earliest Christian congregations. Some adaptation to modern life is required, but how much? To determine this, most churches have developed a distinction between a principle and its

16. The writings of Bart Ehrman are a prominent example of work that assumes great diversity in early Christianity on the basis of noncanonical texts.

application, insisting that while the former ought to remain unchanged, the latter can be modified according to circumstances.

Matters of principle fall under one of three headings: doctrine, discipline, and devotion. All churches agree that they must teach what the apostles taught. They also agree that they must exclude anything that goes against the apostles' teaching, which means that they must make sure that those who are appointed to teach fulfill their function in a way that conforms to what the apostles intended. They must also do what they can to make sure that church members live up to the standards expected of them, and discipline them if they do not. Finally, all churches must meet together for worship, which will normally include acts of praise and thanksgiving as well as prayers for the needs of the church and the world, though the exact content of any particular service is variable.

At the heart of worship is the celebration of the Lord's Supper, though there are many different ways in which its centrality can be expressed. The reading of the Scriptures, followed by preaching and teaching from them, also forms part of the church's worship, though their relationship to it is more complex. For a start, it is perfectly possible to read the Bible and to preach and teach from it *outside* a worship context, and this is frequently done. It is also possible to worship God without including a time of preaching or teaching, particularly if there is no one competent to do it, though even in such cases there would normally be at least a reading from the Bible. But legitimate as these exceptions may be, they are usually recognized as exceptions and not promoted as standard practice. In normal circumstances, preaching and teaching are an important part of regular worship, and in most Protestant churches at least, they occupy the central place.

When we start to apply these criteria to the churches today, what we find is a mixed bag. As far as doctrine is concerned, most churches accept the ancient creeds and the decisions of the first four ecumenical councils as normative, though how much real influence they have in the life of a modern congregation is hard to determine.[17] The creeds are familiar to a wide range of churchgoers, and some congregations occasionally offer courses or study sessions to explain their meaning. Hymns frequently reflect their teaching, or elements of it, and in that way it can be said that the creeds continue to play a significant role in modern church life. The ecumenical councils are much less known, and the fourth one (Chalcedon) remains a point of division

---

17. Many Protestant groups do not use the creeds and are quite unaware of the first four ecumenical councils, but what they teach usually conforms to the creeds, whether they are conscious of this or not.

within the Eastern churches, but their underlying doctrine continues to act as a touchstone of authentic Christian belief, particularly when it comes to determining whether a group like the Jehovah's Witnesses can be recognized as Christian. The Jehovah's Witnesses claim to be biblical, but because they teach a doctrine of Christ that resembles the ancient Arian heresy, which denied his full divinity, the rest of the Christian world does not accept them as orthodox.

It is when we come to doctrines that were formulated in later times that major differences appear over the way in which the New Testament is used. The Roman Catholic Church does not insist that every doctrine that church members are required to believe must have clear scriptural warrant. It claims that its own innate apostolicity gives it the right to proclaim as infallible dogma beliefs that have long been held by church members but that have no written confirmation that can be traced back to an apostle. The belief that Mary remained a virgin all her life is one of these; there is no evidence for it other than popular piety, but the church has made it part of the apostolic faith, and no loyal Catholic is free to reject it on the ground that it cannot be found in the Bible.

Protestant churches reject this sort of claim as a matter of principle. Very few Protestants believe in the perpetual virginity of Mary, but that is not the point at issue. Protestants are free to hold that view if they want to, despite the fact that there is no evidence for it, but they cannot teach it as a doctrine that every Christian must believe in order to be saved. It is not part of the authentic apostolic deposit, and for that reason it cannot be required as an article of faith. The fact that the Roman Catholic Church does so is evidence that it has departed from apostolicity, despite its claims to the contrary. The Eastern Orthodox churches generally try to avoid taking sides in this kind of argument. Most Orthodox believe in the perpetual virginity of Mary, but it has not been defined or canonized by the church and therefore cannot be insisted upon as something that is necessary for salvation. Like the Protestants, the Orthodox tend to think that the Roman Catholic Church has gone too far in demanding acceptance of very precisely defined beliefs from its members and has therefore erred—even if the belief itself is correct.

On the other hand, Protestant churches often have a confession of faith that claims to be based on New Testament teaching but that in fact goes beyond Scripture by insisting on particular positions (regarding baptism, for example) that are not indisputably biblical, though they are claimed as such by those who promote them. The result has been the kind of division that has produced modern denominationalism, and although most theologians today are prepared to accept that some of their confessional positions are too rigid and exclusive as far as the New Testament is concerned, altering what has become traditional is extremely difficult. In practice, they often end up defending beliefs that they know are of secondary importance (at best) but continue to take them seriously because they are an integral part of their denomination's public confession of faith.

One of the main reasons for this behavior is the fear of many conservatives that once a change is introduced to a historic statement of faith like the Westminster Confession, it is impossible to know where the alterations will stop. Many perfectly loyal Reformed people deplore the fact that the confession insists that the pope is the antichrist, but it is often thought to be easier to ignore that clause than to delete it, since abolishing it may lead to demands that other potentially divisive doctrines (like those concerning election and predestination) ought to be dropped as well.[18] These doctrines are regarded by those who take the Westminster Confession seriously as much more central to their church's teaching as well as being a genuine interpretation of the New Testament, and to omit them would be seen as a concession to liberalism and unbelief. The danger, of course, is that someone may try to insist on a literal application of the doctrine that the pope is the antichrist and cause trouble (or at least major embarrassment) as a result. This has actually happened in Northern Ireland, where conservative Presbyterians often have to reassure their Roman Catholic neighbors that they do not agree with that particular statement, even though they are happy to accept the Westminster Confession as their official basis of faith.

One way out of this dilemma is to create new confessions, which is always theoretically possible. Some churches, and several parachurch organizations, have tried to do this, but the difficulties are formidable. One is that the ecumenical spirit of our times is hostile to the idea of making doctrinal statements whose precision would only serve to divide the church still further. Can a single denomination produce a doctrinal statement that will distinguish it from all others without infringing on the spirit of fellowship and cooperation that has recently brought so many different Christian bodies together? If it cannot do so, what is the point of a particular church composing a confession of its beliefs that almost any Christian could happily sign? Such generic statements of faith are frequently produced by interdenominational organizations, one of whose goals is to adopt a position that is as wide-ranging as possible, but in the nature of things this is unlikely to contain anything new. At the same time there are issues ranging from miraculous spiritual gifts to environmental conservation on which it might be desirable for a particular

18. The statement that the pope is the antichrist is found in the Westminster Confession, 25.6.

church or organization to adopt an official position, but agreeing on what that position should be is extremely difficult.

The example of the Roman Catholic Church may serve as a warning here. It has produced three dogmatic definitions in modern times—affirming the immaculate conception and perpetual virginity of Mary (1854), the infallibility of the pope (1870), and the bodily assumption of Mary into heaven (1950)—but it can hardly be said that any of these has furthered the cause of Christian unity. Were these definitions necessary? Have they made any real difference to anybody's faith? It seems best to conclude that the churches today ought to maintain the common heritage that they have inherited from ancient times and seek to reconcile existing differences, rather than create new ones. There may come a time when further doctrinal definition will be possible (as well as desirable), but this would probably best be done by all the main churches acting together, not by individual ones striking out on their own.

It is, however, when we turn from the formulation of doctrine to its application that the most serious problems arise. Since the eighteenth century, all the churches have had to deal with a kind of thinking that maintains that the biblical worldview is outdated, that the early church fathers (and even the sixteenth-century Reformers) were operating with a hermeneutic of Scripture that is no longer valid, and that most of the classical definitions of doctrine were the outcome of (often sordid) church politics, designed to exclude undesirable elements more than to advance the preaching of the gospel. For all these reasons, the claim is made that the classical doctrinal statements cannot be used as criteria for determining what Christians ought to believe now. Even the Bible is only a record of what the church taught in the past and cannot be taken as a guide for its current doctrine or practice, which must be worked out on other principles. This radical critique has been contested many times, but it keeps reappearing in different guises. At the present time, it shows up most often in the common assertion that modern science has disproved a good deal of what the Bible says, so it can no longer be accepted as a reliable authority for living the Christian life today.

At the most fundamental level, this attack has concentrated on the doctrines of creation and the fall, both of which have been denied by a significant number of thinkers in traditionally Christian cultures. It is hard to disagree that the Bible teaches that the world was created by God and that humankind was placed in the world as its crowning glory, but that belief has been attacked by evolutionists and environmentalists alike. Evolutionists deny that man was specially created by God in his own image and likeness, and environmentalists insist that the human race has no business claiming "dominion" over the other creatures, who are in no way inferior to us. As for the fall, it is pointed out that this is nowhere explicitly stated in Genesis and that the received doctrine of original sin is based to some extent on Augustine's faulty interpretation of Romans 5:12.[19] Most people agree that human beings have not reached their full potential, but that is not the same thing as saying that they have fallen away from God—underdevelopment is not to be confused with sin. Would it not be better, the argument goes, to abandon such "unhelpful" ideas as the fall and reconstruct a more positive vision of the human race and its destiny?

This kind of thinking has affected all the major churches one way or another, but their inability (or unwillingness) to produce new doctrinal statements has usually mitigated its effects as far as general public awareness is concerned. Instead, most churches have preferred to leave traditional doctrinal statements as they are and either ignore them or interpret them so broadly that they are virtually meaningless. A few very conservative churches have reacted against this by condemning all forms of modernity, but that kind of "fundamentalism" is relatively rare and is often disliked, even by people who are themselves conservative in their general approach to such matters. In between these two extremes is a spectrum of opinion, of which the most significant is that associated with people who are members of a liberal denomination but hold conservative views, which they insist are what their churches ought to be teaching. On the whole, however, opinions such as these remain the preserve of a concerned minority and seldom impinge on the lives of ordinary people or affect the way a church is governed.

There are, however, two areas where the churches have felt the impact of such modern thinking in recent times, and both have led to divisions that cut across traditional denominational lines. The first concerns the role of women in the life of the church. Until fairly recently, it was universally agreed that the pastoral ministry, and the authority that goes with it, was reserved to men. This is the position of the New Testament, and it has been followed more or less unchanged since earliest times. This is not to say that women's ministry has been denied altogether; there have long been orders of nuns, for example, and many Protestant churches have had deaconesses and women missionaries. But on the whole, the ordained ministry has been closed to women until the past generation or so. Now, largely under the influence of modern ideas of gender equality, many Protestant churches have opened their ministry to women on more or less the same basis as men. As always in such cases, there are a number of variations in practice, and the pace of change has not been

19. Augustine read the verse as saying that human guilt for sin was inherited from Adam, whereas most modern interpreters read it to mean only that death entered the world because of Adam's sin.

the same everywhere, but the general drift is unmistakable in those denominations that have agreed to open their ministry to women.

Some of these churches have tried to justify this change by appealing to the New Testament, which they claim has been misinterpreted over the centuries, but this is not a very plausible argument. The most that can be said for it is that the Bible does not speak about ordination in the modern sense. When it states that women are to keep silent in church and not to teach, the proscription was intended to deal with a particular problem that had arisen in the early church and does not apply to the modern situation.[20] If ordained ministry is a postbiblical development, then it can be argued that what the Bible says about women in general is irrelevant. The churches are free to allow their ministry to develop as times and circumstances change. This is basically the position these churches are obliged to adopt, though some have tried to argue that there were female apostles in New Testament times.[21] Is this a valid argument? Here the real issue is between those who believe that the New Testament lays down a pattern for male-female relations that is of divine origin and cannot be changed and those who say that it is culturally conditioned and can therefore be altered to suit different social patterns. Churches that ordain women have effectively adopted the latter view, whether they admit it or not. Some of them have made provision for the consciences of those who cannot agree with this, in an attempt to preserve unity, but the result has almost always been further division. Women ordained in these circumstances are seldom willing to work with those who disagree with their ordination, and it remains to be seen whether this disagreement can be accommodated within a single church structure. If not, then it must regretfully be said that the ordination of women by most mainline Protestant denominations, but by nobody else, has struck another blow against church unity, and one that is likely to prove to be an insurmountable barrier to further ecumenical cooperation in the future.

Another issue that has come to the fore and is also rooted in the church's doctrine of creation is the question of same-sex relationships.[22] Can two men marry each other with the blessing of the church? The Bible is quite clear that homosexual activity is immoral, which automatically excludes same-sex marriages. In biblical terms, marriage is intended as a form of sanctifying

---

20. Variations of this argument are now commonly found as an interpretation of 1 Timothy 2:11–15. For an excellent, but often overlooked, study of the question, see F. Martin, *The Feminist Question: Feminist Theology in the Light of Christian Tradition* (Grand Rapids: Eerdmans, 1994).

21. The evidence they point to is the case of Junia in Romans 16:7, but it is clear that whoever she was, she was not one of the Twelve and never had any authority over a local church.

22. See L. Nolland, *God, Gays, and the Church* (London: Latimer Trust, 2008), for a good analysis of the issues from the traditional Christian standpoint.

and regulating relations between men and women, including the vitally important reproduction of the human race. The idea that two people who love each other should be allowed to marry, regardless of other considerations, is completely alien to the Scriptures. Both the Old and the New Testaments tell us that we are to love our neighbors as ourselves, but that does not mean that we are expected to marry them. It is a curious limitation of the concept of "love" that has led to this modern interpretation, along with a sense that sexual orientation—something ignored by the Bible—should be allowed to determine conduct. On this issue, most churches have (so far) been more conservative than on the question of women's ordination, but there is a definite trend among liberal Protestants to conform to the prevailing culture of Western secularism, and the battle over same-sex marriage is already tearing some denominations apart. Those churches that have married and ordained practicing homosexuals have undoubtedly caused division, not only in relations with other denominations but within their own churches as well, with dissenters often leaving in protest. It is still too early to say what the long-term effect of this will be, but it is hard to see that it can do anything other than add to the already existing divisions within the wider church.

In the cases of both women's ordination and homosexual marriage, the apostolicity of the church is being directly challenged by an attack on the doctrines of creation and the fall, which are fundamental to the teaching of the Bible that the apostles took for granted. This matters, because the doctrines of redemption and salvation in Christ can only be properly understood against that background.[23] If the diagnosis of what is wrong changes, then the message of how to solve the problem will also change, and the church's message will cease to be what it has been since the time of the apostles. It is the alarm caused by the fear that this is already happening in the mainline Protestant denominations that has led to so many recent splits from them, as well as to the flight of some of their most committed members to Evangelical churches, and in some cases to Rome or to the Eastern Orthodox.

Closely connected to this is the question of discipline, where all churches today face a major problem. In earlier times it was possible to excommunicate those who dissented from the church's teaching and practice. This was done in the New Testament and remained a living part of ecclesiastical life until the Reformation and later. We may recoil at some of the methods used to enforce it—exile at best, burning at the stake at worst—but there can be no doubt that the church took its discipline seriously. The demise of that kind of discipline has seriously affected the internal life of the churches. Theoretically,

23. See 1 Corinthians 15:22, where Paul makes this point.

any denomination can try its members for heresy or misconduct, and until fairly recently, many did. In the nineteenth century, it was not uncommon for university professors to be dismissed for holding unorthodox views or for pastors to lose their charges for the same reason. Moral failure, though less widely publicized, incurred a similar punishment, and in most churches and religious institutions that would still be true today.

Discipline of the clergy—the church's employees, after all—has always been easier and more readily accepted than discipline of the laity. A Protestant church finds it difficult, if not impossible, to exercise any meaningful discipline over its lay members because if it tries to impose its rules on them, they are likely either to stop attending church or to go elsewhere, where they will be more readily accepted. As might be expected, the Roman Catholic and the Eastern Orthodox churches have tried harder to impose discipline, both on the clergy and on the laity, but they too face similar problems where their laypeople are concerned. Whether we like it or not, the church in the modern world has become a body that the average layperson can either join or leave, with little consequence either way. Sectarian groups may be able to exert more pressure on their members, but that is only because they are small and in some cases isolated from wider society. A man or woman who is expelled from an Amish community, for example, may be in a difficult position because that person is then cut off from the only community he or she has ever known, but this is hardly typical of the church as a whole and cannot be taken as the norm in the modern world.

In matters of devotion, a similar anarchy reigns across the denominations. At the time of the Reformation there was a conscious effort in many places to devise forms of public worship that would reflect the teaching of a particular church and be imposed equally on everyone. In the Roman Catholic Church, for example, the Tridentine Mass became the norm and remained so for four centuries. When it was finally set aside in 1970, it left behind a band of diehard loyalists who continue (in ever decreasing numbers, it must be admitted) to plead for its restoration and who regard its abandonment as one of the chief causes of the malaise that has beset the church since the Second Vatican Council (1962–65). Anglicans have the Book of Common Prayer, whose classical form dates from 1662 and has provided the basis for liturgies across the Anglican Communion, but the traditional prayer book is now much less widely used than it was a generation ago, although it still exists and to some extent continues to serve as a kind of "norm" for the conduct of worship and the establishment of doctrine.

The Eastern Orthodox churches cling to their ancient liturgies, which remain virtually unchanged, but in other denominations liturgical traditionalism is much less in evidence. Most Protestant churches, and Roman Catholic ones as well, have undergone sweeping change in the past generation, some of it sparked by genuine liturgical renewal, but much of it inspired by charismatic tendencies and contemporary youth culture. On the whole, it must be said that modern liturgies are uninspiring and often so flexible (with a seemingly endless range of options to choose from) that any sense of unity has been lost. Certainly, as priests and pastors know only too well, it is no longer possible to go into a particular Anglican or Catholic church and lead the worship there without some previous orientation. Even if the broad outline of the service is familiar, the details vary so much from place to place that prior guidance is almost always necessary. It is not even possible to predict which version of the Bible will be read or what form of the Lord's Prayer will be recited.

How far this variety affects the church's claims to apostolicity is hard to say. Liturgical reformers long prided themselves on having recovered primitive forms of worship that went back (so they thought) to apostolic times, and the interdenominational services that they constructed, largely on the basis of a text attributed to Hippolytus (third century), created a sense of unity across denominations that has counterbalanced the factors leading to greater division.[24] However much services may vary from one place to another, lay participants often recognize them when they travel from one denomination to another because the liturgical commissions of their respective churches have worked together to produce broadly similar forms of worship. Not least, the achievement of a common lectionary has been quite remarkable; it is now possible to go into any mainline Protestant or Roman Catholic church and hear the same Scripture readings, something that is bound to encourage a sense of church unity at the grassroots level. In that sense, despite the great variety of outward forms, Christian worship (outside the Eastern tradition) is now much more similar across the different denominations than it was a generation ago.

That much is certainly true, but is it any closer to what the apostles would have recognized? This is a much more difficult question to answer. Leaving aside the incidentals—the apostles would not have known what to make of PowerPoint presentations or even of printed hymn books—perhaps the biggest problem they would have with our modern worship is its relative superficiality. When we read the New Testament, we sense that believers were expected to search the Scriptures, to study them, and to receive deep teaching when

24. It is now known that this attribution is false and that the text used is considerably later in date, probably coming from the fifth century rather than the third, but this does not alter the fact that a large measure of liturgical unity has been achieved.

they gathered together. We also sense that churchgoing was not just one activity among many others but an essential part of the identity of individual Christians. The church was their primary community, in which all the serious business of life was conducted. Joining it was almost like moving to another country, so different from the wider world was it and so demanding were its norms. In this respect, the modern church, whatever form it takes and whatever claims it makes, is a long way from the apostolic model. Many congregations have sensed the need to recover a community feel in the midst of a soulless modern urban life, but how many have taken it seriously? A few have, it is true, but they are the exceptions that prove the rule. Perhaps here, more than anywhere, there is a real challenge and a genuine opportunity for the church to make a difference in the modern world and recover something of what it originally meant to walk in the steps of the apostles, who themselves followed the way of Christ.

A Way Forward?

This chapter began by asking what the church ought to be, and a survey of how this question has been answered by different denominational groups has shown just how difficult it is to come to a common mind on the subject. The Eastern Orthodox churches do not ask it at all, because in their view the church that is is the one that ought to be, and if change is to come it will only be slowly and with general agreement among all those concerned. For years, their leaders have been working toward calling a pan-Orthodox synod that will revise the church's canons and address the questions posed by modernity, but as yet there is no sign of that happening. It may come eventually, but the glacial pace at which the Orthodox move is such that it may still be some centuries down the road. The Roman Catholic Church experimented with change at the Second Vatican Council, whose impact is still being felt and which it is very hard to assess objectively, even at a distance of half a century. What is certain is that the reactionary approach to modern life that started at Trent in the sixteenth century was definitively abandoned at Vatican II, with consequences for the church that have been dramatic. In particular, dialogue with non-Catholic Christians is being promoted as never before, and Catholics are encouraged to work with Protestants and Orthodox in such fields as biblical studies, church history, and systematic theology. But on the basic question of the church and its identity, Rome has not changed its position. What the church should become is what the Holy Spirit will tell the pope that it should be, and he will have to communicate that message to the faithful. Modern communications have turned the popes into media personalities, which makes this task much easier than before, but although a number of Catholics claim to have been inspired by Pope John Paul II (1978–2005) and now by Pope Francis (2013–), it is impossible to say how many of them have actually changed in any way because of them.[25] The papacy will no doubt continue to attract crowds, but what effect it will have on the church at the grassroots level is hard to say and is likely to be much less than media attention might suggest.

For Protestant churches, the possibility of changing the church in order to make it conform to particular principles, whether derived from the New Testament or not, has always been much greater. It can be said without exaggeration that this ideal inspired the Reformation and in that sense is part of Protestantism's DNA—*ecclesia semper reformanda*, as the classic saying goes.[26] But how should this be done? As this survey has indicated, there are many aspects of church life where improvements are desirable, and change of some kind is inevitable—for better or for worse. If they thought it necessary, Protestants could tear down the existing structures of the institutional church and start over again from scratch, and every once in a while some group decides to do just that. The result, all too often, is that another denomination appears, distinguished no doubt by certain shibboleths that are peculiar to it but essentially not very different from the denominations that already exist. Like it or not, experience has shown that real change can only be incremental—one step at a time.

It would be foolhardy in the extreme to predict how this can be done, and no one should be under any illusion that the current state of disarray within the Protestant world can be cured overnight—or at all. Even a dying denomination may take a long time to disappear, and there will always be relics of the past that survive here and there. Nevertheless, the main body of the church can move on and will do so; the challenge is to see that it moves in the right direction. We cannot pronounce dogmatically on what that ought to be, but we can certainly lay down certain things that can serve as a starting point and as a benchmark by which to measure whether any progress is being made.

In a recent book, Professor Norman Doe has outlined fifty principles that he believes are common to all Christian churches.[27] Having looked at ten different denominational traditions that cross the entire spectrum of the

25. Pope Benedict XVI (2005–13) was less media-friendly and therefore less "influential" in those terms, even though he was a more substantial theologian than either his predecessor or his successor.

26. "The church is always in need of reformation."

27. N. Doe, *Christian Law: Contemporary Principles* (Cambridge: Cambridge University Press, 2013), 388–98.

church, he has pinpointed these fifty factors as issues that every church has to face and find some way of dealing with sooner or later. He also concludes that because these factors are shared across the board, the solutions the different churches have found are also broadly similar, even if the terminology used to express them is not the same. The lesson from this study is that whatever happens in the future, these fundamental principles will continue to manifest themselves and that anyone who wants to reform an existing institution, or create a new one, would be well advised to take them into account from the start.

These principles may be summarized as follows:

1–5: All churches are legal bodies that are internally governed by principles or laws that are subject to change but that must be respected and applied fairly to every aspect of their ministry.

6–10: The church is the people of God, and every member of it is equal. Those who are ordained to ministry within it are not imposed from without but emerge from within and are recognized by commonly accepted procedures.

11–15: All churches have responsible officers and practice some form of ordination. Each denomination has a structure of responsibility and authority that extends beyond the local congregation.

16–20: Churches have different forms of government but are usually organized at several different levels—international, national, regional, and local—each of which has structures appropriate to it.

21–25: All churches have some form of discipline, and most have structures for solving disputes and correcting offenses of different kinds. These procedures should be fair and applied equally to all.

26–28: All churches have doctrinal norms that include the duty to preach the faith of Christ and to guard the people of God against error.

29–35: All churches engage in public worship, which will include baptism, Holy Communion, weddings, and funerals, all of which will be organized according to recognized doctrinal and legal norms.

36–40: There is a universal church that is manifested by interdenominational structures and organizations that provide for fellowship at different levels across the spectrum of Christian belief.

41–45: All churches own property and have structures for managing their financial affairs. They have a duty to provide for their ministry and to ensure that everything they do is honest and lawful.

46–50: All churches have a relationship with the wider world. They must
        work out their position with regard to the state, support human
        rights around the world, and accept their share of social respon-
        sibility. They may also participate in public institutions when it is
        lawful and appropriate for them to do so.

These principles are clear and comprehensive, but in themselves they are
like a skeleton that forms the framework of the body without being the body
itself. They may perhaps be compared to the dry bones in Ezekiel 37, which
will live only as and when the Spirit of God blows into them. But when the
Spirit comes, the dry bones do not disappear. Instead, their true purpose is
revealed, and they form the shape that the inspired body will take. This is
the church as it lives in the world, and it is with this goal in mind that those
seeking to advance its cause and reform its structures ought to proceed, to
the glory of the God whom they serve.

APPENDIX

The Ecumenical Councils

The ecumenical councils of the church have played an important part in shaping it down through the centuries. The Roman Catholic Church recognizes twenty-one of them, on the basis that their decisions have been ratified by the pope. The Eastern Orthodox recognize only the first seven because only they were ratified by the whole church.[1] Protestants usually accept the decisions of the first four without question but pick and choose from the rest, using conformity to the Scriptures as the criterion of acceptability. The original texts of the councils' decisions are published, with parallel English translations, in N. P. Tanner, ed., *Decrees of the Ecumenical Councils*, 2 vols. (London: Sheed & Ward; Washington, DC: Georgetown University Press, 1990).

The Eight Ancient Councils

These all met in the East at the behest of the reigning emperor. The pope did not attend any of them, but he sent his representatives and later ratified their decisions. The last of these councils was not recognized by the Eastern church.

1. *The First Council of Nicaea.* This council met from June 19 to August 25, 325, and was summoned by the emperor Constantine I (r. 306–37).

---

1. By "whole church" they mean the West and those Eastern churches in communion with Constantinople. In fact, the Nestorian church recognizes only the first two, and the so-called monophysite (or miaphysite) churches only the first three.

Its acts have not been preserved, but it produced a creed that declared that the incarnate Christ was "consubstantial" (*homoousios*) with the Father, and it sent a letter to Egypt in which it condemned Arius, who did not hold that doctrine. Its twenty canons have survived, most of which regulate the ordination and discipline of the clergy.

2. *The First Council of Constantinople*. This council met sometime in May 381 and held its final session on July 9, 381, though its decisions were not ratified by the emperor Theodosius I (r. 378–95) until July 30, 381. Its acts have not been preserved, but it is generally thought that it produced a statement of faith that we now know as the "Nicene Creed." It also established the hierarchy of five patriarchates (Rome, Constantinople, Alexandria, Antioch, and Jerusalem).

3. *The (First) Council of Ephesus*. This council met on June 22, 431, at the command of the emperor Theodosius II (r. 408–50) and closed sometime in September 431. It is chiefly known for its condemnation of Nestorius, patriarch of Constantinople (r. 428–31), because of his mistaken view that the person of Christ was the result of a conjunction between his divinity and his humanity, rather than being identical with the person of the divine Son.

4. *The Council of Chalcedon.*[2] This council met at Nicaea on September 1, 451, but was transferred to Chalcedon on October 8, 451, at the command of the emperor Marcian (r. 450–57), and closed at the sixteenth session, which was probably held on November 1, 451. It is famous for its christological definition, which stated that the incarnate Son of God was one divine person in two natures, divine and human, "without confusion, without change, without division, and without separation." The council's decision was rejected by the Nestorians and by the church of Alexandria, which insisted that the incarnate Christ had only one nature, not two. Both of these non-Chalcedonian churches continue to exist today; the second is the historic church of Egypt, Ethiopia, Syria, Armenia, and Kerala (South India).

5. *The Second Council of Constantinople.*[3] This council met on May 5, 553, at the command of the emperor Justinian I (r. 527–65) and closed at the eighth session on June 2, 553. Its main purpose was to reconcile

2. See R. V. Sellers, *The Council of Chalcedon: A Historical and Doctrinal Survey* (London: SPCK, 1953); R. Price and M. Gaddis, *The Acts of the Council of Chalcedon*, 3 vols. (Liverpool: Liverpool University Press, 2005).

3. R. Price, ed., *The Acts of the Council of Constantinople of 553* (Liverpool: Liverpool University Press, 2009).

the monophysites of Egypt and Syria to the Chalcedonian faith. In the process, it condemned the writings of Origen (185?–254?), Theodore of Mopsuestia (350?–428), and Theodoret of Cyrus (393?–457?), all of whom were major commentators on the Bible.

6. *The Third Council of Constantinople.* This council met on November 7, 680, and after eighteen sessions closed on September 16, 681. It condemned a compromise attempt to reconcile the monophysites known as monothelitism, which said that there is only one will in the incarnate Christ. It also condemned Pope Honorius I (r. 625–38) because he had favored the monothelites.

   The Council in Trullo.[4] This council was held in the imperial palace of the Trullum in Constantinople at the command of the emperor Justinian II (r. 685–95; 705–11). It met in order to compose disciplinary canons and was generally regarded as an appendix to the fifth and sixth councils, which had not produced any. For that reason it is also called the Quinisext ("fifth-sixth") Council. The canons were never ratified by the Western church but have been the foundation of Eastern canon law ever since.

7. *The Second Council of Nicaea.*[5] This council met on September 24, 787, and closed after eight sessions on October 23, 787. It was summoned by the empress Irene, acting as regent for her son, Constantine VI (r. 780–97). Its main purpose was to declare that it was permissible to paint portraits of Christ because although he was God, he was also a man and was visible to his contemporaries. It was hoped that this would end the iconoclastic controversy, which it did temporarily, although iconoclasm was revived in 811 and was not finally defeated until 843.

8. *The Fourth Council of Constantinople.*[6] This council met on October 5, 869, and closed at its tenth session on February 28, 870. It was summoned by the emperor Basil I (r. 867–86). Its main purpose was to ratify the deposition of the patriarch Photius (r. 858–67; 877–86), who had been accused of fomenting schism between Constantinople and Rome, and to reconcile the Eastern and the Western churches. It reaffirmed papal primacy in the church and was ratified in the West but repudiated in the East.

---

4. See G. Nedungatt and M. Featherstone, eds., *The Council* in Trullo *Revisited* (Rome: Pontificio Istituto Orientale, 1995).

5. The best account of this council in English is in E. J. Martin, *A History of the Iconoclastic Controversy* (London: SPCK, 1930), 92–109.

6. See F. Dvornik, *The Photian Schism* (Cambridge: Cambridge University Press, 1948), for a full discussion of this council and its reception in the later traditions of both East and West.

The Photian Synod in Constantinople.[7] This synod was held in seven sessions from November 1, 879, to March 13, 880, in order to reinstate Photius as patriarch of Constantinople. It was ratified in both East and West, and the suggestion has been made that it should replace the earlier council, held in 870, as the eighth ecumenical one.

The Ten Medieval Councils

These all met under the auspices of the pope, who attended most of them, and are best regarded as synods of the Western church rather than as "ecumenical" in the true sense. The Eastern church was represented at only two (Lyons II and Ferrara-Florence) and later rejected the decisions taken there.

9. *The First Lateran Council.* This council was summoned by Pope Callistus II (r. 1119–24) and met from March 18, 1123, to either March 27 or April 6, 1123. Its main concern was to attack the practice of "lay investiture," a procedure by which the Holy Roman Emperor (in particular) claimed the right to ratify papal appointments to bishoprics. It was at this council that compulsory clerical celibacy was introduced.

10. *The Second Lateran Council.* This council was summoned by Pope Innocent II (r. 1130–43) and met on April 4, 1139. It seems to have closed sometime before April 17, 1139. Its purpose was to end the schism caused by the election of an antipope, Anacletus II (r. 1130–38), and to condemn the heresies of Peter de Bruys (fl. 1117–31) and Arnold of Brescia (1090?–1155).

11. *The Third Lateran Council.* This council was summoned by Pope Alexander III (r. 1159–81) and met from March 5 to either March 19 or 22, 1179. Its purpose was to heal the schism that had produced three antipopes between 1159 and 1178. It also condemned the dualist (Manichaean) heresy of the Albigensians (or Cathars) in southern France.

12. *The Fourth Lateran Council.* This council was summoned by Pope Innocent III (r. 1198–1216) and met in three sessions on November 11, 20, and 30, 1215. It issued far-reaching decrees concerning the reform of the church, including a ban on clandestine marriages and on the purchase of ecclesiastical offices (simony). It promulgated the doctrine of transubstantiation in the Mass and also recognized the place

7. See J. Meijer, *A Successful Council of Union: A Theological Analysis of the Photian Synod of 879–880* (Thessalonica: Patriarchikon Hidryma Paterikōn Spoudōn, 1975).

of Constantinople in the hierarchy of the five patriarchates that had originally been proclaimed at the First Council of Constantinople in 381. Its canons remained the basis of church order in the West until the Reformation.

13. *The First Council of Lyons.* This council was summoned by Pope Innocent IV (r. 1243–54) and met in four sessions from June 28 to July 17, 1245. It tried to legislate for the conformity of the Eastern churches to the Roman rite and to revive interest in crusading, but was largely unsuccessful.

14. *The Second Council of Lyons.* This council was summoned by Pope Gregory X (r. 1271–76) with the assent of the emperor Michael VIII (r. 1258–82). It met from May 7 to July 17, 1274. Its main purpose was to reunite the Eastern and the Western churches. The Eastern emperor accepted its conditions, but his church rejected them, and after he died it repudiated the council.

15. *The Council of Vienne.* This council was summoned by Pope Clement V (r. 1305–14) and met from October 16, 1311, to May 6, 1312. Its main purpose was to condemn the Order of the Templars, which was suppressed at this time. It also sought to regulate excesses that had crept into the Franciscan order of friars.

16. *The Council of Constance.*[8] This council was summoned by Pope Gregory XII (r. 1406–15) and concluded by his successor, Martin V (r. 1417–31). It met in forty-five sessions from December 5, 1414, to April 22, 1418. Its main purpose was to end the great schism of the papacy, which it succeeded in doing, and to condemn the heresies of John Wyclif and Jan Hus. Hus attended the council in person but was arrested, tried, and burned at the stake in defiance of the safe-conduct that he had been granted by the emperor Sigismund.

17. *The Council of Basel-Ferrara-Florence-Rome.*[9] This council was summoned by Pope Eugenius IV (r. 1431–47) and met in Basel from December 14, 1431, to May 7, 1437, then in Ferrara from January 8 to April 9, 1438 (four sessions), in Florence from January 10, 1439, to February 4, 1442 (seven sessions), and finally at the Lateran in Rome from October 14, 1443, to August 7, 1445 (three sessions). Because its most important

8. See P. H. Stump, *The Reforms of the Council of Constance (1414–1418)* (Leiden: Brill, 1994); T. A. Fudge, *The Trial of Jan Hus: Medieval Heresy and Criminal Procedure* (New York: Oxford University Press, 2013); T. E. Morrissey, *Conciliarism and Church Law in the Fifteenth Century: Studies on Franciscus Zabarella and the Council of Constance* (Farnham: Ashgate, 2014).

9. See J. Gill, *The Council of Florence* (Cambridge: Cambridge University Press, 1959).

decisions were taken at Florence, the council is usually known by that name or as the Council of Ferrara-Florence. In its early phase at Basel, it represented the achievement of the conciliar movement, which wanted such councils to meet on a regular basis as a kind of parliament for the church. After its transfer to Ferrara and then Florence, it concerned itself mainly with the reunion of Rome and the different Eastern churches. Reunion agreements were signed in which the East recognized papal supremacy in return for the right to maintain its own traditions. After Constantinople fell to the Turks in 1453, the church there repudiated the union, but it is still the basis used by Rome for reconciling members of the Eastern churches that have chosen to submit to papal authority.

18. *The Fifth Lateran Council.*[10] This council was summoned by Pope Julius II (r. 1503–13) and continued by his successor, Leo X (r. 1513–21). It met in twelve sessions from May 3, 1512, to March 16, 1517, and passed a number of decrees that promised to reform abuses in the church. However, it was eclipsed by the Reformation, which broke out only a few months after it closed, and its canons were almost immediately forgotten.

The Three Post-Reformation Councils

These are councils of the Roman Catholic Church only and are not recognized by any other Christian body.

19. *The Council of Trent.*[11] This council met in three separate stages. The first was summoned by Pope Paul III (r. 1534–49) and lasted from December 13, 1545, to June 2, 1547 (ten sessions). The second was convened by Pope Julius III (r. 1550–55) and went from May 1, 1551, to April 28, 1552 (six sessions). The third was convened by Pope Pius IV (r. 1559–65) and sat from January 18, 1562, to December 4, 1563 (nine sessions).

In the first group of sessions, important decrees were issued on matters dividing Protestants from those loyal to Rome. These included the canon and text of Scripture (April 8, 1546), original sin (June 17, 1546), justification by faith (January 13, 1547), and the sacraments (March 3,

10. See N. H. Minnich, *The Fifth Lateran Council (1512–1517): Studies on Its Membership, Diplomacy and Proposals for Reform* (Aldershot, UK: Variorum, 1993); P. B. T. Bilianiuk, *The Fifth Lateran Council (1512–1517) and the Eastern Churches* (Toronto: Central Committee for the Defence of the Rite, Tradition and Language of the Ukrainian Catholic Church in the USA and Canada, 1975).

11. See J. W. O'Malley, *Trent: What Happened at the Council* (Cambridge, MA: Harvard University Press, 2013).

1547). In the second group of sessions, there were decrees on the sacraments of Holy Communion (October 11, 1551), penance (November 25, 1551), and extreme unction (November 25, 1551). In the third and final group of sessions there was a decree justifying the withholding of the cup from the laity at Holy Communion (July 16, 1562) and another declaring the Mass to be a sacrifice (September 17, 1562).

Further decrees followed that defined and regulated the granting of holy orders (July 15, 1563) and the celebration of marriage (November 11, 1563). Finally, there were decrees on purgatory (December 3, 1563), the veneration of saints and their relics (December 3, 1563), and indulgences (December 4, 1563). It is clear from their content that these decrees were intended mainly as an attack on Protestantism.[12]

20. *The First Vatican Council*.[13] This council was summoned by Pope Pius IX (r. 1846–78) and met in four sessions from December 8, 1869, to July 18, 1870. Its only purpose was to pass the decree on papal infallibility, which it did in the closing session.

21. *The Second Vatican Council*.[14] This council was summoned by Pope John XXIII (r. 1958–63) and was continued by his successor, Paul VI (r. 1963–78). It met in nine sessions from February 2, 1962, to December 7, 1965. The main purpose of the council was to "renovate" the Catholic Church after four centuries in which the decrees of Trent had shaped its teaching and practice. It is the only council to have issued a special decree on the church, known as *Lumen gentium* (November 21, 1964), which was accompanied by *Unitatis redintegratio*, on ecumenism (November 21, 1964), in which non-Catholic Christians were recognized as "separated brethren." The council's interpretation and implementation have been matters of considerable controversy over the years. It is still too early to assess what its long-term impact will be, but there can be no doubt that, superficially at least, the Roman Catholic Church presents a very different face to the world than it did before the council.

---

12. A detailed refutation of the council was made by the German Lutheran theologian Martin Chemnitz (1522–86). See M. Chemnitz, *Examination of the Council of Trent*, 4 vols., trans. F. Kramer (St. Louis: Concordia, 1971–86).

13. See J. J. Hennesey, *The First Council of the Vatican: The American Experience* (New York: Herder & Herder, 1963); F. J. Cwiekowski, *English Bishops and the First Vatican Council* (Louvain: Publications Universitaires de Louvain, 1971).

14. The literature on this council is immense. For some recent studies, see D. Murray, *Keeping Open the Door of Faith: The Legacy of Vatican II* (Dublin: Veritas, 2012); S. Mulligan, *Reaping the Harvest: Fifty Years after Vatican II* (Blackrock, Co. Dublin: Columba Press, 2012); A. Marchetto, *The Second Vatican Ecumenical Council: A Counterpoint for the History of the Council*, trans. K. D. Whitehead (Scranton, PA: University of Scranton Press, 2010).

For Further Reading

I t is impossible to provide a complete or even comprehensive bibliography of books on the doctrine of the church. The following is a list of some important studies that reflect particular denominational backgrounds and concerns and that may be of interest to readers of this book who want to pursue its themes further.

Anglican/Episcopal

Avis, P. *The Anglican Understanding of the Church*. 2nd ed. London: SPCK, 2013.
———. *The Identity of Anglicanism: Essentials of Anglican Ecclesiology*. London: T&T Clark, 2007.

Baptist/Congregational

Allison, G. *Sojourners and Strangers: The Doctrine of the Church*. Wheaton: Crossway, 2012.
Jenson, M., and D. Wilhite. *The Church: A Guide for the Perplexed*. London: T&T Clark, 2010.

Eastern Orthodox

Zizioulas, J. *Being as Communion*. London: Darton, Longman & Todd, 1985.

Lutheran

Bliese, R. H., and C. Van Gelder, eds. *The Evangelizing Church: A Lutheran Contribution*. Minneapolis: Augsburg Fortress, 2005.

Wengert, T. J. *Priesthood, Pastors, Bishops: Public Ministry for the Reformation and Today*. Minneapolis: Fortress, 2008.

Presbyterian/Reformed

Berkouwer, G. C. *The Church*. Grand Rapids: Eerdmans, 1976.

Clowney, E. P. *The Church*. Leicester, UK: Inter-Varsity; Downers Grove, IL: InterVarsity, 1995.

Protestant (General)

Carson, D. A. *The Church in the Bible and the World*. Exeter, UK: Paternoster; Grand Rapids: Baker, 1987.

Roman Catholic

Békés, G., and V. Vajta, eds. Unitatis redintegratio, *1964–1974: The Impact of the Decree on Ecumenism*. Rome: Anselmiana, 1977.

Gaillardetz, R. R. *Church in the Making:* Lumen gentium, Christus Dominus. Orientalium ecclesiarum. New York: Paulist Press, 2006.

Küng, H. *The Church*. London: Search Press, 1968.

Index of Scripture and Other Ancient Sources

Index of Modern Authors

Index of Selected Names

Index of Subjects